INVESTIGATING
WHITE–COLLAR CRIME

ABOUT THE AUTHOR

Lieutenant Howard Williams is a seventeen-year veteran of the Austin Police Department, having joined the department in 1979. He has spent seven years as a patrol officer, eight years as an investigator in theft and narcotics, and two years as a sergeant. He was promoted to Lieutenant in 1996.

Educated in economics and political science at Southwest Texas State University, Lt. Williams has completed courses in financial investigation instructed by the Internal Revenue Service, the Federal Bureau of Investigation, the United States Department of Justice, and ANACAPA Sciences of California. He has over eight years of experience in financial investigations, including embezzlement and fraud. He has been a frequent guest lecturer at criminology classes at the University of Texas.

INVESTIGATING WHITE-COLLAR CRIME

Embezzlement and Financial Fraud

By

LIEUTENANT HOWARD E. WILLIAMS

Austin Police Department
Austin, Texas

CHARLES C THOMAS • PUBLISHER, LTD.
Springfield • Illinois • U.S.A.

Published and Distributed Throughout the World by

CHARLES C THOMAS • PUBLISHER, LTD.
2600 South First Street
Springfield, Illinois 62794-9265

© *1997 by* CHARLES C THOMAS • PUBLISHER, LTD.
ISBN 0-398-06684-1 (cloth)
ISBN 0-398-06685-X (paper)
Library of Congress Catalog Card Number: 96-33550

Printed in the United States of America
SC-R-3

Library of Congress Cataloging-in-Publication Data

Williams, Howard E.
    Investigating white-collar crime : embezzlement and financial
fraud / by Howard E. Williams.
        p.   cm.
    Includes bibliographical references and index.
    ISBN 0-398-06684-1. — ISBN 0-398-06685-X (pbk.)
    1. White collar crime investigation—United States.   I. Title.
HV8079.W47W57   1997
363.2'5968—dc20   96-33550
                                                                          CIP

PREFACE

The law, in its majestic equality, forbids the rich as well as the poor to sleep under bridges, to beg in the streets, and to steal bread.

Jacques-Anatole-François Thibauld
Les Lys Rouge

Thibauld, a 19th century French polemic, reflected the animosity prevalent in his day toward the inequities in the law and the legal system. He believed that criminal laws were repressive, prejudicing the poor while safeguarding the privileges of the rich. Thibauld was not alone in that opinion, and he developed a large following. Such criticisms were not unique to France, but extended worldwide. Eventually, because of the appeal of the masses, it became expedient for the political powers to accord ordinary people protection from the abuses of the upper class. In time, these principles spawned the concept of white-collar criminality. Yet, even today, criticism rages over the inequalities in the enforcement of criminal laws.

In my experience as a police officer, I have had the good fortune to become a white-collar crime investigator. The term unfortunately suggests a degree of expertise and specialization believed uncommon to most property crime investigators. Some investigators have confided to me that cases involving embezzlement or fraud are too complicated or too technical for them to understand or to investigate properly. They know that such investigations are incredibly time consuming. The average investigator is usually responsible for a case load that does not allow sufficient time to investigate complex cases. Questions often arise about whether the allegations under investigation are criminal violations or are civil disputes. There is the additional frustration that investigators waste time investigating white-collar crimes because prosecutors do not vigorously pursue the matter if the case comes to trial.

These fears are not totally warranted. It is true that white-collar criminal investigations pose unique problems for law enforcement officers, but expensive and highly specialized training and education are not necessary to prepare an officer to investigate white-collar criminal activity. Police supervisors and administrators must consider some special qualities, however, when deciding who should investigate such allegations. Some working knowledge of bookkeeping, accounting, financing, and general business principles is beneficial. Organizational skills and a propensity for logical deduction are important. Patience and painstaking attention to detail are vital. The investigator must realize that he cannot rush such investigations. He must stand prepared to understand and contend with the special legal, political, and sometimes social problems inherent in investigating white-collar criminal offenses. Police supervisors and administrators must accept the devotion of man hours and incidental expenses necessary to complete the investigation.

A major problem of enforcing white-collar criminal statutes is that there are elements of proof peculiar to those offenses. The basic investigative technique is, therefore, different from most property crimes. Embezzlement and fraud schemes often extend over a prolonged period. Consequently, the investigator must locate and amass large quantities of documentation. Coordinating and organizing the mass of documents and information is time consuming and difficult. Additionally, it may be difficult to write a report on the investigation presenting all the information concisely and comprehensibly. Such documentation and the organization of those documents are invaluable in presenting a case for prosecution.

The investigator must often research law with which he may not be familiar. Many criminal offenses, particularly white-collar offenses, exist outside the penal codes. The investigator must be prepared to seek advice from experts in whatever field he is investigating. Often, the distinctions between criminal and civil violations of law are nebulous, and victims may be reluctant to accept that criminal law enforcement officials are unable to involve themselves in civil disputes.

In the following chapters we shall briefly review the history of white-collar crime, seeking a working definition of the term, and briefly examining various white-collar offenses. We shall see why it is in the interest of the public generally, and the police service specifically, to pursue and prosecute white-collar criminals. We shall discuss the economic consequences of embezzlement, explain what drives a person to embezzle, and explore why there are rarely prosecutions for embezzlement. We shall define what elements are necessary to prove the offense of embezzlement, outlining techniques to simplify an otherwise difficult and cumbersome investigation. We shall discuss the complexity of fraud, uncovering the multitude of offenses covered by the term and seeking a common definition. We shall define the elements necessary to prove fraud, outlining techniques to simplify the investigation.

We shall discuss the importance of interviews with victims, witnesses, and suspects, highlighting techniques to help the investigator become a more effective interviewer in white-collar criminal cases. We shall note the differences in the primary and secondary stages of the investigation. We shall discover the importance of careful case preparation and of a well written and documented report of the facts. We shall preview some special problems inherent in investigating and prosecuting white-collar crime, discussing ways to avoid and cope with these problems.

We shall examine these problems, concepts, and theories neither as criminologists, nor as sociologists, nor as lawyers, but from the practical view of an investigator who confronts the problems daily. Because of the multitude of acts and omissions covered by the term "white-collar crime," we shall not attempt to discuss details of specific statutes. No one book could address all the legislation, which varies from jurisdiction to jurisdiction, nor could it address the difficulties inherent in investigating each of them separately. Additionally, it is not my intent to divulge specific details of the mechanics of a scheme that may serve only to educate the public in how to perpetrate or conceal certain criminal acts. Instead, we shall discuss principles of investigation specific to embezzlement and fraud, but pertinent to most white-collar criminal activity. By applying these skills, investigators in both law enforcement and private industry will gain a better understanding in detecting, investigating, prosecuting, and preventing white-collar crime.

I have worded many statements in the text with such phrases as "may have," "possibly," or "could have." I have been purposefully vague at such times. Laws vary from jurisdiction to jurisdiction, and laws that apply in one state may not apply in another. Case law citations herein serve only to illustrate a point. I do not purport to be an authority on law, and this book is not a legal treatise. An investigator should direct any questions regarding his legal authority, interpretation of law, or admissibility and sufficiency of evidence to an attorney.

CONTENTS

ix

INVESTIGATING
WHITE-COLLAR CRIME

Chapter 1

WHITE-COLLAR CRIME

Pardon one offense, and you encourage the commission of many.

Publilius Syrus
Maxim 750

Pardoning, excusing, and ignoring white-collar criminal offenses because investigations are too complicated, too time consuming, or too expensive are unacceptable to the modern professional law enforcement organization. A lack of appropriate enforcement action against white-collar criminals fosters an environment that breeds additional activity and more flagrant violations. Where there is no indication that law enforcement authorities within a given geographic or political region are willing to investigate white-collar offenses and to prosecute offenders, a laissez-faire attitude prevails. Conversely, the most potent weapon in the law enforcement arsenal to prevent white-collar criminal activity is an attitude pervasive within society that it will not tolerate such crime. Concrete examples of enforcement action reinforce this attitude.

No investigator can control the course of all legal action during an investigation or prosecution. A prosecutor must consider many factors before bringing a case to trial. Any investigator, however, courageous enough to work a high profile or heavily publicized white-collar case will greatly affect the reputation of his department.

Admittedly, white-collar criminal investigations may be extraordinarily complicated and time consuming. Taking weeks or months to conclude an investigation is usual as investigators research the legal questions involved, subpoena records, and pour over documents of all kinds: letters, contracts, depositions, accounting journals, checks, and bank statements. An investigator may need a great deal of time to find, interview, and take statements from reluctant victims and witnesses. As the investigator obtains more information, it becomes more difficult to organize the documentation. It also becomes more difficult to construct a report of the incident so that it contains all the pertinent information in a concise, logical, and easily understandable form. An investigator may spend

3

much time finding the best way to convey the information to those who will prosecute the case. He spends many hours copying and indexing documents, writing reports, and organizing files. Police administrators and investigators may exploit these complications as convenient excuses not to pursue certain inquiries. With proper training and a proper outlook, however, the investigator will realize these perceived liabilities as true benefits.

Except the Federal Bureau of Investigation and the Internal Revenue Service, few law enforcement agencies have established formal in-house courses or seminars for training white-collar crime investigators. Private sector training programs can be expensive. Smaller law enforcement agencies may not place a high priority on such matters. Administrations may not believe the expenditures to be cost effective. Many police administrators hold to the historic but antiquated idea that police officers should deal with crime on the streets. They believe that regulatory agencies or federal authorities should investigate crimes in the suites. Even in larger departments where funds may be available, owing to the complexities of white-collar crimes investigations, comprehensive training may not be readily available. Thus, investigators may receive training sporadically, attending schools or lectures with limited scope or instruction. Consequently, many investigators are reluctant to attempt or to participate in white-collar crimes investigations. Identifying measures and procedures to simplify these arduous investigations without lengthy and costly training is, therefore, important.

Due to the diverse violations encompassed in the generic classification of white-collar crime, defining techniques and procedures unique to each is not feasible. Such an undertaking would require an encyclopedic effort. The practical alternative, then, is to develop functional outlines that are applicable to the investigation of a variety of offenses.

Perhaps the most difficult task of outlining such investigative procedures lies in defining the scope of white-collar crime. White-collar crimes include violations of ethics laws, purchasing regulations, voting laws, banking codes, insurance regulations, labor relations laws, pure food and drug laws, consumer protection laws, commerce codes, and a host of others. The concept encompasses many state and federal statutes and regulations. Such laws and regulations vary from jurisdiction to jurisdiction. Government bodies tailor these statutes to meet particular social or economic needs. The need for such diversity is obvious. Regulations concerning working conditions in West Virginia coal mines would hardly be necessary or applicable in the state of Florida.

Consequently, any analysis of investigative technique must begin, not by listing pertinent legislation, but by developing a workable definition of the concept. Even this most basic approach is difficult since there exists no uniform definition of white-collar crime.[1] Criminologists and the public have expressed differing opinions on what to include in the definition. In the debate over white-collar crime, much discussion is had over whether to include noncriminal acts within the definition. For the criminal investigator, this argument is merely an academic exercise. Whether an act or omission should be criminal instead of civil or administrative is irrelevant. Unless a law exists making specific acts or omissions a criminal violation, no crime exists. Consequently, no criminal investigation is necessary.

The concept of white-collar crime is not static. In an evolving society the perceptions of what should be criminal activity changes. Abortion, which was until recently forbidden in many states within the United States, since the celebrated Supreme Court decision in Roe v. Wade, is now legally acceptable within defined limits. Even so, public debate on the issue still rages. During World War II, the government closely regulated typical daily business transactions such as the selling of butter, meat, and shoes. Violations of such controls were subject to severe sanction. Such were the necessities in a nation at war. As technology progresses, and as economic and social conditions change, so do the laws and regulations that govern. Thus, over time, changing social and legal standards have refined the definition of white-collar crime.

The problems of white-collar crime are not new. The 19th century French polemic Jacques-Anatole-François Thibauld recognized that law protected the business dealings of the upper class at the expense of the less fortunate. Witness the exploitations of labor and consumers by the "robber barons" of the late 19th century American railroad and steel industries.[2] In 1931, the *New York Times* reported four cases of embezzlement in the United States where losses exceeded $1 million each. The total loss in the four cases was more than $9 million.[3] In 1938 the men listed as one through six on the Federal Bureau of Investigation's Most Wanted list derived $130,000.00 through criminal activity, mostly burglary and robbery. By comparison, during the 1930s, Swedish financier and promoter Ivar Krueger defrauded some $250 million from investors in Sweden, France, and the United States.[4]

Defining White-Collar Crime

In the 1930s, the prevailing view of American sociologists was that criminal behavior was essentially the result of cultural conflicts, the weakening of the forces of the privileged upon the less privileged members of a society. They viewed the consequential social disorientation as a struggle between contradictory moral and ethical standards. Coupling of such conditions with concomitant materialistic values, they believed, led individuals, particularly those of lower intelligence or those who were mentally or emotionally unstable, to satisfy their needs or desires by criminal or otherwise deviant or antisocial behavior.[5]

Edwin H. Sutherland contended that contemporary theories of criminality were insufficient. He noted that criminologists based such theories on data from studies of individuals imprisoned for some offense. Sutherland contended that these data excluded from consideration professional people, business and industrial leaders, and corporations who rarely, if ever, faced criminal sanctions and imprisonment. Consequently, Sutherland argued, theories based on socioeconomic deprivation, low intelligence, or psychopathic states were incomplete and did not address the full gambit of criminal activity.[6]

Sutherland first introduced the term "white-collar crime" in a presidential address to the American Sociological Society in 1939. Later, he formally defined it as "a crime committed by a person of respectability and high social status in the course of his occupation."[7] Sutherland noted that, because members of the upper socioeconomic classes committed these crimes while doing business, they caused serious injury to society by undermining public confidence in the economic and financial institutions of that society. He also contended that such lack of confidence and trust created low morale and social disorganization. Consequently, Sutherland's definition included acts violating any law or regulation, criminal or civil, he felt were harmful to society.[8] "Sutherland concluded that such crime existed because of differential association, a process whereby behavior is learned in association with those defining the behavior favorably and in isolation from those defining it unfavorably."[9] He argued that corporate crime would become self-propagating as corporate officers defined their own limits of acceptable behavior.[10]

Gilbert Geiss criticized Sutherland's work, claiming that the major difficulty with *White Collar Crime* as criminological research was in Sutherland's inability to differentiate between the corporations and the actions of the corporations' executive and management personnel.[11] Geiss did not fully accept Sutherland's conclusions because Sutherland asserted that corporations as individual entities could be guilty of criminal action. Geiss contended that any criminal action could only be the responsibility of the individuals directing, administrating, and managing the corporation.[12]

For the criminal investigator, including violations of civil law or administrative regulations as criminal activity is unacceptable. The criminal investigator must try to familiarize himself with the differences in criminal and civil law, but he must avoid entanglement in purely civil disputes. It is neither the investigator's duty nor his responsibility to decide who may be right or wrong in a civil dispute. It is his duty to serve as an impartial witness to the facts and to enforce the encoded criminal laws. The investigator should refer any questions regarding civil recourse or civil responsibility to proper legal practitioners. This is not to imply that law enforcement officers cannot use civil action to enhance criminal enforcement. Civil law may be a most useful supplement to criminal law, as in forfeiture proceedings or suits at common nuisance. Clearly, however, the investigator must base the action upon a criminal violation, as in civil forfeitures of the tools and proceeds of narcotics trafficking. If the investigator decides that no criminal violation has occurred, the investigator should leave any civil remedy for the injured parties to pursue.

Such shortcomings do not invalidate Sutherland's ideas. Sutherland's theories formed the basis for more extensive sociological research, and, as in any scientific research, subsequent research expanded and refined the basic theory. The need for a more restrictive definition, however, was evident. Criminologist Don C. Gibbons defined white-collar crime as an offense that represented a violation of legal rules constructed to govern business affairs and occupational practices, but only as far as those violations took place in furtherance of the conduct of regular business or occupational activities.[13] Thus, Gibbons associated white-collar crime not with the social status of the offender, but with the activities within the professions. He was mainly concerned with violations of federal regulatory statutes and regulations of administrative agencies.[14]

Gibbons' definition was more restrictive than Sutherland's, but it failed to include acts individuals commit against legitimate business such as embezzlement and insurance fraud. Thus, Gibbons' definition excluded important aspects of white-collar crime.

In their discussions, sociologists Marshall B. Clinard and Richard Quinney emphasized that the crucial point in defining white-collar crime was that the behavior included in the concept had to be directly related to those occupations regarded as legitimate in society. Thus, Clinard and Quinney defined what they termed occupational crime as violations of legal codes during activity within an otherwise legitimate occupation.[15] August Bequai added that such violations had to be committed by means of guile, deceit, or concealment.[16]

Clinard, Quinney, and Bequai raised the important points that the criminal activity had to be involved with a legitimate and legal business or occupation. They added these violations must include elements of fraud and deception. Their definitions specifically excluded acts of violence or coercion. Thus, extortion, robbery, narcotics trafficking, gambling, and vice are excluded, no matter the socioeconomic stature of the actor. The actions of a banker or lawyer who helps in laundering the proceeds of such activity, however, may be involved in white-collar crime.

In 1979, a United States Congressional Subcommittee on Crime derived what is, for the criminal investigator, perhaps the most functional definition of white-collar crime. The Subcommittee defined white-collar crime as "an illegal act or series of illegal acts committed by nonphysical means and by concealment or guile, to obtain money or property, to avoid the payment or loss of money or property, or to obtain personal or business advantage."[17]

Types of White-Collar Crime

One difficulty of the white-collar crime concept is that white-collar criminality exceeds the normal limits of traditional crime.[18] English common law recognized larceny as a criminal offense, but it had no provisions to govern complex fraud or embezzlement. Embezzlement was legally undefined in England until 1799.[19] The lack of trust that accompanied the growth of the banking profession led to the definition of criminal embezzlement.[20] This social consciousness and reaction to a perceived threat to the society's economic and social well-being are the basis for legislation defining white-collar criminal activity.

Similar problems developed with the growth of other industries and professions. As professions such as insurance, banking, and medicine grew in importance and complexity, lawmakers faced the need to protect the public from unscrupulous and dangerous practices. Subsequently, legislators enacted laws and regulatory statutes that branded as criminal certain acts unique to these professions. Racketeering laws were a result of the intermingling of organized crime with otherwise legal businesses in the early 1900s. Special criminal laws regulated labor relations and the growth of labor unions. Such laws, written to regulate specific areas of business relations, were highly technical and severely limited in scope. Such statutes creating and defining new criminal activity became the basis for the concept of white-collar crime.

In recent years legislators have defined criminal acts in such areas as stocks and securities exchange, electronic data storage and communications, government ethics, and government services such as welfare and social security. The list of new criminal acts is ever growing as lawmakers attempt to maintain control over various aspects of a growing and evolving society. The problem with white-collar crime, however, is that the antisocial behavior that so disturbed Sutherland often comes far ahead of laws restricting or prohibiting that behavior. White-collar criminal statutes are reactive rather than proactive. It is only after a condition has developed to the point where it shocks the social conscious or poses a serious threat to the welfare of society do legislators devote their time and attention to the problem.

White-collar criminal activity falls into three general categories:

1) crimes by individuals, for personal gain or profit, in the course of their legitimate occupations, but in violation of the loyalty or fidelity of an employer or client,
2) crimes in furtherance of, and for the benefit of, otherwise legitimate business; and
3) criminal activity disguised as legitimate business.

Table 1 contains a list of some common white-collar criminal activities grouped into each of the three categories.

In the first category, crimes by an individual, the individual is seeking personal profit or gain. He works against legitimate businesses and institutions, or against the trust and fidelity of employees or clients. Credit fraud and fraud in insolvency are directed against banks and

Table 1. White-Collar Criminal Activity.

I. Crimes by an individual
   A. Credit fraud
      1. False statements to obtain credit
      2. Purchasing on credit with no intent to repay
      3. Hindering a secured creditor in repossessing property
   B. Fraud in insolvency
   C. Tax fraud
      1. Tax evasion
      2. Fraudulent tax returns
   D. Government services fraud
      1. Unemployed insurance fraud
      2. Welfare fraud
      3. Social security fraud
   E. Insurance fraud
   F. Embezzlement
   G. Commercial bribery and kickbacks
   H. Securities fraud
   I. Banking regulation violations
   J. Petty larceny by employees
   K. Computer fraud
II. Crimes in furtherance of business or occupation
   A. Professional regulatory violations
      1. Banking violations
      2. Insurance violations
   B. Embezzlement
      1. Bank officers and directors
      2. Fiduciaries
   C. Securities fraud
      1. Market manipulation
      2. Insider training
   D. Commercial bribery
      1. Kickbacks
      2. Collusion
   E. Antitrust violations
   F. Conflicts of interest
   G. Computer fraud
   H. Tax violations
      1. Employment taxes
      2. Sales or professional taxes
   I. Credit fraud
      1. False financial statement to obtain credit
      2. Fictitious or overvalued collateral
   J. Deceptive business practices
      1. False advertising
      2. False weights and measures
      3. Adulterated or mislabeled products

Table 1. (Continued)

    K. Labor violations
    L. Commercial espionage
        1. Theft of trade secrets
        2. Copyright violations
    M. Environmental code violations
        1. Toxic and hazardous waste disposal
        2. Air and water quality violations
    N. Health and safety violations
        1. Occupational Safety and Health Act (OSHA) violations
        2. Building and fire code violations
    O. Political and professional ethics violations
    P. Food and drug violations
    Q. Truth-in-lending violations
III. Crime as a business
    A. Health or medical fraud
    B. Fraudulent public contests
    C. Advance fee scheme
    D. Bankruptcy fraud
    E. Securities fraud
    F. Real estate fraud
    G. Third party leasing scheme
    H. Charity contribution fraud
    I. Personal improvement schemes
        1. Mail order diploma
        2. Correspondence schools
    J. Insurance fraud rings
    K. Vanity schemes
        1. Publishing schemes
        2. Modeling schools
    L. Ponzi scheme
    M. Corporate raiding
    N. Employment agency fraud
    O. Mail order swindles
    P. Pyramid schemes
    Q. Confidence games
    R. Phone solicitation schemes

other financial or lending institutions. An individual may file false reports or statements to deceive the lender into providing credit he would not otherwise have provided. He purchases merchandise on credit, refuses to pay for it, then secrets the property from the creditor, thus prohibiting the creditor from enforcing a secured interest in the property. He may also purchase a great deal of property on credit, convert it or transfer title to another, then declare bankruptcy, thus prohibiting the creditor from repossessing the property.

Tax and government services fraud exist at all levels of government. Everyone has heard of individuals who file fraudulent tax returns, understating income, overstating deductions, or finding ways to avoid completely paying taxes. In 1989, a New York federal jury convicted hotelier and socialite Leona Helmsley of tax evasion for failing to pay $1.2 million in taxes.[21] Individuals also file claims for government services to which they are not rightfully entitled, such as social security or welfare benefits, or they convert legitimate services, such as selling food stamps.

Other acts are most damaging to legitimate businesses. Employees embezzle from their employers, taking pains to alter or distort company records. Albert Miano, a middle level manager at *Reader's Digest*, embezzled $1 million from his employer between 1982 and 1987.[22] Individuals defraud insurance companies by filing claims for casualty losses that never occurred, or by filing multiple claims against different policies for the same incident.

In the second category, crimes in furtherance of business or occupation, the actor, as an agent for the business, or within his occupation, may be seeking to increase the company's profits or prestige, or he may be trying to salvage a failing business. The business or occupation itself is a legitimate and legal enterprise, but certain acts by the individual, incidental to the operation of the business, are criminal. These acts may adversely affect an individual, another business, or a governmental agency.

Officers of banks and savings and loan institutions have endangered their depositors' funds because of violations of banking regulations, lending money on fictitious or overvalued collateral; a situation witnessed by the devastating corruption of the savings and loan industry that appeared in the late 1980s.[23] Insurance agents write phony policies to make quotas, or to sell the phony policies to other companies. People in positions of trust, such as bank officers, public officials, attorneys, and executors of estates, embezzle funds to which they have access only because of their positions. The former president of the Philippines, Ferdinand Marcos, was indicted in a U.S. federal court for racketeering under allegations he used $123 million embezzled from the Philippine government to purchase real estate in New York.[24] Marcos died before the case could come to trial.

Brokerage firms have attempted to manipulate various stocks or to profit from collusion and insider trading. In 1988, the securities firm of Drexel Burnham Lambert Inc. pled guilty to six criminal charges, which included insider trading and manipulation, and paid $650 million in penalties.[25] Ivan Boesky profited millions of dollars by insider trading on Wall Street in the mid 1980s.[26]

To increase profits or prestige, company officials bribe government employees or pay kickbacks to other company officials to obtain contracts or preferential treatment. Operation Ill Wind, a joint investigative effort of the Federal Bureau of Investigation and the Naval Investigative Service, resulted in several indictments in 1988 alleging kickbacks and bribery regarding the administration of purchasing contracts for the U.S. military.[27] Company directors collude on prices or competitive bidding violating antitrust legislation. Public officials vote or rule in favor of a company or firm in which they have some financial interest, by that violating conflict of interest laws.

Business owners attempt to save money by filing falsified employment and sales tax reports, or by evading taxes entirely. A businessman looking to secure a line of credit files a false financial statement with his bank. Some businessmen seek to increase profits by deceptive business practices such as false weights and measures, or selling adulterated or mislabeled products. In 1988, a federal jury convicted Niels L. Hoyvald and John F. Lavery, the former president and vice-president, respectively, of Beech-Nut Nutrition Corporation, on criminal charges of selling adulterated apple juice.[28] Some business managers resort to unfair labor practices to reduce operating costs. Countless dollars are lost each year to commercial espionage or copyright infringements.

To save money in costly waste disposal, industry officials seek ways to avoid complying with federal and state regulations detailing the manner in which they must dispose of hazardous, toxic, and nuclear wastes. Health and safety regulations designed to protect the worker in the workplace are also expensive. Company officials seek to bypass the regulations to increase profit margins.

In the third category, crimes as a business, the actor corrupts a business enterprise. He takes a legal and legitimate business, and uses it to defraud his victims. These businesses are not inherently illegal. Only the evil intent of the individual makes these enterprises illegal. The actor has no intention of behaving as an honest businessman. These acts most often affect individuals, although they may damage other businesses or institutions.

This category includes many acts. "Miracle cures," psychic surgery, and similar medical frauds not only defraud victims of money, but pose serious threats to the public health and safety. The fixing of public contests spurs interest and increases sales in a product or service, but the organizer never awards a prize. Advance fee schemes cause victims to pay for services or products they will never receive.

Financial advisory businesses front for securities fraud rings. Realty offices cover for real estate schemes. Third party leasing brokers defraud unsuspecting victims, promising titles they cannot deliver.

Nonprofit charitable organizations accept donations only to fill the pockets of their organizers. Mail order diploma firms and correspondence schools swindle victims anxious to improve their lot in society.

Companies promising to publish novels, poems, or songs take advantage of people who believe their work is worthy of publication. The writer finds he has paid an exorbitant fee to have his work printed in a worthless periodical or book. Employment agencies promise high paying jobs to applicants who, after paying a fee to the agency, discover the jobs never existed.

Corporate raiders take over businesses, sell the company assets, convert the money to some alternate use, then drive the company into insolvency. Ponzi schemes attract investors into a variation of a pyramid scheme that must ultimately collapse. Mail order and phone solicitation schemes swindle many people over a wide geographical area without risking a face-to-face confrontation with a victim.

Some acts directly affect others individually. Confidence games aimed at swindling victims into investing in nonexistent or shell businesses, or pyramids devised to defraud others in "get rich quickly" schemes are examples of such crimes.

The examples above are hardly a comprehensive listing of white-collar criminal activity, but they do show how broad the study of white-collar crime can be. Recent history proves the diversity of motives involved with white-collar crime. A Texas jury found Rocky J. Mountain and his political consulting firm, Southern Political Consulting, guilty of forgery, falsifying signatures on petitions for the Texas presidential primary elections in 1988.[29] A federal jury convicted ex-presidential aid Lyn Nofzinger on charges of influence peddling.[30]

White-collar crime is, of course, not limited to the United States. In 1988, Lucio Gelli, an Italian financier, was extradited from Switzerland to Italy to face charges relating to his alleged role in the collapse of Banco Ambrosiano, the largest private bank in Italy. Legal controversies arose about whether a Vatican Archbishop and two other Vatican Bank officials should be required to face charges also.[31] Yury M. Charbanov, the son-in-law of the late Soviet Premier Leonid Breshnev, and eight other officials faced charges of accepting more than $1.3 million in gifts and bribes to protect corrupt police officials in the former Soviet Union.[32] Swiss authorities arrested two suspected computer hackers for the unauthorized electronic transfer of about £15 million in Eurobonds from a Japanese investment bank in London.[33]

These examples serve to emphasize the phenomenal financial, economic, political, and social implications of white-collar criminal activity. The confusion about the white-collar crime concept is an expected byproduct of an evolving and complex society. Many specialized statutes define criminal acts and restrict or prohibit activities. These statutes are constantly changing because of various social, economic, and legal pressures.

Enforcement of White-Collar Crime

Despite some progress and success in recent years investigating and prosecuting white-collar criminal offenses, large segments of the population still view the police as agents for the status quo. "Through both the nature of the law and its differential patterns of enforcement, the interests of the more powerful segments of the community are supported more actively by the police than are the interests of the less powerful."[34] This perceived class bias, noted a century ago by Thibauld and still true today, helped create an adversarial relationship between the police and groups of the socially and economically disadvantaged.

"Wealthy people's criminality includes fraud, embezzlement, income tax cheating, and the like, crimes costing vast sums but not likely to be monitored by local police. The police concentrate on poor people's crimes, a selective bias that points to a basic contradiction in the nature of law enforcement in our society.

A similar point can be made about crimes against the person. The police deal with the important crimes of rape, homicide, and aggravated assault. Few would argue they should not. But the police infrequently deal with white collar, illegal behaviors that cause even more death and illness than the preceding crimes, such as illegal safety violations in the workplace, or air and water pollution. The result is that overall, the police deal with illegal behavior of the poor much more than they deal with the illegal behavior of the wealthy."[35]

Such a view may seem cynical. The public expects the local police to deal with emergency response calls and so called "street crimes." In recent years, economic factors have constrained municipal, county, and state budgets. The public appears unable, even unwilling, to bear the proportionate increase in taxes necessary to fund the work force and incidental expenses required to deal effectively with such violations. Additionally, in many jurisdictions, such violations are subject only to administrative actions or civil fines. Nevertheless, the point that a segment of society believes that the police apply their power inequitably is not lost on the observant police administrator or investigator.

Such inequalities in enforcement increase tension in social and economic class struggles. These disparities reinforce the negative attitudes about law enforcement prevalent in lower socioeconomic classes and racial minority groups. The disadvantaged lose faith in the laws, and in the ability of the police to enforce those laws fairly and impartially. The simplest and most effective means of combating these inequalities and inherent social discontent are an honest and open effort by law enforcement authorities adequately to investigate and prosecute white-collar criminal activity.

Notes

[1]Sue Titus Reid, *Crime and Criminology, Third Edition* (New York: Holt, Rinehart & Winston, 1982), p. 230.

[2]Edwin H. Sutherland, *White Collar Crime: The Uncut Version* (New Haven, CT: Yale University Press, 1983), p. 7.

[3]Ibid., p. 9.

[4]Ibid.

[5]Reid, op cit.

[6]Ibid., pp. 230–231.

[7]Edwin H. Sutherland, *White Collar Crime* (New York: Holt, Rinehart & Winston, 1959), p. 31.

[8]Reid, op cit., p. 16.

[9]Charles H. McCaghy, *Deviant Behavior: Crime, Conflict, and Interest Groups* (New York: MacMillan Publishing Co., Inc., 1976), pp. 173–174.

[10]Ibid.

[11]Walter C. Reckless, *The Crime Problem, Fourth Edition* (New York: Merideth

Publishing, 1967), p. 358, quoting Gilbert Geiss, *Sociological Inquiry,* Volume XXXII, Number 2 (Spring, 1962), p. 162.

[12]Ibid.

[13]Don C. Gibbons, *Society, Crime, and Criminal Careers: An Introduction to Criminology, Third Edition* (Englewood Cliffs, NJ: Prentice Hall, 1977), p. 322.

[14]Reid, op cit., p. 231.

[15]Marshall B. Clinard and Richard Quinney, eds., *Criminal Behavior Systems: A Typology* (New York: Holt, Rinehart & Winston, 1967), p. 131.

[16]August Bequai, "Wanted; The White-Collar Ring," *Student Lawyer,* No. 5 (May 1977), p. 45.

[17]42 United States Code § 3701, et seq.

[18]Richard D. Knudten, *Crime in a Complex Society; An Introduction to Criminology* (Homewood, IL: The Dorsey Press, 1970), pp. 218, 219.

[19]Ibid., p. 56.

[20]Ibid.

[21]Maynard Parker, ed., "At Last, a Verdict Fit for a Queen," *Newsweek,* Vol. CXIV, No. 11 (September 11, 1988), p. 61.

[22]Brian Dumaine, "Beating Bolder Corporate Crooks," *Fortune,* Vol. 117, No. 9 (April 25, 1988), p. 193.

[23]Ashby Bladen, "The Texas S&L Massacre," *Forbes,* Vol. 141, No. 6 (March 21, 1988), p. 199.

[24]John Bierman, "A dictator on trial," *Macleans,* Vol. 101, No. 45 (October 31, 1988), P. 31.

[25]Pamela Sherrid, "The deal Drexel could not resist," *U.S. News and World Report,* Vol. 106, No. 1 (January 1, 1989), p. 46.

[26]Patrick E. Cole, "Tennis Anyone? Ivan Boesky Does Time," *Business Week,* No. 3049 (April 25, 1988), p. 70.

[27]William Lawther, "Scandal in the Pentagon," *Macleans,* Vol. 101, No. 27 (June 27, 1988), p. 25.

[28]Duncan Chappell, "Crime, Law Enforcement, and Penology," *1988 Britannica Book of the Year* (Chicago: Encyclopedia Britannica Inc., 1989), p. 146.

[29]Fred Bonavita, "Political consultant fined $7,600, gets probation for petition forgery," *The Houston Post,* June 24, 1988, B15.

[30]Michael Kinsley, ed., "Nofzinger's Complaint," *The New Republic,* Vol. 198, No. 10 (March 7, 1988), p. 8.

[31]James M. Wall, ed., "Vatican Challenge," *The Christian Century,* Vol. 105, No. 1 (January 6, 1988), p. 9.

[32]Andrew Bilinski, "A Former Era on Trial," *Macleans,* Vol. 101, No. 39 (September 19, 1988), p. 18.

[33]Chappell, op cit.

[34]Louis Radelet, *The Police and the Community, Fourth Edition* (New York: MacMillan Publishing Co., Inc., 1986), p. 129.

[35]Ibid.

Chapter 2

EMBEZZLEMENT

Now as through this world I ramble,
I see lots of funny men,
Some will rob you with a six gun,
And some with a fountain pen.

Woody Guthrie
"Pretty Boy Floyd"

Law enforcement officials are beginning to realize the severe economic and social implications of white-collar criminal activity. The pen has proven to be a mighty weapon in the hands of the criminal element. According to San Francisco Assistant District Attorney John Carbone, who heads that office's special prosecution unit, the annual cost of white-collar crime exceeds $200 billion nationally, a total more costly than nearly all other crime combined.[1] Statistics from the Federal Bureau of Investigation reveal that the typical bank robber steals approximately $3,000 in a given robbery, and stands about a 61 percent chance of apprehension. On the other hand, the average embezzler steals approximately $42,000, and stands a slim chance of apprehension and prosecution.[2]

Embezzlement is a serious and growing economic problem. One major bonding company, United States Guaranty Company, estimates that 30 percent of all business bankruptcies are attributable to employee dishonesty.[3] In 1982, embezzlement and fraud charges accounted for between 25 and 30 percent of the total criminal case load in such federal district court jurisdictions as New York City, Chicago, Philadelphia, and Los Angeles, according to statistics of the Administrative Office of the Court.[4] It also appears that embezzlement is increasing by approximately 15 percent per year.[5] The estimated loss to embezzlement is more than $4 billion annually.[6]

Embezzlement permeates every level of business and industry from labor unions, to multinational corporations, to the Girl Scouts of America. Yet, although the Federal District Court caseload is burdened with

18

embezzlement and fraud cases, the potential for financial loss is enormous, and the economic consequences are staggering, the rate of arrests for embezzlement (the number of arrests for embezzlement per 100,000 inhabitants) is incredibly small. According to Federal Bureau of Investigation uniform crime reporting statistics, embezzlement has the lowest arrest rate of any category of crime, including murder and arson.[7] Table 2 is a synopsis of the 1992 Federal Bureau of Investigation reported arrests statistics.

Arrests for embezzlement are rare for many reasons. Embezzlements are usually difficult to detect and even more difficult to prove. Street criminals know the victim will soon discover the crime. The criminal's best chance to avoid capture is to protect his identity. In embezzlement, the opposite is true. The crime is such that the perpetrator need not conceal his identity. He must, however, conceal both the evidence and the effect of the crime. A well-designed scheme may succeed for years before the victim ultimately discovers it. When the victim does uncover embezzlement, he often chooses not to report it to law enforcement authorities. Consequently, law enforcement officials investigate less than 60 percent of all embezzlements and frauds.[9] For many reasons, such as the victims' fear of publicity and loyalty to straying employees, only about 1 percent of all trust violations result in criminal prosecution.[10] Even when the authorities investigate a victim's report of embezzlement, insufficient evidence may prevent the investigator from filing a criminal complaint or obtaining an indictment. Records and information may be incomplete, missing, or inconclusive. Witnesses and victims may be unwilling to continue with criminal prosecution.

Defining Embezzlement

Uniform crime reporting statistics differentiate between larceny/theft and embezzlement, because embezzlement has specific elements not common to larceny or theft. The offenses are quite different.

English common law developed a flaw in defining larceny. The law did not consider it larceny for a person, to whom another had entrusted money or property, to convert the goods to his own use before the goods reached the possession of the intended owner. To correct this defect, the English Parliament passed a statute in 1799 creating the crime of embezzlement.

"Obtaining possession of property by fraud, trick, or device with

Table 2. Crime in the United States.

Offense Charged (1992)	U.S. Total 10,962 agencies reporting Population 213,392,000
Total	11,877,802
Rate	5,566.2
Murder and non-negligent manslaughter	19,491
Rate	9.1
Forcible Rape	33,385
Rate	15.6
Robbery	153,456
Rate	71.9
Aggravated assault	434,918
Rate	203.8
Burglary	359,699
Rate	168.6
Larceny—theft	1,291,984
Rate	605.5
Motor vehicle theft	171,269
Rate	80.3
Arson	16,322
Rate	7.6
Other assaults	912,517
Rate	427.6
Forgery and counterfeiting	88,649
Rate	41.5
Fraud	346,314
Rate	162.3
Embezzlement	11,707
Rate	5.5
Stolen property; buying, receiving, possessing	136,765
Rate	64.1
Vandalism	262,477
Rate	123.0
Weapons; carrying, possessing	204,116
Rate	95.7
Prostitution and commercialized vice	86,988
Rate	40.8
Sex offenses (except forcible rape)	91,560
Rate	42.9
Drug abuse violations	920,424
Rate	431.3
Gambling	15,029
Rate	7.0
Offenses against family and children	84,328
Rate	39.5

Table 2. (Continued)

Driving under the influence	1,319,583
Rate	618.4
Liquor laws	442,985
Rate	207.6
Drunkenness	664,236
Rate	311.3
Disorderly conduct	605,367
Rate	283.7
Vagrancy	29,004
Rate	13.6
All other offenses (except traffic)	2,954,440
Rate	1,384.5
Suspicion (not included in totals)	15,351
Rate	7.2
Curfew and loitering violations	74,619
Rate	35.0
Runaways	146,170
Rate	68.5[8]

preconceived design or intent to appropriate, convert, or steal is larceny."[11] In larceny, the actor takes possession of property without the owner's knowledge or effective consent. An element of trespass is present in the act. The owner or possessor of the property has not granted to the taker any right of possession or ownership.

Theft and larceny are roughly synonymous. Theft is "the fraudulent taking of corporeal personal property belonging to another, from his possession, or from the possession of some person holding the same for him, without his consent, with the intent to deprive the owner of the value of the same, and to appropriate it to the use or benefit of the person taking."[12]

Larceny and theft imply that no special relationship exists between the owner of the property and the taker. Theft, however, is a broader term than larceny. Theft includes larceny, swindling and embezzlement.[13] Anyone who obtains possession of property by lawful means, but afterwards appropriates the property to the taker's own use is guilty of theft.[14] The courts have found, however, a distinction between theft and embezzlement. In theft, title to the property taken never passed. In embezzlement, title to the property taken did pass.[15]

In theft, the taker is acting knowingly and with larcenous intent at the time he comes into possession of the property in question. "(L)arcenous intent exists where a man knowingly takes and carries away the goods of another without any claim or pretense of right, with intent wholly to deprive the owner of them or convert them to his own use."[16]

In embezzlement, however, the actor first comes into possession of the property with the permission of the owner. Embezzlement is "the fraudulent appropriation to his own use or benefit of property or money intrusted to him by another, by a clerk, agent, trustee, public officer, or other person acting in a fiduciary character,"[17] or "the fraudulent appropriation of property by a person to whom it has been entrusted, or to whose hands it has lawfully come."[18] "It is common-law larceny extended by statute to cover cases where the stolen property comes originally into the possession of the defendant without a trespass."[19]

"Embezzlement is a species of larceny, and the term is applicable to cases of furtive and fraudulent appropriation by clerks, servants, or carriers of property coming into their possession by virtue of their employment. It is distinguished from 'larceny' properly so called, as being committed in respect of property which is not at the time in the actual or legal possession of the owner. That is to say, that in embezzlement the original taking of the property was lawful or with the consent of the owner, while in larceny the felonious intent must have existed at the time of the taking."[20]

"Both words, however, may be used, as in a bond, as generic terms to indicate the dishonest and fraudulent breach of any duty or obligation upon the part of an employee to pay over to his employer, or account to him for any money, securities, or other personal property, title to which is in the employer, but which may come into the possession of the employee."[21] "Under statute declaring guilty of a felony an officer or clerk of a state bank who 'embezzles, abstracts, or willfully misapplies' its funds, 'embezzle' refers to acts done for benefit of the actor as against the bank, 'misapply' covers acts having no relation to pecuniary profit or advantage to the doer, while 'abstract' means only to take and withdraw from the possession and control of the bank; and while 'embezzlement' may include the offenses of abstraction and willful misapplication, either of these offenses may be committed without embezzlement."[22]

Note that the courts apply different standards of proof as to the intent of the actor. For theft, the requirement is for proof of larcenous intent at the time the actor takes the property. For embezzlement, the courts do not require proof of larcenous intent at the time the property is originally transferred. The courts do require proof of intent when the actor converts the property to his own use. The distinction is vital.

Under statutes defining embezzlement, the following elements are present:

1) the fraudulent appropriation or conversion,
2) of personal or corporeal property of another,
3) by a person who came into lawful possession of the property by virtue of a relationship of trust and confidence,
4) with the intent feloniously to convert or use the property inconsistently with the nature of the possession.[23]

Problems in Investigating Embezzlement

A definite relationship between the owner of the property and the taker exists in embezzlement. The owner usually knows the taker personally, and the owner has granted the right of possession to, but not ownership of, the property to the taker. It is this grant of possession that makes embezzlement possible, and, consequently, makes it difficult to detect and to prove. This relationship also allows for defenses to prosecution.

An additional difficulty in investigating embezzlement is the hesitancy of many victims. When a victim discovers embezzlement, he has a natural reluctance to believe that such a thing could happen, or that the suspect could have done such a thing. The actor is often a friend or trusted employee, and the victim may feel a reluctance to report the loss to law enforcement officials. The victim may feel guilty about getting the suspect in trouble with the law. Additionally, the victim may fear he is mistaken and may unjustly accuse a friend or trusted employee.

The victim's initial disbelief that a person is an embezzler is understandable. People who rise to a position of financial responsibility are not usually classical criminal types. They have not been delinquent as juveniles, and they usually have no criminal record as adults. They are generally better educated than the ordinary street criminal, and they are often respected members of their communities.[24] They are often long-term employees who are active in company and civic events.

It often takes many years of hard work before an employee achieves the levels of success and trust to go undetected while stealing on a daily basis. He may start as one of several bookkeepers in an office. After he has proven he is capable in that position, he earns a promotion to a position where his work is more independent of others and subject to less supervision. After a few more years of dedicated work, he obtains a position where his work is subject to little scrutiny by his supervisors. He may become a vice-president in charge of finance, the comptroller, or the chief accountant. It is because he has given the company many years of faithful service that he holds such a position of trust. Once he has attained that trust, his work is virtually free from verification. No one checks his work regularly. By the time the employee reaches this position, his superiors usually have neither the time nor the expertise to check the accuracy of his work. He is now responsible for checking the accuracy of other employees in his charge. When questioned how embezzlement could succeed undetected for a long period, victims invariably explain, "I trusted him."

Victims of robbery or burglary are seldom hesitant to contact law enforcement authorities, because they were victims of strangers. The victim feels no allegiance to or sympathy for the suspect. In embezzlement, this is not so. The victim usually knows the suspect. They have often met not only on the job, but in social situations. With a personal interest in the suspect, the victim often does not want to feel as though he got the suspect in trouble by calling the police.

Embezzlers

Embezzlers, as noted above, are not average criminal types. They are usually well educated, and at least moderately successful. The question arises about why such people would turn to crime. Donald R. Cressey did the first study on the social psychology of embezzlers. He concluded that a trusted employee becomes an embezzler when he meets three conditions:

1) he develops a financial problem that he believes he cannot share with anyone,
2) he becomes aware that he can resolve the problem secretly by violating the financial trust reposed in him, and
3) he can adjust his self-conception to rationalize his use of the funds or property.[25]

The nonshareable financial problem refers to difficulties the individual feels he must keep secret, because he is ashamed of the underlying problems, or because he cannot adjust to some inadequacy. The embezzler will realize, while pondering solutions to his financial dilemma, that he can use funds entrusted to him, and no one will know. Finally, the embezzler employs what Cressey calls "vocabularies of adjustment" to rationalize the use of the funds.[26] The embezzler excuses his actions by reasoning that he is not stealing funds. He rationalizes that he is borrowing funds, and that he will repay them in better times, or that the victim owes him the money anyway because of any number of perceived wrongs.

Gwynn Nettler, however, in a study of six large scale embezzlers in Canada, found that a meeting of desire and opportunity was more often the motivation for an employee to embezzle that was Cressey's unshared financial problem.[27]

The two positions are reconcilable. Either way, the embezzler first seeks to satisfy some need. Need is primarily of two kinds:

1) financial need, where the employee must have the money to satisfy an immediate and real responsibility, such as paying an overdue mortgage or medical expenses, or
2) manufactured need, where the employee first convinces himself that the money is necessary to satisfy a presumed need, such as the purchase of a new car or jewelry, to satisfy his greed, or to obtain revenge against an unrepentant employer.

Any number of factors can influence a trusted employee to embezzle from his employer: alcoholism, drug abuse, gambling debts, extravagant living standards beyond his means, catastrophic illness in the family, death of a spouse, divorce, greed, or vengeance for some perceived wrong.

When he meets one or more of the above conditions, the employee comes to the rationalization that he can obtain the money he needs if he violates a trust. He then finds a way to rationalize his predicament by convincing himself that he is not stealing, that he is merely "borrowing" or "using" the money for a short time. By doing this, he convinces himself that he is not a criminal. He is convinced that no one would understand his problems, so he refuses to seek help from his family or friends. Even if he feels that they could help him, he is too ashamed to admit that he cannot handle his own finances. The employee convinces himself that he will repay the money somehow, once he resolves his problems.

An employee seeking revenge or vengeance convinces himself that the company should be paying him more money. He may also believe that he must punish a superior, or the company, as redress for some injury. In this way, the employee convinces himself that he is not committing a crime, but is exacting justice on a tyrant.

Next, the employee must devise a plan to take the money and hide that fact in the bookkeeping. He has many ways to do this: by destroying documents, altering documents, changing numbers on receipts or ledgers, debiting expense accounts, or fabricating an entire set of fictitious ledgers. By then the employee is well trained in the accounting procedures of the company, and he knows the flaws in the system. He can devise a plan to abstract funds, but not arouse suspicions.

Once the employee has devised the plan, he will ponder the situation, weighing the potential rewards against the risks, until he develops the nerve to test his plan. Several factors may compel the employee to try out his plan:

1) extreme pressure from creditors,
2) fear of bankruptcy,
3) anxiety and the feeling that he has nothing to lose, or
4) any combination of disappointments at work or at home that act as the proverbial "last straw."

Embezzlers often carefully plan and rehearse their schemes. Embezzlements usually start in small amounts. The employee takes a small amount of money, alters the books or ledgers to disguise the theft, then waits to see if anyone discovers it. If someone does notice the discrepancies, it is a simple matter to explain a small bookkeeping error. The embezzler may repeat the experiment, in small amounts, once each week or month. If no one discovers the theft, the way is open for larger and more frequent thefts along the same format. After the employee has tried a few experiments and is assured that no one will detect his plan, he can begin to embezzle funds at whatever rate he deems necessary.

It may take years for an employee in a trusted position to discover the loopholes through which he can hide his activities. Even when he discovers the flaws in the accounting system, it may take some time before he develops the need or the fortitude to carry forth his plans. Consequently, an employee will begin to embezzle only when he develops:

1) a trusting relationship with his employer or beneficiary,
2) a perceived need, either financial or manufactured,

3) an awareness of a solution for that need which involves the use of entrusted funds,

4) a rationalized adjustment of his self-conception,

5) a plan designed to conceal the theft in the bookkeeping or accounting,

6) the fortitude or desperation to put the plan into effect, and

7) a test to learn whether the plan can succeed.

If he devised the plan well, is careful in its operation, and does not bring excess suspicion on himself by a sudden change in his lifestyle or spending habits, the embezzlement may succeed for years.

Elements of an Embezzlement

When an investigator receives a report of embezzlement, he must carefully examine all aspects of the allegation and of the relationship between the parties involved. The business and personal relationships between the victims and the suspects become either an element of the offense or proof that no criminal offense has occurred. In what manner and at what time the actor takes possession of the property may be more important than the mere fact that he took the property. What actions the victim takes after discovering an offense are also important and pertinent to the investigation of embezzlement.

Many states have consolidated theft offenses, incorporating shoplifting, theft by false pretext, theft by appropriation, conversion by bailee, and embezzlement into general theft statutes.[28] This has simplified prosecution by eliminating the necessity of categorizing offenses, then presenting those cases within a rigid technical framework. Courts often overturned convictions upon appeal for purely technical reasons, such as whether a case was more properly, for example, a theft by false pretext rather than a conversion by bailee. Perhaps no other area of law has seen more cases overturned on grounds unrelated to guilt or innocence.

The consolidation of theft offenses may have eliminated the technical distinctions in theft statutes and, consequently, some associated prosecutorial difficulties, but the basic elements of proof have not changed. Common law and case law dictate what evidence is necessary to prove each type of theft offense. While embezzlement may no longer be a separate and distinct criminal offense, the elements necessary to prove the offense still exist.

As in any criminal offense, the questions of motive, means, and opportunity are paramount. In any theft offense the motive is, superficially at least, obvious—financial or economic gain. Motive may go deeper, however, to include revenge or vengeance. Surprisingly, many embezzlements are not committed for the economic benefit of the embezzler.[29] An investigator must pay attention not only to suspects in financial distress, but also to those who harbor some animosity toward a company official or toward the company itself.

To prove means, the investigator must show that the offender has the knowledge to manipulate the records and abstract the property. The suspect must have either training or education in the bookkeeping and accounting procedures to disguise the theft in the company records.

To prove opportunity, the investigator must show that the offender had access to the property, could physically or electronically remove it, and avoid detection. Simultaneously, the offender must have access to the business records, and he must alter or falsify records without detection.

Additionally, to prosecute embezzlement successfully, the investigator must prove the following elements:

1) a person
2) fraudulently appropriates,
3) to his own use or benefit,
4) money or property
5) entrusted to him by another
6) without the effective consent of the owner.[30]

A Person

In most businesses, employees who handle money have no responsibility for maintaining the company records and vice versa. This is a cardinal rule in securing company funds and preventing thefts. At some point in the system, however, these functions may meet in one person. That person becomes responsible for the money and the accounting for it. It is at this point that means meets opportunity in one person. Consequently, this person is the most likely candidate to be a successful embezzler.

To be an embezzler, the employee need not handle cash. Any employee responsible for writing disbursement, payroll, or expense checks has the same opportunity to embezzle funds as has any employee who handles cash. Any employee who is responsible for writing checks and posting ledger entries is also a likely candidate to be a successful embezzler.

By examining the remaining elements of embezzlement, the investigator can gather the evidence and facts to expose the suspect. In any embezzlement, the paper trail is vitally important. The investigator should watch for discrepancies and alterations in the bookkeeping and ledgers. He should watch for missing receipts, checks, or documents. Verifying when the changes occurred, entries in ledgers were falsified, or when documents disappeared will narrow the list of suspects to those people, or that one person, responsible for the records at that point in the accounting process. That person, responsible for the paperwork, becomes the primary suspect.

As in any criminal offense, the charge must specifically and properly identify the accused. Narrowing a field of suspects to a few individuals, then filing complaints on one or any combination of suspects without producing evidence of that individual's culpability and responsibility, is never permissible.

Fortunately, in cases of embezzlement, the victims usually know the suspects. If a personal relationship exists between a victim and suspect, the victim may give the investigator the suspect's name, race, sex, address, and date of birth. In an internal theft from a large company, the company records often contain job applications or insurance forms that will provide most of the necessary identification information. Other employees may provide information lacking in the company's records. If the suspect is a licensed professional, such as a lawyer or accountant, then licensing authorities such as the State Bar or Board of Accountants may provide identification information.

When obtaining personal identification information on suspects, the investigator should always obtain the full name, including the maiden name of a married woman suspect, nicknames, race, sex, date of birth, social security number, drivers' license number, and physical description including height, weight, hair color, and eye color. All these identifiers are necessary to enter suspect information into the National Crime Information Center (NCIC) if a judge issues a warrant or a grand jury returns an indictment for a criminal offense.

Fraudulently Appropriates

The investigator must prove that the suspect maintains possession of money or other property to which he is not entitled, and to which he has no pretense of right. Appropriate means "to make a thing one's own; to make a thing the subject of property; to exercise dominion over an object to the extent, and for the purpose, of making it subserve one's own proper use or pleasure."[31]

Fraudulent includes "all acts, omissions, and concealments involving a breach of a legal or equitable duty and resulting in damage to another."[32] "It consists of some deceitful practice or willful device, resorted to with intent to deprive another of his right, or in some manner to do him an injury. As distinguished from negligence, it is always positive, intentional."[33] Thus, proving only that a person is responsible for missing money or property is not sufficient for criminal prosecution. The investigator must prove the actor maintains possession by some deceitful act or acts intentionally and specifically undertaken to deprive the owner of his rightful possession of the property.

The actor may take possession by physically removing the property, electronically transferring money, or altering documentation to show an alleged transfer of title in some property. The investigator needs to prove that the actor maintained possession of the property contrary to an agreement under which the actor held the property, or grossly inconsistent with commonly accepted business procedures.

If the property is held under an agreement, the investigator must establish the terms of the agreement. If the agreement is a written contract or court order, the investigator must obtain a copy of the agreement or court order and study it carefully. Once the investigator has determined exactly how the actor took the property or money, the question arises whether the taking is a criminal act or merely a breach of contractual obligation. Generally, if the suspect is acting strictly as a bailee, having possession of the property by bailment, then the fraudulent appropriation of the property may be a criminal act. Bailment "imports a delivery of personal property by one person to another in trust for a specific purpose, with a contract, expressed or implied, that the trust shall be faithfully executed and the property returned or duly accounted for when the specific purpose is accomplished or kept until bailor claims it."[34] If, however, the agreement is an oral understanding, validating the victim's claims about the terms of the agreement is necessary. The investigator must find witnesses to prove the victim's claims. Without verification, the entire case may disintegrate into a "my word against yours" dispute, preventing successful prosecution.

Often the taking of property is not violating any specific agreement, but runs contrary to established business procedures, such as embezzlement by an accountant, company official, or bank officer. It is a generally accepted and understood principle that employees of a business have no right to dispose of property or to remove it without authorization from corporate officials or the owners of the business.

It is not sufficient for prosecution, however, to show only that property in the possession of an individual is missing. The investigator must show fraudulent intent. Seldom during an embezzlement investigation will the investigator find direct evidence of fraudulent intent. Witnesses will seldom claim to see the suspect committing overt criminal acts or converting property to his own use. The key to proving the fraudulent intent lies in the paper trail of business records, contracts, and other documents.

Proof of fraudulent appropriation may be in evidence of cash shortages between ledger entries and bank deposits made by the same suspect. Such evidence is sufficient to support a conviction for theft.[35] The courts have held that evidence of several discrepancies between bank deposits and cash received into a cash register, which was operated by the same employee who prepared most of the deposit slips and made the deposits, is sufficient proof of fraudulent appropriation.[36] Also, the courts have held that evidence in an acknowledgment made by a suspect that he falsified payroll vouchers to cover what he believed to be a cash shortage, and that he held back or discarded sales tickets where there was not enough money to cover such sales, is sufficient to establish a fraudulent intent in prosecutions for embezzlement.[37]

The investigator must look for discrepancies in the bookkeeping, ledgers, deposit slips, and vouchers. He must attribute these discrepancies to one suspect. The discrepancies must be of sufficient number and degree to establish the suspect knew, or obviously should have known, that the entries were fraudulent and were not merely the products of mistake or negligence. The investigator must also stand prepared to prove that the actor did not merely misplace records or documents, but that he destroyed or removed them with deliberate design.

To One's Own Use or Benefit

Perhaps the most difficult element of proof in embezzlement is conversion. Even when the investigator can properly prove that a suspect is directly responsible for the loss of money or property, it remains to show he converted it for his own use or benefit. Even proof that an accused suspect did not return property, possession of which he had obtained by bailment, is not sufficient to show a conversion.[38] Additional evidence beyond the suspect's possession of missing money or property must exist.

Seldom will an investigator find direct evidence of a conversion. In a prosecution for embezzlement, however, the prosecutor may prove conversion by circumstantial evidence. Concealment and denials, coupled with the failure of a defendant to properly account for property held in trust may be sufficient to support a conviction for embezzlement.[39] Evidence of conversion may be in a suspect's bank records where deposits far exceed his expected or anticipated income. However, as long as a person entrusted with money or property of another acts according to the terms of the trust, he is not guilty of embezzlement. He could deposit money in the bank in his own name and account without being guilty of appropriating it. However, a withdrawal by him for purposes of his own could constitute appropriation.[40] Those same bank records may show for what purposes he expended those funds. Evidence may also appear as a sudden change in a suspect's lifestyle, or as an extraordinary increase in spending far beyond the suspect's means on his income.

Probably the most obvious evidence of embezzlement on a large scale is a significant and unexplained increase in net worth, such as a new home, new cars, jewelry, and clothes. Evidence of unexplained wealth is admissible in some prosecutions for embezzlement.[41] It may even be permissible for a prosecutor to cross examine a defendant on an unexplained increase in net worth.[42]

It is imperative to show that the suspect is not only responsible for the loss of the money or property, but that he applied it to his own benefit, did not return it to the rightful owner, or apply it to another cause that directly benefitted the owner of the property.

If the property embezzled is other than money, the investigator must locate or track the property and discover its ultimate disposition. The actor may have sold the property and returned the proceeds to the owner. Even if the actor sold the property without the owner's knowledge or consent, if the actor tenders the proceeds to the owner, no embezzlement may have occurred. The actor may have embezzled property, however, if he secrets it from the rightful owner, has it in his possession, it provides him some use, and he is maintaining it contrary to the agreement under which it came into his possession. Once the prosecutor can show the misappropriation, claims by the accused of an intent to repay the funds may not be a defense.[43]

Money or Property

Commonly, embezzlers take money. This is not always the case, however. An embezzler can also steal securities, cars, jewelry, or other corporeal property. Nevertheless, the problems facing the investigator remain the same; prove the existence of the property, track the property to its ultimate destination and disposition, and prove the value of the property.

If the property in question is other than money, identifying the property specifically is necessary. Stocks, bonds and securities are normally on certificates bearing serial numbers. The investigator can identify these instruments by the name of the issuing authority and the serial numbers. Such documents generally are worth their nominal value, although market values may fluctuate. Cars have vehicle identification numbers or VIN's, and there are publications in use by automobile dealers and insurance companies that set the market values for cars. A gemologist can appraise jewelry to identify it specifically and establish its fair market value. For all property, state and federal laws set rules for establishing the value, then defining levels of offenses and punishment accordingly. Various statutes even designate a degree of offense when the courts cannot deduce a value for the property.

Obviously, the value of money is the face value of the money. It is much more difficult, however, to distinguish specifically one individual's money from another's. It is true that bills issued by the Treasury Department of the United States Government all have unique serial numbers. Except for some bait money, however, few people keep track of the serial numbers on their money. Accounting, bookkeeping, banking, and business records, however, do document the flow of cash funds and the diversion of those funds from the normal course of business.

Embezzlement is rarely a single incident. Most often, the course of the embezzlement involves several occurrences of appropriation over a long period. In most states, the criminal law allows the aggregation of the amounts taken. Aggregation allows the court to consider one charge that includes the total appropriated. The test the courts apply in such cases is whether the entire taking was governed by a single intent and a general illegal design.[44] Such factors as common ownership of the stolen property, similarity of the property, and the proximity of the time and place of the various incidences of theft may properly show the existence of such a scheme or continuing course of conduct.[45]

Entrusted to Him by Another:

The trust between the suspected embezzler and the victim is important. It is this trust that enables the embezzler to gain possession of the property, and it is this trust that allows him to convert it to his own use undetected by the victim. It is, therefore, essential particularly to describe that trust, the conditions and limitations set on that trust, and by what exact means the actor violated that trust. Where there is no trust relationship, no embezzlement exists.[46]

A person holding the character of a trustee, or a character analogous to that of a trustee, in respect to the trust and confidence involved in it and the scrupulous good faith and candor it requires, is a fiduciary.[47] The term fiduciary, moreover, is not limited to technical or express trusts, but includes such offices or relationships as an attorney, a guardian, an executor, a broker, a director of a public corporation, or a public officer.[48]

Often there are contracts between business associates. These contracts describe the conditions of the business relationship, detailing how and for what purposes the parties may use or disburse money or goods. In such cases, when one party fraudulently appropriates property, it should be a simple matter for the investigator to show that the party violated the trust, provided, of course, that those contracts are available. Without the contracts, establishing the terms of the trust may be difficult or impossible.

If the nature of the trust is employer-employee, there are commonly accepted limitations on the employee's authority to dispose of the employer's property. Still, to avoid any future argument, exploring written personnel directives, accounting procedures, and office rules may be necessary.

Usually, partners in a partnership cannot be guilty of embezzlement for taking partnership funds. A partner is entitled to use the property. He is only civilly liable if he converts the property to his own use.[49] In a corporation, however, the officers and directors are only agents of the corporation. The fact that officers and directors of a corporation constitute a majority does not render it impossible for them to embezzle corporate funds.[50]

It is important to note that during routine business the owner may entrust property to another, and possession of the property may change hands, but title to the property remains with the original owner. Title to the property passes to the accused only after the fraudulent conversion. Consequently, failure to repay a loan properly obtained, or refusal to surrender property owned by the suspect and claimed by another, is not embezzlement, since title to the property was vested with the accused at the time the property was transferred.

Without the Effective Consent of the Owner

The evidence must show that the owner of the property never gave his consent for conversion of the property. If the owner gave his consent for the conversion or transfer of title, there can be no embezzlement. If the actor gained consent by deception or duress, the offense may be fraud, extortion, or robbery, but not embezzlement.

Should the owner, not having originally consented, discover the embezzlement, but says or does nothing to prevent the taking of the property or to recover it, he may be consenting to the taking of the property.

The most basic proof of the lack of consent rests in the testimony of the owner. Other factors, however, such as the owner's conduct in previous similar transactions or his actions upon discovery of the embezzlement may also be determinate. If the owner confronts the embezzler, then agrees to allow restitution in installment payments or future contractual obligations, he is giving his effective consent for the embezzler to have the property.

Notes

[1]Dennis J. Opatrny, "Women committing more white-collar crime, statistics show," *Austin American-Statesman*, (Austin, TX: Sunday, November 22, 1987), A3.

[2]Ibid.

[3]William W. McCullough, *Sticky Fingers: A Close Look at America's Fastest Growing Crime* (New York: Amacon, 1981), p. 7.

[4]Kenneth Mann, *Defending White-Collar Crime: A Portrait of Attorneys at Work* (New Haven, CT: Yale University Press, 1985), pp. 19–20.

[5]Wayne K. Bennett and Karen M. Hess, *Criminal Investigation* (St. Paul, MN: West Publishing Co., 1981), p. 361.

[6]Ibid.

[7]———, *Crime in the United States—1992* (Washington, D.C.: The Federal Bureau of Investigation, 1993), p. 218.

[8]———, *Crime in the United States—1992*, op cit.

[9]Peter W. Greenwood, Jan M. Chaiken, and Joan Petersilia, *The Criminal Investigation Process* (Lexington, MS: D.C. Heath and Company, 1977), p. 110.

[10]Charles H. McCaghy, *Deviant Behavior: Crime, Conflict, and Interest Groups* (New York: MacMillan Publishing Co., Inc., 1976), p. 183.

[11]John v. U.S., 65 App.D.C. 11.

[12]Quizlow v. Texas, 1 Tex.App. 65.

[13]Kidwell v. Paul Revere Fire Ins. Co., 294 Ky. 833.

[14]Kidwell v. Paul Revere Fire Ins. Co., 294 Ky. 833.

[15]Akers v. Scofield, 167 F.2d. 218.

[16]Wilson v. Texas, 18 Tex.App. 274.

[17]4 Bl. Comm. 230, 231.

[18]American Life Insurance Co. v. U.S. Fidelity & Guaranty Co., 261 Mich. 221.

[19]Moody v. People, 65 Colo. 339.

[20]Tredwell v. U.S., C.C.A. Va., 266 F. 350, 352.

[21]National Surety Co. v. Williams, 74 Fl. 446.

[22]Ferguson v. Texas, 80 Tx.Cr.R. 383.

[23]Gwynn Nettler, *Explaining Crime* (New York: McGraw-Hill, 1984), p. 258.

[24]Robert D. Pursley, *Introduction to Criminal Justice, Second Edition* (Encino, CA: Glencoe Publishing Co., 1980), p. 45.

[25]Donald R. Cressey, *Other People's Money: A Study of the Social Psychology of Embezzlement* (Glencoe, IL: The Free Press, 1953).

[26]Ibid. p. 114.

[27]Gwynn Nettler, "Embezzlement without problems," *British Journal of Criminology,* 1974.

[28]George E. Dix and M. Michael Sharlot, *Basic Criminal Law and Cases, Second Edition* (St. Paul, MN: West Publishing Co., 1980), p. 379.

[29]Bennet and Hess, op cit.

[30]Henry Campbell Black, *Black's Law Dictionary, Fourth Edition* (St. Paul, MN: West Publishing Co., 1968), p. 614.

[31]People v. Ashworth, 222 N.Y.S. 24.

[32]Coppo v. Ashworth, 163 Misc. 249.

[33]Maher v. Hibernia Insurance Co., 67 N.Y. 292.

[34]Commonwealth v. Polk, 256 Ky. 100.

[35]McCarron v. Texas, 605 S.W.2d 587.

[36]Clay v. Texas, 592 S.W.2d 609.

[37]Carranza v. Texas, 499 S.W.2d 140.

[38]Smith v. Texas, 501 S.W.2d 657.

[39]Larkin v. Texas, 248 S.W.2d 134.

[40]Parnell v. Texas, 339 S.W.2d 49.

[41]U.S. v. Crips, 435 F.2d 354.

[42]U.S. v. Hockridge, 573 F.2d 752.

[43]Nesbitt v. Texas, 144 S.W. 944.

[44]People v. Cox, 36 N.E.2d 84.

[45]Zaiontz v. Texas, 700 S.W.2d 303.

[46]Berdell v. Texas, 87 Tx.Cr.R. 310.

[47]Svanoe v. Jurgens, 144 Ill. 507.

[48]Templeton v. Blocker, 73 Or. 494.

[49]O'Marrow v. Texas, 147 S.W. 252.

[50]Parnell v. Texas, 339 S.W.2d 49.

Chapter 3

FRAUD

> The great masses of the people ... will more easily fall victims to a big lie
> than to a small one.
>
> Adolf Hitler
> *Mein Kampf*

Adolf Hitler, despite his propensity for distorted and demented logic, was correct in one respect. The bigger the deception, the greater is the likelihood it will succeed. Fraud is a multimillion dollar problem, not only in the United States, but worldwide. Fraud extends across all businesses and professions, from small private enterprises, to multinational corporations, to public service. According to Federal Bureau of Investigation crime reporting statistics, fraud is a prevalent crime in the United States.[1] A study by the National Association of Certified Fraud Examiners determined that the average business loses about 6 percent of its total annual revenue to fraud and abuse by its own employees.[2] Based on the estimated Gross Domestic Product of $7.01 trillion, U.S. businesses will lose $435 billion in 1995.[3] Table 3 shows the median loss for various U.S. industries as determined by the study.

In 1978, noted criminologists Edwin Sutherland and Donald Cressey claimed that, if the legal standards of fraud that applied to individuals also applied to corporations, approximately 90 percent of all large corporations in America would be habitual violators.[5] The biggest lies and the biggest frauds appear, anecdotally at least, the most successful. Unfortunately, history is rife with examples.

Examples of Fraud Cases

Fraud can greatly affect business and the economy. In the 1930s, through fraudulent business practices, Philip Mariano Fausto Musica brought down the powerful pharmaceutical house of McKess and Robbins, Incorporated.[6] The result was a financial loss to investors and a loss of jobs as a major employer ceased to do business.

Table 3. Fraud Losses.

Median Dollar Loss Per Fraud Case in Various U.S. Industries
1985–1995

Real Estate Financing*	$475,000.00
Manufacturing	$274,000.00
Banking	$200,000.00
Oil and Gas	$173,000.00
Construction	$142,000.00
Health Care	$105,000.00
Retail	$100,000.00
Service	$ 95,000.00
Insurance	$ 72,000.00
Government	$ 50,000.00
Utility	$ 50,000.00
Education	$ 32,000.00

*The large median loss in the real estate financing is due primarily to the savings and loan problems of the 1980s.[4]

The results of fraud in the business community can have extensive effects on the economy and on society. A federal jury convicted Currier J. Holman of bribery and conspiracy for his participation in a scheme to salvage his business, Iowa Beef, at the time the largest meat processing firm in the world. The scheme resulted in the retail prices of meat worldwide rising five cents a pound.[7] The Equity Funding Corporation conducted a decade long fraud of issuing false policies, selling those policies to other companies, then killing off the pretended policy holders. This fraud resulted in a $143 million loss to investors.[8] Ted Wolfram and the brokerage firm of Bell and Beckwith, by fraudulent transactions and investments, defrauded $47 million from more than seven thousand investors. One large loser was the city of Toledo, Ohio.[9] Jim Bakker, a popular television evangelist with an international following in the millions, was convicted in 1989 on twenty-four counts of wire fraud, mail fraud, and conspiracy for defrauding his followers of more than $3.5 million.[10]

It is no surprise that fraud exists even at the higher levels of government in the United States. Congressman John Dowdy was convicted of fraud in the Monarch Construction Corporation case. That case, which involved a home improvement fraud in Washington, D.C. from 1963 to 1965, resulted in a loss to American taxpayers of $4.5 million.[11] Possible fraudulent activity in the United States Congress check kiting scandal that became known in 1992 helped create such voter dissatisfaction that many members of the House of Representatives either retired or were replaced in that year's election.

Perhaps the largest known fraud in United States history was the operation of OPM, a business machine and computer leasing firm. This fraud culminated in a loss of over $200 million to investors and in the following convictions for fraud, conspiracy, mail fraud, wire fraud, and false statements to banks: Myron Goodman, sixteen counts; Mordecai Weisman, nine counts; Marty Schulman, five counts; Allen Ganz, four counts; Steve Lichtman, three counts; Mannes Friedman, three counts; and Jeff Resnick, two counts.[12]

"This is an extraordinary case in which a business was built and maintained for ten years in a foundation of pervasive fraud. During the ten-year period, Myron Goodman and Mordecai Weisman . . . resorted to multimillion dollar frauds to meet cash flow problems . . . frequently did business through the payment of commercial bribes . . . and utilized false financial statements as suited their needs.

This pattern of criminal activity culminated with the Rockwell [International] fraud, in which over nineteen lending institutions were fraudulently induced to lend OPM over $190,000,000. This crime . . . standing alone would constitute one of the largest white collar frauds in the history of the country. . . . "[13]

These examples illustrate the vastness and complexity of fraud. According to the Federal Bureau of Investigation uniform reporting statistics, law enforcement authorities make several arrests for fraud yearly. In 1992, the arrest rate was 162.3 arrests per 100,000 inhabitants.[14] While the arrest rate may seem high, particularly when compared with embezzlement, it is important to remember that, for FBI reporting purposes, fraud includes several offenses. It is also true, however, that investigations of fraud are becoming more commonplace.

Most law enforcement officers can easily detect gross forms of fraud, but expert investigators are necessary to deal with subtler forms of fraud that are flourishing in many areas of business and the professions. As investigators gain such expertise, what they have at times considered mere chicanery, they now interpret and deal with as criminal fraud.[15]

Forms of Fraud

Fraud takes many forms, but generally falls into one of four categories:

1) abuse of trust,
2) business fraud,
3) government fraud, and
4) investment fraud.

Table 4 lists some common forms of fraud in each of the four categories.

Abuse of Trust

Abuse of trust is the misuse of one's position, or the misuse of privileged information gained by virtue of that position, to acquire money, property, or privilege to which one is not entitled. The victims of such abuse are those who rely, to their detriment, on the individuals who abuse trusted positions.

Becoming a victim of fraud without knowing it is easy. A person donating to a charity does not expect delivery of any service or any return of profit from his contribution. Consequently, he will seldom check to see if his gift benefited those he intended to help.

Corporate officers and directors, executors of estates, and lawyers are obligated to act in the best interest of their stockholders or beneficiaries. The degree of care and diligence required depends on individual circumstances, but fiduciaries are not entitled to secret profits or special advantage due to their positions.

Landlord/tenant frauds normally include schemes to avoid the return of a security deposit, or the leasing of property to which the lessor has no claim to right. Medical frauds arise from the provision of bogus, questionable, or dangerous medical services, cures, or medications. Such frauds include quackery and misrepresentation of medication and treatment.

A pigeon drop is one of a large variety of street con games. The actor persuades the victim to withdraw a large sum of cash from a bank account. This is to show good faith and financial responsibility regarding the sharing of a supposedly serendipitous discovery of a large cache of money. During the con, the "discovered" money and the victim's money disappear, along with the con artist.

Business Fraud

The most prevalent and multifarious forms of fraud are found in the business world where victims are making a living or purchasing some good or service.

Table 4. Forms of Fraud.

I. Abuse of Trust
   A. Charity and Religious Frauds
   B. Fiduciary Fraud
   C. Landlord/Tenant Fraud
   D. Medical Fraud
   E. Pigeon Drop
II. Business Fraud
   A. Banking Fraud
      1. Check Kiting
      2. Collateral Fraud
   B. Insurance Fraud
      1. False Claims
      2. False Policies
   C. Consumer Fraud
      1. Advance Fee Scheme
      2. Repair Services Fraud
      3. Guilt Inducement Fraud
      4. Vanity Schemes
   D. Merchandising Fraud
      1. Bait and Switch Schemes
      2. Directory Advertising Schemes
      3. False Advertising
      4. False Weights and Measures
   E. Anti-Trust Violations
      1. Price Fixing
      2. Restraint of Trade
III. Government Fraud
   A. Fraud Against Government Services
      1. Tax and Revenue Fraud
      2. Welfare Fraud
      3. Voting Fraud
      4. Equity Skimming
   B. Public Corruption
      1. Bribery
      2. Procurement Fraud
IV. Investment Fraud
   A. Chain Referral Schemes
      1. Ponzi Schemes
      2. Pyramid Scheme
   B. Franchising Fraud
   C. Securities Fraud
      1. Insider Trading
      2. Market Manipulation
   D. Pension Fraud
   E. Bankruptcy Fraud
   F. Money Laundering

The late 1980s provided many examples of fraud in the banking and savings and loan industries. Check kiting is a species of fraud that relies for success on the time it takes for checks to clear the banking system. The actor circulates checks between various accounts fraudulently building up balances. Once he builds up balances, the actor withdraws funds from one account, the shortage going undetected for a few days until all the checks have cleared for redemption.

Collateral fraud occurs when a borrower pledges fraudulent security for a loan. The borrower may not own the security. He may steal it, or it may be borrowed, subjected to a previous lien, or grossly overvalued. Common credit rating schemes include the sale of a good credit rating to a high risk applicant, false statements in credit applications, or the creation of false credit accounts.

Frauds perpetrated by insurance companies against their clients include failure to provide promised coverage, failure to reimburse on claims, and manipulation of risk categories. Frauds against insurance companies include bogus or inflated claims, the filing of multiple claims for a single loss, and false statements on claims and applications.

Consumer fraud in the marketplace involves seller misrepresentation to buyers. Advance fee schemes involve assurances of some future benefit with full compensation to the provider upon the service being rendered. In actuality, the provider is interested only in obtaining the victim's good faith deposit.

Repair frauds include overcharging for services performed, charging for unnecessary services or parts, and doing unnecessary repairs. Guilt induced frauds rely on feelings of guilt or anxiety in a victim concerning obligations or relationships to others. Vanity schemes involve eliciting fees from individuals on the promise to promote or develop nonexisting talent.

Merchandising fraud encompasses a variety of consumer frauds. Bait and switch schemes involve advertising a bargain that is, in reality, nothing more than an inducement to lure a customer into a store. Once in the store, the promoter presents the customer with similar but more expensive merchandise. Directory advertising schemes involve sending bills to legitimate businesses. The bills are deceptively similar to bills the business is accustomed to receiving for the purchase of goods or services. However, the promoter has delivered no goods or services related to the deceptive bill.

False advertising is the use of untrue or deceptive promotions to defraud victims. False weights and measures include delivering fewer goods than the purported amount sold.

Antitrust violations create inequalities in the marketplace, increasing prices. Price fixing is an illegal combination of sellers to administer the price of a good or service. Restraint of trade involves any combination of schemes, including kickbacks and commercial bribery, to interfere with marketplace transactions.

Government Fraud

Government fraud consists of actions against government and abuses by government officials. Tax and revenue violations occur when individuals, businesses, or corporations seek to deprive a taxing authority of the revenue to which it is entitled. Many white-collar crimes, such as embezzlement and financial fraud, obligate the offender to commit tax fraud as the offender does not wish to report illicit income.

Individuals have historically plagued government welfare programs by claiming benefits to which they are not entitled. Doctors and other health care providers make claims for fictitious Medicare and Medicaid expenses. Voters stuff ballot boxes by voting more than once, or by voting under fictitious names.

Equity skimming involves an investor assuming home mortgages guaranteed by agencies of the United States government. The investor leases the home and accepts the rent, but never makes a mortgage payment. When the lender forecloses on the property, the government must pay any deficiency.

Government officials commit fraud by taking bribes to influence their official decisions. Procurement fraud is the manipulation of the contract process and includes bid rigging and bid fixing.

Investment Fraud

Investment frauds are schemes in which victims, induced by propositions of capital growth and high rates of return, invest money in imprudent or bogus business ventures. Chain referral is any scheme in which a victim invests money or property on the representation that he will make money by inducing others to pay into the same scheme. Such schemes include Ponzi Schemes and pyramids.

Franchising frauds arise out of business opportunities. A victim invests his time, money and talents to obtain a business, relying on a franchiser to supply specified goods and services along with a territorial market area. The franchiser then refuses to perform, taking the victim's original investment.

Securities fraud involves the sale, transfer, or purchase of securities or other interests in the business activities of others. Insider trading is a major cause of bank failures and involves corporate officers and directors trading in the stock of their own company based on privileged information.

Pension fraud includes violations of fiduciary duties by the managers of pension funds, poor investments, self-dealing and commercial bribery. Bankruptcy fraud consists of planned bankruptcies where the actor systematically sells the assets of a business. He then conceals the cash or other assets so they cannot be sold for the benefit of creditors.

Money laundering involves any number of activities by which the perpetrator spends or invests money in an attempt to conceal the unlawful source of the funds. The suspect may also launder the funds to finance an ongoing illegal enterprise.

Problems in Investigating Fraud

The complexities of fraud create many difficulties for a fraud investigator. One difficulty is dealing with the ability level of the suspect who initiated the fraud. In major fraud cases, the suspect is much like the embezzler. He is often well educated, occupies a position of trust and respect in the community, and has seldom, if ever, been in trouble with the law. For a major fraud to succeed, the suspect must have the trust and respect of his intended victims. Unless they trust the suspect, victims are unlikely to part with their valuable property or money.

Unraveling a fraud of the suspect's design is difficult since the suspect can design impediments to the investigation into the scheme at its inception. The more education and training a suspect has, the more difficult it is to discover, investigate, and prosecute a fraud.

A suspect designing, implementing, and perpetrating a fraud relies on misconception and deceit. A street criminal, knowing the victim will discover the crime, seeks to conceal his identity from witnesses and law enforcement officials. An embezzler, knowing his identity is already known, attempts to conceal the fact that he has committed a crime. The actor in a fraud, however, may conceal his identity and the fact that a crime has been committed. The actor may assume a fictitious name, or he may develop any number of shell companies or corporations through which to channel his transactions and conceal his involvement. A suspect, too, may try to convince victims and investigators that any number of problems, not of the actor's making, are responsible for any loss the victims may have suffered. Additionally, the actor will use deceit, misdirection, and lies to placate protests of wrongdoing. Discovery of each deceit requires another to take its place. The truth will cause even the most carefully constructed fraud to unravel. Each misrepresentation becomes a new problem for the investigator, as he must prove the representations are false. Even after the investigator proves the representations are fraudulent, the actor will try to persuade the victims and the investigator that his actions are a misunderstanding, not a crime.

The primary difficulty in investigating fraud is that fraud is an ambiguous term, and great confusion arises in discriminating between civil and criminal fraud. Instances of misrepresentation may occur in many complex or long lasting relationships. This does not mean that such relationships are fraudulent. For criminal fraud to exist, the relationship must be built upon and permeated with fraud.

Fraud is a nonviolent crime involving elements of intentional deceit, concealment, corruption, misrepresentation, and abuse of trust to gain the property of another. The willing cooperation of unwary or unknowing victims often facilitates the act of fraud.[16]

Defining Fraud

To prove fraud, the investigator must first distinguish honest from dishonest promoters by showing the promoter's intent and knowledge. The intent to defraud is often difficult to prove. To show what the promoter knew or believed to be true or false at the time of his representations may be equally difficult. Second, many representations yield mixed results, and, therefore, may not be demonstrably true or untrue. Consequently, proving fraudulent intent may be impossible. Additionally, many illegitimate promoters use legitimate principles of marketing, promotion and sales, so an intent to deceive is not always evident in the promotion of the fraud.

"In cases of embezzlement, apprehension usually follows detection because of the readily available tangible evidence that audits and law enforcement techniques can reveal. The fact of fraud, on the other hand, places the offender and the victim in . . . ambiguous positions and allows for greater opportunity to engage in a wide variety of petty or gross illegal operations."[17]

Obviously, to alleviate the ambiguity, defining the elements of fraud is important. This is necessary to decide whether, in any given set of circumstances, a criminal fraud exists. Fraud is "an intentional perversion of the truth for the purpose of inducing another in reliance upon it to part with some valuable thing belonging to him, or to surrender a legal right. It is false representation of a matter of fact, whether by words or by conduct, by false or misleading allegations, or by concealment of that which should have been disclosed, which deceives and is intended to deceive another so that he shall act upon it to his legal injury."[18]

Unlike embezzlement, fraud is not a technical and limited definition. "It is a generic term, embracing all multifarious means which human ingenuity can devise, and which are resorted to by one individual to get advantage over another by false suggestions or by suppression of truth, and includes all surprise, trick, cunning, dissembling, and any unfair way by which another is cheated."[19] "It includes anything calculated to deceive, whether it be a single act or combination of circumstances, whether it be done by direct falsehood or by innuendo, by speech or by silence, by word of mouth, or by look or gesture."[20] As with embezzlement, however, fraud is never a product of simple mistake or negligence. "As distinguished from negligence, fraud is always positive and intentional."[21]

Fraud is a broad ranging concept, but it falls within two classifications, actual or constructive. "Actual fraud consists in deceit, artifice, trick, design, or some direct and active operation of the mind. It includes cases of the intentional and successful employment of any cunning, deception, or artifice used to circumvent or cheat another. It is something said, done, or omitted by a person with the design of perpetrating what he knows to be a cheat or deception."[22] "Constructive fraud consists of any legal or equitable duty, trust, or confidence justly reposed which is contrary to good conscience and operates to the injury of another. It is an act, statement, or omission which operates as a virtual fraud on an individual, or which, if generally permitted, would be prejudicial to the public welfare, and yet may have been unconnected with any selfish or evil design."[23]

Elements of Fraud

The most basic element of fraud is deceit. Deceit is "a fraudulent and cheating misrepresentation, artifice, or device, used by one or more persons to deceive and trick another who is ignorant of the true facts, to the prejudice and damage of the party imposed upon."[24] "A deceit may be either: (1) the suggestion, as a fact, of that which is not true, by one who does not believe it to be true; (2) the assertion, as a fact, of that which is not true, by one who has no reasonable ground for believing it to be true; (3) the suppression of a fact, by one who is bound to disclose it, or who gives information of other facts which are likely to mislead for want of communication of a fact; or (4) a promise made without any intentions of performing it."[25] "To constitute deceit the statement must be made untrue, made with knowledge of its falsity or reckless and conscious ignorance thereof, especially if the parties are not on equal terms, made with intent that the victim act thereon or in a manner apparently fitted to induce him to act thereon, and the victim must act in reliance on the statement to his injury."[26]

Criminal fraud is based on deceit and maintained on false pretenses. "A false pretense is a designed misrepresentation of an existing fact or condition whereby a person obtains another's money or goods."[27] "It is a false representation of past or existing fact, made with knowledge of falsity, with intent to deceive and defraud, and which is adapted to deceive the person to whom it is made."[28] "A pretense is the holding out or offering to others something false or feigned. This may be done either by words or actions which amount to false representations. In fact, false representations are inseparable from the idea of a pretense. Without a representation which is false there can be no pretense."[29]

Generally, false pretenses may exist in oral or written representations. Contractually, an oral agreement is just as valid as a written agreement, except for some statutory exceptions. There are certain advantages to proving or disproving representations made in written agreements as opposed to oral statements. First, establishing the existence and nature of the representations in a written agreement is easier since the agreement is its own proof of terms. The investigator must establish the representations in an oral agreement through witness testimony that may be conflicting, inconclusive, or lacking in corroboration. Second, oral evidence cannot ordinarily change the representations of a written agreement. This rule, known at the parol evidence rule, limits the terms of the representations to the actual written instruments.

"It is a well-established general rule that when contracting parties embody their agreement . . . in writing, evidence of a prior or contemporaneous oral agreement is not admissible to vary or contradict the agreement."[30] Evidence of oral fraudulent misrepresentations designed to obtain consent to the written agreement may be admissible as an exception under certain circumstances. Consequently, the courts consider the written agreement to be the entire body of the agreement. Arguments of oral assurances or agreements contrary and subsequent to the agreement, while they may appear fraudulent, may not be admissible.

Not all instances of fraudulent representations or deceit, however, are criminal fraud. Civil remedies for actionable fraud are extensive. Criminal statutes, however, are more strictly constructed. Criminal fraud statutes must define the limits of the forbidden conduct.

The criminal offense of fraud is strictly statutory, created as a remedy for defects in the common law offense of larceny. Many statutes throughout the United States define fraud, though the language may vary from state to state. In 1962, the American Law Institute published a Model Penal Code. Many states have adopted various sections of the Model Penal Code. The American Law Institute defined Theft by Deception as follows:

"A person is guilty of theft if he obtains property of another by deception. A person deceives if he purposely:

a) creates or reinforces a false impression, including false impressions as to law, value, intention, or other state of mind; but deception as to a person's intention to perform a promise shall not be inferred from the fact alone that he did not subsequently perform the promise; or

b) prevents another from acquiring information which would affect his judgment of a transaction; or

c) fails to correct a false impression which the deceiver previously created or reinforced, or which the deceiver knows to be influencing another to whom he stands in a fiduciary relationship; or*

d) fails to disclose a known lien, adverse claim, or other legal impediment to the enjoyment of the property which he transfers or

---

*The laws regarding fraud are heavily influenced by the common law concept of caveat emptor. The law requires parties to the contracts to demonstrate and exercise common business sense in their dealings. Consequently, "the general rule is that silence in the absence of a duty to speak does not constitute fraud."[31] There are accepted exceptions:

1) there is a duty to disclose information when parties to the agreement or contract stand in a fiduciary relationship;

2) there is a duty to reveal information based on justice, equity, and fair dealing, such as when a manufacturer or vendor is aware of a latent flaw or defect in a product; and

3) there is an obligation of the parties of an agreement to correct previous misstatements or misunderstandings when such are discovered.

encumbers in consideration for the property obtained, whether such impediment is or is not valid, or is or is not a matter of public record.

The term 'deceive' does not, however, include falsity as to matters having no pecuniary significance, or puffing by statements unlikely to deceive ordinary persons in the group addressed."[32]

A Person

As with embezzlement, or any other criminal allegation, it is never permissible to file a criminal complaint for fraud without proof of a specific individual's responsibility and culpability. Unlike embezzlement, the identity of the suspect of a fraud may not be so easily determined. Unfortunately, in cases of financial fraud, the victims may have no idea who the suspect is. There is seldom any personal relationship between the suspect and the victim, although there may be a business relationship. Often the suspect hides behind aliases or a veil of shell businesses or corporations. The suspect may use several identities and addresses simultaneously, or he may change them from time to time, through different towns or states. The investigator may have to conduct extensive background investigations on the suspect and all of his corporate affiliations. Even then, the actual identity of the suspect may remain unknown.

The best leads to establishing the identity of such suspects may be in his social contacts. Such sources may know the suspect personally, may have heard stories about the suspect, or may have met family members or other friends who can divulge information about the suspect. Victims, too, may have conducted their own inquiries, and they may have pertinent information to share.

In any case, the investigator should gather all the necessary National Crime Information Center (NCIC) information: name, nicknames, race, sex, date of birth, social security number, and physical description. He should also note all known aliases and corporate associations. Such information may prove invaluable in proving the suspect acted with fraudulent intent.

Occasionally, an officer or director of a bank or a well-established corporation may be a suspect in a fraud. If so, the suspect's identity may be well known. Corporate personnel files may contain all the information to identify the suspect properly. Other employees can probably provide any missing information. If the suspect of the fraud is in a licensed profession, such as a lawyer or certified public accountant, then licensing authorities such as the State Bar or Board of Accountants can provide the necessary information.

Often in a fraudulent enterprise, the person making the fraudulent representations to the victims may not be the culpable party. He may be an employee of the enterprise, trained to make the representations, but not knowing such representations are fraudulent or willfully misleading. In such instances, the investigator must trace the source of the representations. The originator of such fraudulent representations is the suspect of the fraud.

Obtains the Property of Another by Deception

The gist of the fraud offenses is the element of deception, but since deception is so broad a term, the American Law Institute's Model Penal Code defined specific acts and omissions that constitute criminal fraud in cases of theft. Deception is not an all encompassing term. Statements of mere exaggeration, made by a seller promoting his wares, to induce a seller to buy, do not amount to false pretenses within the meaning of fraud. Also, misrepresentations lacking pecuniary interest do not amount to fraudulent misrepresentation.

Criminal statutes for fraud often contain various elements particular to the forbidden conduct, some examples being wire fraud, stock fraud, tax fraud, and banking fraud. In each instance, however, allegations of fraud are present, and the prosecution must prove that:

1) representations were made,
2) the representations were knowingly and designedly false,
3) the representations were made with intent to defraud,
4) the representations did defraud,
5) the representations were related to existing fact or past events, and
6) the party to whom the representations were made, relying on their truth, was thereby induced to part with his property.[33]

Representations Were Made

To prove any degree of fraud, proving that the suspect made certain representations is necessary. In criminal prosecutions, building a case around a victim's presumptions and speculations is never permissible. The investigator must produce evidence of each representation, fraudulent or not, which constitutes the whole of the agreement and suspected offense. Such evidence exists in several forms such as contracts, letters, depositions, and statements, either written or oral. However, since evidence to corroborate a victim's allegations of specific oral representations may often be difficult to produce, oral representations are difficult to prove.

Because of the difficulties inherent in proving and disproving oral representations and agreements, the English Parliament, in 1677, passed an Act for Prevention of Frauds and Perjuries.[34] Parliament designed the statute to prevent fraud by excluding from consideration by the courts legal actions on certain types of contracts and agreements, unless there was written evidence of the agreement signed by the defendant in the suit or by his duly authorized agent. Generally, these limitations include contracts to be liable for another person's debts, contracts involving real property, and agreements that cannot be performed within one year from the date of making the agreement.[35] All states have now enacted a statute of frauds similar to the early English statute.[36]

While the statute of frauds applies to civil, not criminal, cases of fraud, the greater standards of proof in criminal cases make it even more difficult to prove a fraud, especially absent documentation of the representation. Even so, misrepresentation need not necessarily be written or spoken. "Verbal assertions or direct representations [are] not required to show false pretenses or representations as they could [be] shown by the party's conduct and acts."[37] "A misrepresentation may be made by conduct as well as by language."[38]

Equally, the conditions under which representations occur are crucial. The credibility of a representation may rest on the way the suspect made the representation, the place he made the representation, and the conduct and actions of the parties involved.

Representations Were Knowingly and Designedly False

Ways by which parties to an agreement may be mistaken about an agreement include:

1) a mistake as to the nature of the transaction,
2) a mistake as to the subject matter of a contract,
3) a mistake as to the identity of the parties,
4) a mistake by one party only, or
5) a mistake in motive.[39]

Such matters are, as the definition denotes, merely mistakes, common errors of judgement or understanding. No intent to deceive exists.

To be fraud, the suspect must make the misrepresentations knowing that the representations are not true. An honest belief that a representation is true, even if it is not, constitutes a mistake, not fraud. However, "a false representation [made] without belief as to its truth is intentionally false."[40] Interestingly, though, "a statement that is partially or even literally true may be fraudulent in law if it was made in order to create a substantially false impression."[41] Additionally, if the representation is not false, it is immaterial that the promoter believed it to be false at the time he made it.

Representations Were Made with Intent to Defraud

Should a party to an agreement make intentional misrepresentations, the law considers those misrepresentations to be fraudulent. If, however, the representations are not intentional, there is no fraud, merely an innocent misrepresentation. In either case, of course, the victim may have an available civil remedy to rescind the contract, as the loss is the same, despite whether the misrepresentations were intentional or innocent.[42]

In criminal prosecutions, the requirement is for proof of intentional misrepresentation made with the intent to defraud. Innocent misrepresentation is not criminal fraud. To be a crime, the accused must intend to defraud the victim.

Proof of intentional misrepresentation may take many forms: statements made by a party to the contract that are contrary to established fact, conflicting statements of fact to different parties or witnesses to the same agreement, and deliberate efforts to falsify or fabricate documents. Additionally, the investigator may prove knowledge of falsity, or scienter, in circumstances other than intentional misrepresentations. The investigator can show scienter when there has been a concealment of a material fact or a nondisclosure of such a fact.[43] A fraudulent misrepresentation made when an actor's intent is to enforce a previous agreement or to collect a just debt, however, does not constitute an intent to defraud.

The inability to perform an agreement, absent proof of a deliberate fraudulent intent in forming the agreement, is not sufficient to support a prosecution for fraud. "Mere failure to return or pay back money after being unable to perform a contract, which has been paid for in advance, without more, [does] not constitute theft by false pretext."[44]

Representations Did Defraud

It is not sufficient to show that, while negotiating a contract or agreement, a suspect made misrepresentations, even when the evidence is overwhelming that such misrepresentations were intentional. The representations must, by law, defraud the victim. If the victim knew the representations to be false, or if the victim does not believe the representations to be true, there is no fraud. "Thus the offense is not committed if the victim is not in fact deceived but rather transfers the property for some other reason."[45]

It follows logically, if the misrepresentation must defraud the victim, the misrepresentation must be believable. A fraud is not possible if the victim finds the pretenses to be absurd or irrational.[46]

Even when the pretenses are plausible and rational, the victim may have an obligation to conduct reasonable research. "Some courts have indicated that if all the information is readily available for ascertaining the truth of statements, blind reliance upon the misrepresentation is not justified."[47]

If the pretenses are too remote there can be no conviction for fraud. The pretenses need not be the immediate cause of the transfer of property, but if the pretenses are too far removed from the intent to defraud, there is no criminal fraud.

Representations Related to Existing Fact or Past Events

"The misrepresentations must be of present or past fact."[48] False statements of opinion, of conditions to exist in the future, or of promissory matters will not, even if the other factors are present, constitute fraud.[49] Thus, it is not fraud to obtain money or property on a conditional promise to do something in the future, even when the suspect does not keep that promise. In some jurisdictions, it is not criminal fraud if at the time the suspect made the promise he had no intention of keeping it.[50] This will, of course, depend on individual fraud statutes and prevailing judicial opinions. Not all deceit rises to the level of fraud. A false statement of existing fact is no less a false pretext, however, because it is coupled with a promise or a statement as to the future.

Statements of opinion are not statements of fact, and, accordingly, are not usually an element of fraud. There are exceptions, however, as when the person making the fraudulent misrepresentation is an expert, such as a physician, or when a fiduciary relationship exists between the parties.[51]

Whether a particular representation is one of fact or opinion is often a matter for the trier of fact to decide.

In some jurisdictions, misrepresentations of current law are not elements of fraud. The law is presumed to be a matter of common knowledge, so such misrepresentations may not defraud a victim. Specific guidance on that point is a matter of law and judicial opinion.

Party to Whom the Representations Were Made, Relying on Their Truth, Was Thereby Induced to Part with His Property

"The misrepresentations must be the cause of the victim's transferring the title to the offender. Thus, there is no offense if the victim is not deceived, but transfers the property for another reason. Nor is it an offense if the victim is deceived, but the false impression does not play a significant role in his decision to give the property to the other."[52] "If the injured party knew, or by the exercise of ordinary prudence should have known, at the time he parted with possession of the property that the pretext was in fact false, the offense could not arise."[53] "In a prosecution for fraud, the state cannot rely on a false pretext used by a defendant where the person from whom the defendant procured the property did not believe the pretext to be true, and therefore was not induced by such a pretext to deliver the property to the defendant."[54]

In any case, the issue about whether the reliance is justified is for a jury to determine.[55]

The interest to be obtained must be the title to the property and not merely possession of the property.

Once the investigator proves all the elements of a fraud, when there is no doubt about the fraudulent intent of a defendant, there is no necessity to show what the defendant did with the property once he had it, and proof of appropriation in such cases is satisfied by mere proof of the taking.[56] In a criminal prosecution for fraud, however, to show that the offender did fraudulently appropriate the property, proving the ultimate disposition of the property is preferable, though there may be no legal requirement to do so. Additionally, in his attempts to conceal or dispose of unlawfully acquired property, the offender may have violated other criminal laws.

Notes

[1] ——, *Crime in the United States—1992* (Washington, D.C.: Department of Justice, Federal Bureau of Investigation, 1993), p. 218.

[2] Lori Hawkins, "Employees steal billions, study says," *Austin American-Statesman* (Austin, TX: Tuesday, October 3, 1995), E1.

[3] Ibid.

[4] Ibid.

[5] Edwin H. Sutherland and Donald Cressey, *Criminology, 10th ed.* (Philadelphia, PA: J. B. Lippencott Co., 1978), p. 96.

[6] Isadore Barmash, ed., *Great Business Disasters: Swindlers, Bunglers, and Frauds in American Industry* (Chicago, IL: Playboy Press, 1973), p. 13.

[7] Jonathan Kevitney, "Necessary Payoffs—But Who Really Pays?" *Swindled! Classic Business Frauds of the Seventies* (Princeton, NJ: Dow Jones Books, 1976), p. 155.

[8] Lee J. Seidler, Frederick Andrews, and Marc K. Epstein, *The Equity Funding Papers* (Santa Barbara, CA: John Wiley & Sons, 1978), p. vii.

[9] Homer Brinkley, Jr., *Master Manipulator* (New York: AMACON, 1985), p. 149.

[10] ——, "PTL head gears up for appeal, Baaker to suspend storefront ministry," *The Austin American-Statesman* (Austin, TX: Saturday, October 7, 1989), A4.

[11] Jean Carper, *Not With a Gun* (New York: Grossman Publishers, 1973), p. 202.

[12] Stephen Fenichell, *Other People's Money: The Rise and Fall of OPM Leasing Services* (Garden City, NY: Doubleday, 1985), p. 280.

[13] Ibid., p. 282, quoting from a government sentencing memorandum written by Audrey Strauss.

[14] ——, *Crime in the United States—1992,* op cit.

[15] Edwin H. Sutherland and Donald R. Cressey, *Principles of Criminology* (New York: J.B. Lippencott Co., 1966), p. 16.

[16] Wayne K. Bennett and Karen M. Hess, *Criminal Investigation* (St. Paul, MN: West Publishing Co., 1981), p. 412.

[17] Dorothy Zeits, *Women Who Embezzle or Defraud: A Study of Convicted Felons* (New York: Praeger Publishers, 1981), p. vii.

[18] Brainard Dispatch Newspaper Co. v. Crow Wing County, 196 Minn. 194.

[19] Johnson v. McDonald, 170 Okl. 117.

[20] People v. Gilmore, 345 Ill. 28.

[21] Alexander v. Church, 53 Conn. 561.

[22] Jackson v. Jackson, 47 Ga. 99.

[23] Jackson v. Jackson, 47 Ga. 99.

[24] People v. Chadwick, 143 Cal. 116.

[25] Civil Code of South Dakota, Section 1293.

[26] Corley Co. v. Griggs, 192 N.C. 171.

[27] People v. Gould, 363 Ill. 343.

[28] State v. Alick, 62 S.D. 220.

[29] State v. Joaquin, 43 Iowa 132.

[30] Hathaway v. Ray's Motor Sales, 247 A.2d 512.

[31] Robert N. Corley and William J. Robert, *Principles of Business Law* (Englewood Cliffs, NJ: Prentice-Hall, Inc., 1975), p. 213.

[32] ——, *The Model Penal Code,* American Law Institute, 1962, quoted by George Dix and M. Michael Sharlot, *Basic Criminal Law: Cases and Materials, Second Edition* (St. Paul, MN: West Publishing Co., 1980), pp. 381–382.

[33]Diamond v. State, 52 Ga.App. 184.
[34]Corley and Robert, op cit.
[35]Ibid.
[36]Ibid.
[37]Hogan v. Texas, 393 S.W.2d 898.
[38]Corley and Robert, op cit.
[39]William C. Wermuth, "Contracts," *Modern American Law* (Chicago, IL: Blackstone College of Law, 1955), Vol. 1, Sect. III, pp. 35–37.
[40]Corley and Robert, op cit., p. 172.
[41]Ibid.
[42]Joss v. Shodle, 498 P.2d 787.
[43]Corley and Robert, op cit.
[44]Bearden v. Texas, 487 S.W.2d 739.
[45]Dix and Sharlot, op cit., p. 379.
[46]Nickson v. Texas, 180 S.W.2d 161.
[47]Corley and Robert, op cit., p. 175.
[48]Dix and Sharlot, op cit.
[49]Corley and Robert, op cit., p. 172.
[50]Dix and Sharlot, op cit.
[51]Corley and Robert, op cit.
[52]Dix and Sharlot, op cit.
[53]Kinder v. Texas, 477 S.W.2d 584.
[54]McCain v. Texas, 158 S.W.2d 796.
[55]Capital Dodge v. Haley, 288 N.E.2d 766.
[56]Cameron v. Hauck, 383 F.2d 966.

Chapter 4

ACCOUNTING THEORY FOR INVESTIGATORS

I hate definitions.

Benjamin Disraeli
Earl of Beaconsfield
Vivian Grey

A difficult truth for white-collar crime investigators is that, except those Special Agents of the Federal Bureau of Investigation and the Internal Revenue Service whom those agencies hire for their knowledge of accounting, few have had any formal education or training in book-keeping or accounting techniques and terminology. Yet, financial investigation is an indispensable tool for the modern law enforcement officer.

Accountants, as with other professionals, have developed a specialized vocabulary. Consequently, a brief review of common accounting terms and principles is necessary since white-collar crime investigations often involve the interpretation of accounting data. The review is to help the investigator learn what various accounting statements mean, and to aid in understanding how transactions flow through an accounting system. Such an understanding will help the investigator detect abnormal or fraudulent entries and transactions.

During the investigation of some offenses, the investigator may find he needs an expert, such as a certified public accountant, to conduct a detailed and thorough examination of the records related to the investigation. It is important to remember, however, that while accountants are trained to audit the financial books and records, they are seldom trained to collect evidence of embezzlement and fraud. They also lack the author-ity to obtain subpoenas and search warrants.

For many local and state agencies, professional accounting services are not readily available. The investigator may have to seek assistance from an accountant or bookkeeper whom the agency or the victim has hired. Therefore, the investigator needs a basic understanding of accounting concepts and terminology to understand the work of the accountant or bookkeeper, and to help him locate needed evidence. The investigator, too, must conduct complete and meaningful interviews with victims, witnesses, and suspects of white-collar crimes. These individuals often use common accounting terminology in relating their experiences to the investigator. Further, the investigator must present the facts of the case before a grand jury, a trial court, a prosecutor, or a defense attorney. Without a working understanding of accounting concepts and terminology, explaining the circumstances surrounding the case is difficult.

The art of accounting is more than three thousand years old.[1] Archaeologists have discovered stone and clay tablets containing financial data in several sites throughout the world. The Roman Empire, which developed methods of recording and summarizing numerical data, kept elaborate records for keeping track of its military forces and payrolls.[2] American Indians used notches on sticks and strings of beads to note accounting data.[3]

As trade and business grew more complicated and complex, accounting naturally grew more sophisticated. During the Industrial Revolution businesses needed large pools of capital to finance the purchase of machinery and equipment. Partnerships, joint stock companies, and corporations evolved to meet this need. New accounting procedures developed to meet the needs of new, more complex business organizations.[4] Accounting has become the chief method of accumulating, measuring, and communicating economic data about an enterprise. The American Institute of Accountants defines accounting as "the act of recording, classifying, and summarizing in a significant manner, and in terms of money, transactions and events which are, in part at least, of a financial character, and interpreting the results thereof."[5]

Accounting Personnel

As business and accounting became more complex, a three-tier hierarchy developed throughout accounting staffs. At the top of the accounting pyramid is the chief financial officer. This individual may have one of several titles: president, vice president, treasurer, or comptroller. When making the initial contact to investigate a claim of criminal activity, it is a good policy for the investigator first to approach the chief financial officer. The investigator can explain the investigation to the chief financial officer and seek his approval and cooperation, assuming, of course, that the chief financial officer is not the target of the investigation. Additionally, should the investigator later obtain a summons or subpoena, serving such legal documents on the chief financial officer will probably be necessary.

The chief accountant supervises the secondary level, the accounting and bookkeeping staffs. The chief accountant can relate general information about the company's accounting records, systems, and procedures. He can also provide access to the employees who are most knowledgeable about them.

At the third level are the accounting and posting clerks. These employees are most familiar with the day to day entries in the books. These employees are most helpful in tracing specific items or explaining apparent discrepancies.

Many businesses also employ outside accountants or accounting firms to verify the accuracy of their financial statements. If, for whatever reason, the records of a company or of an individual are unobtainable from the target of the investigation, obtaining them from the target's accountant may be possible for the investigator. The accountant's files may contain not only ledger accounts and journals, but may also contain comments on the target's financial position, accounting procedures, and internal controls.

Forms of Business Organizations

There are many forms of business organizations, each with its advantages and disadvantages, and each with different bookkeeping and accounting requirements.

A proprietorship is the simplest form of business organization. One owner is responsible for business operations. The proprietorship is also the most common form of business organization. There are few legal impediments to starting a proprietorship, except certain licenses required for particular activities.[6]

When two or more people enter an agreement to do business together, they form a partnership. In a general partnership, each partner in the business bears the full liability for the partnership. The partners divide the profits and losses equally, and each partner bears the responsibility and authority to participate in the management of the business, unless the partnership agreement specifies other arrangements.[7]

A limited partnership allows the partners to limit their risks to the amount of their individual investments in the partnership. A limited partnership agreement must be in writing. The partners usually file the agreement in the county courthouse with the County Clerk or Recorder. In a limited partnership one general partner assumes liability for the partnership. The limited partners may not participate in the management of the partnership, but they may meet periodically to vote on the general policies of the operations.[8]

A corporation is a legal entity separate from the people owning it. Corporations exist under the laws of a state or of the federal government. The actions taken by the corporation are restricted to what is allowed by law and authorized by the corporate charter. Stockholders own the corporation. The stockholders elect officers who run the corporation. A corporation can own property, buy, sell, enter agreements, borrow money, or take any other business action an individual can take, subject to the restrictions of law and the corporate charter. Stockholders' liabilities for the debts of the corporation are limited.[9]

A shell corporation has no assets or liabilities. It simply has a charter to do business. The names of the persons responsible for the original application for the charter to the State government are usually on record with the Secretary of State, but subsequent directors or officers of the corporation may not be.

A cooperative is a corporation in which profits are distributed to shareholders in proportion to how much business each shareholder does with that business, as opposed to the number of shares of stock he holds.[10]

A mutual company is a type of corporation with no stockholders. The customers, such as policy holders or depositors, own the corporation. Mutual companies are prevalent in the fields of life insurance and savings investment. If the company distributes profits, they distribute them proportionately to the size of the policy or the size of the deposit.[11]

Accounting Systems

The objective of any system of accounting is to record, in summary form, the results of all transactions conducted in the course of business. There are many ways to accomplish this, but two systems are in common use today: single-entry recording and double-entry bookkeeping.[12]

The single-entry recording system has been in use for most of the three thousand year history of accounting. It is the simplest form of noting a financial transaction. Because of the advent of more complex financial organizations, single-entry recording has declined in use, although it is still prevalent in many small businesses. Even in its most sophisticated form, single entry recording is merely the entering of information from all sources in one place, usually in columnar form. With single-entry recording no effort is made to balance the records.[13]

The double-entry bookkeeping concept of accounting is that every transaction affects two or more accounts with equal debits and credits. The name double-entry derives from the fact that two or more adjustments must occur with each transaction, never just one. The object of the double-entry system is to show, in summary form, the results of the transactions and forces affecting the business.[14]

One basic idea of the double-entry system is that someone owns or claims every item of value.[15] Thus, the total of items of value is equal to the total of claims.

Assets are the various items of value that a company or an individual owns. Assets include such tangible items as cash, supplies, furniture, fixtures, raw materials of production, inventory, and land. Assets also include such intangibles as accounts receivable, copyrights, patents, and investments. To be an asset, an item must have some value to the owner. If an item has no value, it is of no concern to the accounting system.

There are two kinds of claims against assets. The first is the claim of the owners for their investments. These claims are known as capital, equity, or net worth. These claims represent the original investments of the owners, less any losses, plus any retained profits. In a proprietorship, the net worth belongs to the proprietor. In a partnership, the net worth belongs to each partner as designated in the partnership agreement. A corporation's net worth is divided into two accounts, surplus, also known as retained earnings, and capital stock. The capital stock account may also be divided into common stock and preferred stock.

The second kind of claim against the assets of a business arises from those who have extended credit to the business. These claims come from suppliers, banks, investors, and mortgagors. The claims of the creditors are known as liabilities.

The idea that someone owns or claims every asset of a business translates into the fundamental accounting equation: Assets = Liabilities + Capital. This equation has been the cornerstone of accounting since Luca Pacioli first developed it in 1494.[16]

Though the various financial transactions affect the composition of one or more items in the equation, the equation must always be in balance. When the value of an asset increases, for instance, there must be either a corresponding decrease in another asset, an increase in a liability, or an increase in an item of net worth. Table 5 shows the cause and effect relationships between the items in the fundamental accounting equation.

Table 5. Balancing the Fundamental Accounting Equation.

The Change	The Result
Increase in an asset	Decrease in another asset, or Increase in a liability, or Increase in an item of net worth
Decrease in an asset	Increase in another asset, or Decrease in a liability, or Decrease in an item of net worth
Increase in a liability	Increase in an asset, or Decrease in another liability, or Decrease in an item of net worth
Decrease in a liability	Decrease in an asset, or Increase in another liability, or Increase in an item of net worth
Increase in an item of net worth	Increase in an asset, or Decrease in a liability, or Decrease in another item of net worth
Decrease in an item of net worth	Decrease in an asset, or Increase in a liability, or Increase in another item of net worth

All business transactions are classified into various types of accounts. An account is a title, or heading, for various categories of assets, liabilities, or factors affecting net worth. Increases and decreases in each account, expressed as money, are recorded in columns under each heading.

Accounting Methods

There are two basic methods of accounting: cash basis and accrual basis. The cash and accrual methods may be used alone or in combination, known as the hybrid method.[17] Cash basis means that all revenues are recorded in the period when payments are received, and expenses are recorded when they are paid. Accrual basis means that revenues are recorded in the period when they are earned, and expenses are recorded when they are incurred.

The difference between the cash and accrual basis is a matter of timing. Most accountants describe the process of determining periodical net income as a matching of revenues and expenses within a given period. The accrual basis achieves this matching, but the cash basis does not achieve it unless all transactions are completed within the same period.

The hybrid method of accounting is a combination of the cash and accrual methods. It is useful only when it is consistently applied and clearly reflects income. The hybrid method is most often applied to business inventories in small businesses where the delay between earning and collecting income and accruing and paying expenses is short. Larger businesses, as a rule, due to the complexity of business transactions and the need to predict future business, analyze cash flows, and analyze costs, use the accrual basis.

The Balance Sheet

The balance sheet is the basic financial document completed at the end of each accounting cycle. The balance sheet depicts the total assets, liabilities and capital of a business organization at a specified point of time.[18]

The balance sheet has two basic forms, the report form (Table 6) and the account form (Table 7). There are no changes in the figures or the designation of the groupings in the report or account forms. All that changes is the placement of the groupings on the presentation.

Assets and liabilities appear in a definite order on the balance sheet. Assets appear in order of liquidity, the quickness to which an asset can be converted into cash. The most liquid assets are listed first. The least liquid assets are listed last. The liquidity of a liability is that which falls due or matures first. The most liquid liabilities are listed first. The least liquid liabilities are listed last.

Both sections of the balance sheet must balance. Assets must equal liabilities plus owners' equity. Under the assets heading is a list of all the property and goods owned by the business, and the company's claims against others that are yet to be collected. Under the liabilities heading are all the debts due. Equity includes all the claims of the owner or owners against the business.

Current assets include cash, marketable securities, accounts receivable, and inventories. Cash includes the bills and coins in the business plus any money on deposit with a bank. Marketable securities are investments of excess or idle cash that is not normally needed for the operation

Table 6. Report Form.

Widgets, Inc. Balance Sheet
December 31, 19XX

ASSETS

Current assets

Cash	$ 45,000
Marketable securities	85,000
Accounts receivable	200,000
Less allowance for bad debt	
Inventories	270,000
Total current assets	$600,000

Fixed Assets

Land	$ 45,000
Building	380,000
Machinery	95,000
Office Equipment	10,000
	530,000
Less: accumulated depreciation	180,000
Net fixed assets	350,000
Prepayments and deferred charges	10,000
Intangibles	10,000
Total Fixed Assets	$370,000
Total Assets	$970,000

LIABILITIES

Current liabilities

Accounts payable	$100,000
Notes payable	85,000
Accrued expenses payable	33,000
Federal income taxes payable	32,000
Total current liabilities	$250,000

Long-term liabilities

First mortgage bonds	$270,000
Total Long-Term Liabilities	270,000
Total liabilities	$520,000

STOCKHOLDERS' EQUITY

Capital stock

Preferred stock	$ 60,000
Common stock	150,000
Capital surplus	70,000
Accumulated retained earnings	170,000
Total stockholders' equity	$450,000
Total liabilities and stockholders' equity	$970,000

Table 7. Account Form.

Widgets, Inc. Balance Sheet December 31, 19XX			
ASSETS		**LIABILITIES**	
Cash	$ 45,000	Accounts payable	$100,000
Marketable securities	85,000	Notes payable	85,000
Accounts receivable	200,000	Accrued expenses payable	33,000
Inventories	270,000	Federal income taxes payable	32,000
Land	45,000	Long-term liabilities	270,000
Building	380,000	Total liabilities	$520,000
Machinery	95,000		
Office Equipment	10,000		
	1,130,000		
Less: accumulated depreciation	180,000		
Net fixed assets	$ 950,000	**STOCKHOLDERS' EQUITY**	
Prepayments/deferred charges	10,000	Preferred stock	$ 60,000
Intangibles	10,000	Common stock	150,000
		Capital surplus	70,000
		Accum. retained earnings	170,000
		Total equity	$450,000
Total assets	**$ 970,000**	**Total liabilities and equity**	**$970,000**

of the business. These investments are usually in commercial paper or government securities.

Accounts receivable include the amounts not yet collected from customers to whom goods have been delivered or services rendered prior to payment. An allowance of a percentage of the accounts receivable is usually made for debts that, for whatever reason, will be uncollectible. This percentage varies according to the nature of the business.

Inventory includes the raw materials of production, partially completed goods in the process of manufacture, and finished goods ready for sale. Inventories are generally valued at cost or market value, whichever is lower.

Fixed assets are often called property, plant, and equipment. Fixed assets are not intended for sale, but are used to manufacture, display, warehouse, and transport a product. The generally accepted and approved method for valuation of fixed assets is acquisition cost minus accumulated depreciation. Depreciation is the decline in the useful value of a fixed asset due to wear and tear from use or the elements or due to obsolescence. Land is not subject to depreciation.[19]

Depletion is a term used primarily in mining or oil and denotes a reduction in natural resource wealth.

Prepayments are payments made in advance for which the company has not yet received the benefits, but for which it will receive the benefits in the next accounting period. Deferred charges are large expenditures of cash for such things as research and development charged off over several years. Intangibles include franchise rights, patents, and goodwill.

Current liabilities include all debts that fall due within the coming year, such as accounts payable, notes payable, accrued expenses payable, and taxes payable. Accounts payable represent the amount a company owes to its regular creditors from whom it has purchased merchandise or goods on open account. Notes payable represent money owed to a bank or commercial lender evidenced by a written promissory note. Accrued expenses payable represent debts owed by the company for various expenses such as salaries, insurance premiums, interest on borrowed funds, legal expenses, and pensions that have accrued but are unpaid at the end of the accounting period. Taxes payable constitute the same type of liability, but, because of the amount and legal importance of the tax factor, are usually stated separately.

Long term liabilities are debts due that will not be paid within one year from the date of the financial report. Long-term liabilities include bonds or mortgages.

Equity is the owner's interests, or the net worth of the business. It represents the difference between assets and liabilities at cost and not at fair market value.[20] The balance sheet for a proprietorship will show the owner's equity. The balance sheet for a partnership will show the proportionate equity for each partner. The balance sheet for a corporation will show equity in three categories: capital stock, capital surplus, and accumulated retained earnings.

Capital stock is divided into two categories, preferred stock and common stock. Preferred stocks have some preference to other shares regarding dividends, or in distribution of assets upon liquidation, or both. Ownership of preferred stocks does not normally endow voting rights. Common stock pays dividends after holders of preferred stocks. Holders of common stock are usually the last paid if the corporation liquidates. Normally, preferred stock dividends are limited to a percentage of the par value of the stock each year, while dividends on common stock have no such limitation and may vary according to the profits of the corporation. Each share of common stock normally endows the holder with one vote for directors.

Capital surplus is the amount over the par or legal value of each share the various shareholders pay. Accumulated retained earnings, sometimes called earned surplus, are the amounts of profit a corporation earns, less declared dividends.

What the Balance Sheet Shows

A business expends considerable time compiling accounting data to produce a balance sheet. It remains for the investigator, however, to interpret the significance of the figures. The preliminary lines of a balance sheet can reveal a great deal about the financial health of a company.

One very important calculation available from the balance sheet figures is the net working capital. Net working capital is the difference between current assets and current liabilities. Net working capital often determines the ability of a company to meet its current obligations, expand its volume, and to take advantage of business opportunities.[21]

Current Assets	$600,000
Less Current Liabilities	$250,000
Net Working Capital	$350,000

The current ratio, or ratio of current assets to current liabilities, may also be a helpful calculation. Analysts generally agree that a business should maintain a 2:1 current ratio, that is $2 in current assets for each $1 in current liabilities.[22] This generalization, however, requires modification depending on the business. The investigator can find typical current ratios by comparing the ratios of similar other businesses.

Another important calculation from the balance sheet is the net book value of a company's securities. The book value represents the business's assets backing or protecting bonds or each share of common and preferred stock.[23] To state this figure for bonds, subtract from the total assets the value of intangible assets and current liabilities. This yields the net tangible assets. The net asset value of the bond is the net tangible assets divided by the number of outstanding bonds.[24]

Total Assets	$970,000
Less Intangible Assets	10,000
Total Tangible Assets	960,000
Less Current Liabilities	250,000
Net Tangible Assets	$710,000

$710,000 Net Tangible Assets/270 Bonds = $2,629 Net Asset Value per $1,000 Bond

To state the book value of preferred stock, subtract from the total assets the value of the intangible assets, current liabilities, and long term liabilities. This yields the net realized assets. The net asset value of the preferred stock is the net realized assets divided by the number of shares of outstanding preferred stock.[25]

Total Assets	$970,000
Less Intangible Assets	10,000
Total Tangible Assets	960,000
Less Current Liabilities	250,000
Net Tangible Assets	710,000
Less Long Term Liabilities	270,000
Net Realized Assets	440,000

$440,000 Net Realized Assets/600 Shares of Preferred Stock = $733 Net Asset Value per Share of Preferred Stock

The book value of common stock is the amount of money each share would receive if the company liquidated at balance sheet values. Subtract from the total assets the intangible assets, current liabilities, long term liabilities, and par value of the preferred stock. The net book value of common stock is the net assets divided by the number of shares of common stock.[26]

Total Assets	$970,000
Less Tangible Assets	10,000
Total Tangible Assets	960,000
Less Current Liabilities	250,000
Net Tangible Assets	710,000
Less Long Term Liabilities	270,000
Net Realized Assets	440,000
Less Preferred Stock Value	60,000
Net Assets	380,000

$380,000 Net Assets/30,000 Shares of Common Stock = $12.67 Book Value per Share of Common Stock

The investigator must be careful not to be misled by book value figures, especially of common stocks. Most profitable companies often show a low net book value but substantial earnings. If the directors of a corporation declare large dividends on the stock, the net assets are lowered, and the book value of the stock declines, although each share results in large returns for the investor.

Income Statement

An income statement, also known as a profit and loss statement, reflects the money earned and expenses incurred by a business for a designated period, usually a calendar or fiscal year. While the balance sheet reflects the financial position of a business on a given date, the income statement shows the record of the business's operating activities over the whole reporting period. The income statement matches the amounts received from selling goods and services and other sources of income against the costs incurred to operate the company. The result is the net profit or net loss.[27] Table 8 is an example of a simplified Income Statement.

The most important source of revenue for a business is the first item on the income statement. It represents the primary source of revenue from customers for goods sold or services rendered. For Widgets, Inc., the hypothetical company in Table 8, this is Gross Sales. For other concerns this item may be operating revenues or fees received. The net sales operating revenue or net fees received is the gross amount received less returns and allowances for damaged or defective merchandise. Additional sources of revenue may include interest received on investments of retained earnings.

The expenses of a manufacturing business are usually listed in three categories:

1) costs of goods sold,
2) operating expenses, and
3) administrative expenses.

The costs of goods sold represent the total costs incurred to obtain raw materials for production, including the costs of the raw material, plus freight-in, less returns. To calculate the costs of goods sold, make allowances for inventory at the beginning and end of the reporting period.

Operating expenses are those expenses incurred in manufacturing, marketing, storing, and selling a product. These expenses include sales and manufacturing salaries, depreciation of manufacturing equipment, freight-out, delivery expenses, and disposable supplies.

Administrative expenses are those expenses incurred which are not directly related to the costs of goods sold or operating expenses. These expenses include insurance expenses, executive office salaries and expenses, depreciation of office equipment, and expenses for stocks and bonds.

Table 8.

Widgets, Inc.
Consolidated Income Statement
For the Year Ending December 31, 19XX

Revenue			
Gross Sales			1,130,000
Less: Sales Returns and Allowances			30,000
Net Sales			1,100,000
Interest Revenue			5,000
Net Revenue			1,105,000
Costs of Goods Sold			
Merchandise Inventory			
Jan. 1, 19XX		250,000	
Purchases	835,000		
Less: Purchase Returns and Allowances	20,000		
Net Purchases	815,000		
Add: Freight-In	25,000		
Net Cost Purchases		840,000	
Goods Available for Sale		1,090,000	
Merchandise Inventory			
Dec. 31, 19XX		270,000	
Costs of Goods Sold			820,000
Gross Profits from Sales			285,000
Operating Expenses			
Selling Expenses:			
Sales Salaries	63,000		
Mortgage Expense/Selling Space	10,000		
Advertising Expense	16,000		
Freight-out/Delivery Expense	5,000		
Store Supplies	6,000		
Depreciation/Store Expense	20,000		
Total Selling Expenses		120,000	
General and Administrative Expenses:			
Office Salaries	25,000		
Mortgage Expense/Office Space	8,000		
Insurance	2,000		
Office Supplies	5,000		
Depreciation/Office Equipment	10,000		
Interest on Bonds	13,500		
Total General and Administrative Expenses		63,500	
Total Operating Expenses			183,500
Net Income Before Taxes			101,500
Less: Provision for Taxes			48,000
Net Income			53,500

Allowances for taxes could be an administrative expense, but, considering the importance of taxes in the accounting system, they are usually noted separately.

What the Income Statement Shows

The income statement, much like the balance sheet, will tell a lot more about the position and profitability of a company after a few detailed comparisons.

To find the operating margin of profit, subtract from the net sales the costs of goods sold, the operating expenses, and general and administrative expenses (except interest paid on bonds issued by the company). The result, operating profit, is calculated as a percentage of the net sales.[28]

Net Sales		$1,100,000
Less: Costs of Goods Sold	820,000	
Operating Expenses	120,000	
General and Administrative Expenses		
(except Interest on Bonds)	50,000	
		− 990,000
Operating Profit		$ 110,000

$110,000 Operating Profit/$1,100,000 Net Sales = 10% Margin of Profit

By comparing the margin of profit for preceding years, it is possible to determine whether the business is becoming more or less profitable.

The complement of the margin of profit is the operating cost ratio. The margin of profit for Widgets, Inc., is 10 percent. The operating cost ratio is 90 percent.

The net profit ratio is the net profit of the business as a percentage of net sales.[29] For Widgets, Inc., the net profit ratio is:

$53,500 Net Profit/$1,100,000 Net Sales = 4.9% Net Profit Ratio.

This means that for every $1 in sales, $0.049 in profit ultimately went to the company.

There is also a definite relationship between items on the company's balance sheet and the income statement. A change in any item on the balance sheet must be directly related to some item on the income statement.[30] The correlations can become complicated, depending on the nature of the changes. Table 9 illustrates some examples of the relationships between the balance sheet and the income statement sheet.

Table 9. Table of Relationships.

Balance Sheet Account	Income Statement Account
Current Assets:	
Cash	Sales; Cash Paid Out; Expenses; Petty Cash
Notes Receivable	Interest Income
Accounts Receivable	Sales
Allowance for Bad Debt	Bad Debt Expense
Merchandise Inventory	Costs of Goods Sold
Prepaid Expenses	Various expense accounts, i.e., Rent; Insurance; Supplies
Fixed Assets:	
Furniture and Fixtures	Depreciation; Interest Expense; Repairs; Sales of Furniture and Fixtures
Allowance for Depreciation	Depreciation; Sales of Furniture and Fixtures
Machinery	Depreciation; Repairs; Sales of Machinery
Building	Depreciation; Repairs; Property Taxes; Insurance Expense
Current Liabilities:	
Notes Payable	Interest Expense
Accounts Payable	Various Expenses and Purchases
Accrued Expenses	Payroll Expense; Payroll Tax Expense
Long Term Liabilities:	
Mortgage Payable	Interest Expense; Property Taxes; Insurance Expense
Capital:	Net Profit or Loss

Statement of Source and Application of Funds

The Statement of Source and Application of Funds identifies a business's sources and uses of cash over the reporting period. This statement is extremely useful for identifying how a company is funding operations, whether from owner investments, earnings or borrowings. It also shows what the company is doing with its money, whether it is being distributed to the owners, being used to make additional investments, or being used to operate the business. Table 10 is a sample of a simplified income statement for the hypothetical Widgets, Inc.

In the Statement of Cash Flows, net income is usually converted to cash flow by allowing some adjustments. These adjustments are necessary because some accounts effect net income in the Income Statement, but they are not cash receipts or expenditures.

1) Depreciation is added to the net income because it is a noncash expense that reduces net income, but does not reduce cash.

Table 10.

Widgets, Inc. Statement of Source and Application of Funds For the Period Ending December 31, 19XX		
Funds Were Provided By		
Net Income	$53,500	
Depreciation	30,000	
Total		$83,500
Funds Were Used For		
Dividends on Preferred Stock	$ 3,000	
Dividends on Common Stock	12,000	
Plants and Equipment	30,500	
Sundry Assets	1,000	
Total		46,500
Increase in Working Capital		37,500
Analysis of Changes in Working Capital		
Changes in Current Assets		
Cash	15,000	
Marketable Securities	39,000	
Accounts Receivable	10,000	
Inventories	(30,000)	
Total		$34,000
Changes in Current Liabilities		
Accounts Payable	6,000	
Notes Payable	(15,000)	
Accrued Expenses Payable	3,000	
Federal Income Taxes	3,000	
Payable		
Total		$(3,000)

2) Any increase in receivables is subtracted from net income because receivables do not represent a cash asset. The cash is received only when the account has been paid, not when the sale is made and recorded for the reporting period.

3) Any decrease in inventories is added back to the net income because the sale of inventory results in a cost of goods sold expense that consequently reduces net income. However, since inventories purchased in prior reporting periods were sold, the inventory sold during this period did not require an outlay of cash.

4) Any increase in accounts payable is added to net income. These expenses were recognized on the Income Statement, consequently reducing net income. Since they have not yet been paid, no cash has been expended for the expense incurred.[31]

Journals and Ledgers

Many businesses conduct thousands of transactions a day, and, consequently, it is impossible to prepare a balance sheet or income statement each day. Instead, the thousands of daily transactions are recorded in the accounting record, and, at the end of the reporting period, a balance sheet and income statement are prepared.

An account is a systematic arrangement of the increases and decreases affecting the same person or thing. In an accounting system, there are separate accounts for each individual asset, liability, and capital account. When each of these accounts are grouped together, either in a loose leaf notebook or computer program, it is known as a ledger. A ledger is simply the book in which the accounts are kept.[32]

In accounting there are different types of ledgers, including the General Ledger and Subsidiary Ledgers. Ledgers are periodical postings into a series of numbered accounts. The postings are entries from the journals in summary form.

The General Ledger consists of all asset, liability, capital, income, and expense accounts. Each account has a number. This number comes from a document known as the Chart of Accounts. The Chart of Accounts is a listing of the accounts in balance sheet order. The number is a reference to classify the various transactions in the journals. Table 11 is a sample Chart of Accounts.

The Subsidiary Ledgers are a group of accounts that support a single account in the General Ledger. The Subsidiary Ledgers include separate records for accounts receivable, accounts payable, and equipment. These ledgers show specific names, invoice numbers, and descriptions of the transactions. For example, the General Ledger has an Accounts Receivable Control Account that is an aggregate of all money owed to the business. This aggregate amount comprises many different individuals and companies. While the total dollar value appears in the General Ledger in the Accounts Receivable Control Account, the individual dollar breakdown by customer is found in the Accounts Receivable Subsidiary Ledger.

Table 11. Chart of Accounts.

ASSETS		REVENUE	
101	Cash on Hand	301	Sales
102	Cash in Bank	302	Sales Returns and Allowances
103	Accounts Receivable	303	Sales Discount
105	Merchandise Inventory	304	Purchases
106	Prepaid Insurance		
117.0	Delivery Equipment	OPERATING EXPENSES	
117.5	Accumulated Depreciation—		
	Delivery Equipment	401	Delivery Expenses
118.0	Office Furniture	402	Depreciation Expenses—
118.5	Accumulated Depreciation—		Delivery Equipment
	Delivery Equipment	403	Salaries Expenses
119.0	Office Equipment	404	Payroll Expenses
119.5	Accumulated Depreciation—	405	Miscellaneous Selling Expenses
	Office Equipment	407	Depreciation Expenses—
120	Goodwill		Office Furniture
		408	Depreciation Expenses—
LIABILITIES			Office Equipment
		409	Insurance Expenses
201	Accounts Payable	410	Office Supplies Expense
202	Salaries Payable	411	Rent Expense
204	Employees' Income Tax Payable	412	Bad Debt Expense
205	F.I.C.A. Tax Payable	413	Miscellaneous General Expenses
206	Sales Tax Payable		
207	State Unemployment Tax Payable	OTHER INCOME	
208	Notes Payable		
		501	Gain on Disposal of Plant Assets
NET WORTH		502	Interest Income
251	Capital, John Public	OTHER EXPENSES	
252	Drawing, John Public		
253	Profit and Loss	601	Interest Expenses

There are two additional ledgers of interest to the white-collar crime investigator, the Corporate Minutes Book and the Corporate Stock Book. The minutes book contains minutes and resolutions of corporate stockholder or board of directors meetings. It may also reflect persons authorized to sign on checking accounts, nominee agents of the corporation, and functions of responsible corporate officials. The corporate stock book shows the stocks issued by the company, the date of sale, who purchased the stocks, and the amount paid for each share.

The journal is the book of original entry. It is a chronological record that shows for each day the debits and credits from each transaction.[33]

The accountant records and classifies all the information from the source documents in the proper journal. The journals include:

1) Cash Receipts Journal — The cash receipts journal will show the source and amounts of all cash the business receives.
2) Cash Disbursements Journal or Check Register — The cash disbursement journal and the check register will show the dates, amounts, and recipients of payments made by the company. They will also show the balance sheet or income statement account to which the payment is recorded.
3) Sales Journal — The sales journal lists all sales invoices in date or numerical order.
4) Purchases Journal — The purchases journal records all acquisitions of services or merchandise for cash.
5) Accounts Payable Journal — The accounts payable journal records all acquisitions of services or merchandise on credit.
6) General Journal — The general journal records all transactions not covered by the specific purpose journals.

Although it is possible to enter each transaction directly in the ledger, it is more feasible to record initially each transaction into the journal. Continually recording each transaction directly to the ledger would fail to produce an entire record of each transaction. A credit would be in one account and a debit in another. A second problem encountered by recording directly to the ledger would be the absence of a chronological listing of each transaction. To reconstruct the activities of a given business day would require researching the entire General Ledger. To alleviate these problems, transactions are recorded originally into the journal.

Following is the sequence of steps by which information flows through the accounting system:

1) A business transaction occurs.
2) Business documents are prepared to document the transaction.
3) Information from the transaction is summarized and recorded into the journal.
4) Information is transferred from the journal to the ledger.
5) Adjusting entries are made.
6) Financial statements, such as the balance sheet and net income statement, are produced from the ledgers.
7) Closing entries are made.

At the end of the reporting period, adjusting entries are made to ensure the accuracy of the financial statements. Due to changes in the value of accounts such as insurance and depreciation, the records do not always reflect the correct values. Before financial statements can be accurately prepared, consideration must be given to those accounts that do not appear or are not correctly stated in the various accounts.[34]

Closing entries are necessary to close the books on income and expense accounts at the end of a reporting period. This is done to start a new reporting period with zero balances in income and expense accounts. The process of closing the books is accomplished by transferring the balances of all income and expense accounts to a summary account, usually known as the Profit and Loss (P&L) Summary or the Income and Expense Summary. Closing the books is accomplished through the following four steps:

1) transferring the balances from all Income Accounts to the P&L Summary,
2) transferring the balances from all Expense Accounts to the P&L Summary,
3) transferring the P&L Summary balance to the Drawing Account, and
4) transferring the balance of the Drawing Account to the Capital Account.

At the completion of the closing entries, which are recorded in the General Journal, the only accounts that remain open are the assets, liabilities, and capital accounts.[35]

It is important for white-collar crime investigators to understand the way entries are posted to the ledgers and journals. It is during this phase of the record keeping that an embezzler is best able to alter the records to disguise his activity.

Source Documents

Source documents record each business transaction. They are the pieces of paper, whatever the form, that affect the business operation. The source documents are the basic documents from which all transaction entries and financial statements are compiled. They include cash register tapes, sales slips, credit card slips, checks, deposit tickets, invoices, purchase receipts, notes payable, insurance policies, leases, and a host of others. These documents are usually maintained and stored separately from the journals and ledgers. Source documents are usually the best source of evidence and information when tracing fraudulent entries in the books.

It is important for the white-collar crime investigator to remember that embezzlement and fraud investigations are initiated by indicators, a composite of small events that point to a pattern of deception. The investigator must look for those indicators in the financial documents and statements. Table 12 is a list of some common indicators of fraud.

Table 12. Indicators of Fraudulent Financial Transactions.

1. Maintaining two sets of books and records.
2. Concealing assets.
3. Destruction of books and records.
4. Large or frequent currency transactions.
5. Payments to fictitious companies or persons.
6. False or altered entries and documents.
7. Photocopies on file instead of original documents.
8. False invoices or billings.
9. Use of nominees.
10. Large company loans to employees or other persons.
11. Frequent cashing, instead of depositing, checks received.
12. Frequent use of cashiers' checks.
13. Purchases or sale of underpriced or overvalued assets.
14. Personal expenses paid with corporate funds.
15. Payees' names on checks left blank and inserted at a later date.
16. Excessive billing discounts.
17. Excessive spoilage or defects.
18. Double payments on billings.
19. Unnecessary use of collection accounts.
20. An individual negotiating checks made payable to a corporation.
21. Second or third party endorsements on corporate checks.
22. Excessive use of exchange checks or clearing accounts.

Notes

[1] ———, *Financial Investigative Techniques* (Washington, D.C.: Internal Revenue Service, Department of the Treasury, 1986) p. 3-1.

[2] ———, "Introduction to Books and Records," *Narcotics Related Financial Investigative Techniques* (Washington, D.C.: Department of Justice, Federal Bureau of Investigation, 1992) p. 14.

[3] Ibid.

[4]——, *Financial Investigative Techniques,* op cit., p. 3-1.

[5]Ibid., p. 3-3.

[6]Ibid.

[7]Ibid.

[8]Ibid.

[9]Ibid.

[10]Ibid., p. 3-5

[11]Ibid.

[12]Ibid.

[13]Ibid. p. 3-6.

[14]Ibid.

[15]Ibid.

[16]Joseph T. Wells, W. Steve Albrecht, Jack Bologna, Gilbert Geis, and Jack Robertson, *Fraud Examiners' Manual* (Austin, TX: National Association of Certified Fraud Examiners, 1989) Section III, p. 1.

[17]——, *Financial Investigative Techniques,* op cit., p. 3-6.

[18]——, "How to Read a Financial Report," *Narcotics Related Financial Investigative Techniques* (Washington, D.C.: Department of Justice, Federal Bureau of Investigation, 1992) p. 8.

[19]Ibid., p. 10.

[20]——, *Financial Investigative Techniques,* op cit., p. 3-18.

[21]——, "How to Read a Financial Report," op cit., p. 13.

[22]Ibid., p. 14.

[23]Ibid., p. 16.

[24]Ibid., p. 17.

[25]Ibid.

[26]Ibid., p. 18.

[27]——, *Financial Investigative Techniques,* op cit., p. 3-20.

[28]——, "How to Read a Financial Report," op cit., p. 22.

[29]Ibid.

[30]——, *Financial Investigative Techniques,* op cit., p. 3-24.

[31]Wells et al., Section III, pp. 21–22.

[32]——, "Introduction to Books and Records," op cit., p. 19.

[33]Ibid.

[34]——, *Financial Investigative Techniques,* op cit., p. 3-43.

[35]——, "Introduction to Books and Records," op cit., p. 49.

Chapter 5

AUDITING THEORY FOR INVESTIGATORS

Never tell people how to do things. Tell them what to do and they will
surprise you with their ingenuity.

George S. Patton
War as I Knew It

A white-collar crime investigator will rarely, if ever, need to review or
to reconstruct a complete set of business records. He will, however,
be working daily with financial records and documents. Unfortunately,
there exist no step-by-step rules or formulas to guide an investigator in
researching the records of questionable financial transactions. Considering the complexity of modern financial records, dictating rules to prove
fraudulent transactions would be impossible.

Accountants, however, have created auditing procedures and techniques to help them in checking and verifying financial data. Audit
techniques are tools that can help investigators, too, in connecting financial transactions to various kinds of criminal activity. Audit techniques
are based on three key terms—analyze, scrutinize, and compare.

Remember that as an investigator looking beyond the obvious is
necessary. Investigating books and records requires the same cautious
skeptical approach applied to the investigation of any other criminal
activity.[1] The investigator can analyze ledger entry records by breaking
a ledger balance into its component parts, listing those figures that make
up the balance, and checking to see if they are comparable with the
account to which they were charged. The investigator should scrutinize
those documents used to derive the figures in the ledgers, looking for
alterations or for lack of a legitimate business purpose. The investigator
can then compare and evaluate different sources for accuracy or proper
recording while looking for any items that appear irregular or out of the
ordinary.

It cannot be too strongly emphasized that company records of any
kind, to be useful in an analysis or investigation, must be compared.[2]
The comparison may be to copies of records in the hands of others, other
records of the same company, records from previous reporting periods,

records of other companies in a similar business, records of the industry as a whole, to nonfinancial data, or to eyewitness accounts.

Auditors analyze and compare the financial records of a company in three ways to reveal fraud and other types of errors. First, they compare financial statement data from the current reporting period with results from prior reporting periods to discover any unusual relationships. Second, they compare financial statement data from the company in question with data from similar industry statistics to discover any unusual relationships. Third, they associate financial statement data with non-financial data to see if the numbers on the statements are rational and sensible.[3]

Financial Statement Analysis

When a company's financial statements are prepared with integrity, changes in account balances from one reporting to another have logical explanations. If a company is built or operated on fraud, however, the perpetrators may attempt to disguise that fact by manipulating financial statements to conceal missing assets or to understate liabilities. When fraud becomes so large that it affects not only specific assets or liability accounts, but also results in misleading or incorrect financial statements, an analysis of the financial statements of the company may identify potential problem areas. Auditors often use ratio and trend analysis to identify unusual relationships within a financial statement, thereby suggesting areas of errors or irregularities that require further research. Auditors have found that using financial statement analysis to look for unexpected fluctuations in the financial statements is the single best audit technique for discovering material errors.[4]

Auditors use three techniques in comparing financial statement data:

1) ratio analysis,
2) vertical analysis, and
3) horizontal analysis.[5]

Ratio Analysis

Ratio analysis involves computing key ratios to compare significant financial statement relationships between reporting periods. Three of the most helpful ratios in analyzing financial statements are:

1) Current Ratio = Current Assets/Current Liabilities
2) Quick ratio = (Cash + Securities + Receivables)/Current Liabilities
3) Cash Ratio = (Cash + Securities)/Current Liabilities.[6]

Since most internal thefts and embezzlements involve the theft of cash or inventory, or the manipulation of receivables, the investigator can analyze these three current or short-term accounts using the above ratios. Many factors, including ever changing economic conditions, simple accounting errors, changes in management strategy, or manifest fraud, may cause significant variations in these ratios between reporting periods. The investigator's responsibility is to use these ratios to identify significant and unexplained fluctuations, and then to find out whether those fluctuations have logical explanations. Lacking any logical explanation, it is possible that someone may be manipulating financial data to conceal criminal activity. Remember that these ratios only suggest potential problem areas. They do not incriminate anyone or prove conclusively that embezzlement or fraud exists.

If the current, quick, or cash ratios suggest potential problems in either receivables or inventory, five additional ratios may be used to identify problem areas further:

1) Accounts Receivable Turnover = Sales/Average Receivables
2) Days to Collect Receivables = 365/Accounts Receivable Turnover
3) Inventory Turnover = Cost of Goods Sold/Average Inventory
4) Days to Sell Inventory = 365/Inventory Turnover
5) Days to Convert Inventory to Cash = Days to Sell Inventory + Days to Collect Receivables.[7]

Unexplained changes in the ratios can signal problems. If, for example, receivable turnover is increasing and days to collect receivables are increasing, it may be a sign of a recession, financial problems within the industry, or financial problems with specific customers. If no such reasonable explanation is apparent, it is possible that someone is stealing cash or compromising short-term receivables, and manipulating the account receivables to balance the financial statements.

Six additional ratios, not as sensitive to embezzlement and fraud as the current asset ratios, may help identify problem areas in cases of large scale fraud:

1) Debt to Equity Ratio = Total Liabilities/Total Equity
2) Times Interest Earned = Net Income/Interest Expense

3) Profit Margin Ratio = Net Income/Net Sales
4) Asset Turnover = Net Sales/Average Total Assets
5) Return on Equity = Net Income/Average Equity
6) Earnings Per Share = Net Income/Numbers of Shares of Stock.[8]

Vertical Analysis

Vertical analysis is a technique for analyzing the relationships between items appearing as lines on the income statement or balance sheet by expressing all the components as percentages. In a vertical analysis, the total assets line on a balance sheet is assigned a value of 100 percent. On an income statement, the net sales line is assigned a value of 100 percent. All other items on the statements are then expressed as a percentage of those two numbers.[9] As with ratio analysis, vertical analysis is useful only if embezzlement or fraud is large enough materially to affect the balances on the financial statement. Table 13 contains a sample of a vertical analysis of a simplified income statement.

Table 13.

Widgets, Inc.
Vertical Analysis of Income Statement for the Year Ending December 31, 19XX

	Year 2		Year 1	
Net Sales	$100,000	100%	$ 80,000	100%
Cost of Goods Sold	(60,000)	(60)%	(40,000)	(50)%
Gross Margin Expense	40,000	40%	40,000	50%
Selling Expenses	(15,000)	(15)%	(12,000)	(15)%
Administrative Expenses	(10,000)	(10)%	(8,800)	(11)%
Income Before Taxes	15,000	15%	19,200	24%
Income Taxes	(6,000)	(6)%	(8,000)	(10)%
Net Income	9,000	9%	11,200	14%

The vertical analysis for the hypothetical Widgets, Inc. reveals that the cost of goods sold increased from 50 percent of sales in year one to 60 percent of sales in year two. There are several possible legitimate reasons for the increase. The costs of raw materials may have risen or there may have been spoilage in the factory. If no reasonable explanation exists, it is possible that someone is stealing inventory. When inventory is stolen, the ending inventory balance is lower and the cost of goods sold appears higher. It is possible, too, that the inventory is being sold, the sales are not being documented, and someone is diverting the proceeds.

Horizontal Analysis

Horizontal analysis is a technique for analyzing the percentage change in individual income statement or balance sheet items from one reporting period to the next. Horizontal analysis supplements ratio and vertical analysis, and allows an auditor to learn whether any particular item has changed in an unusual way in relation to the change in net sales or total assets from one period to the next.[10] Table 14 contains a sample of a horizontal analysis of a simplified income statement. As with vertical analysis, the horizontal analysis may show a potential problem area, but it does not explain the variance. As with any other financial statement analysis, the horizontal analysis, by itself, does not incriminate anyone or prove that fraud or embezzlement exists.

Table 14.

Widgets, Inc.
Horizontal Analysis of Income Statement for the Period Ending December 31, 19XX

	Year 2	Year 1	$ Change	% Change
Net Sales	$100,000	$ 80,000	$20,000	25%
Cost of Goods Sold	(60,000)	(40,000)	20,000	50%
Gross Margin Expenses	40,000	40,000	0	0%
Selling Expenses	(15,000)	(12,000)	3,000	25%
Administrative Expenses	(10,000)	(8,800)	1,200	14%
Income Before Taxes	15,000	19,200	(4,200)	(22)%
Income Taxes	(6,000)	(8,000)	(2,000)	(25)%
Net Income	9,000	11,200	(2,200)	(20)%

Statement of Cash Flow

Because embezzlers often target cash, the statement of cash flow is very useful for identifying potential embezzlement or fraud.[11] The statement of cash flow is often quite complicated. Table 15 contains an analysis of a simplified cash flow statement.

The cash flow statement for Widgets, Inc. in Table 15 shows a net increase of $100,000 in cash. That cash should exist somewhere in some form, either in a bank account where the amount is verifiable, or in a safe or cash drawer where the amount should be countable. Additionally, if the cash amount increased by $100,000 during the reporting period, there seemingly were ample cash reserves to run the business.

Table 15.

Widgets, Inc. Statement of Cash Flow for the Period Ending December 31, 19XX		
Cash Flows from Operations		
Net Income	$ 90,000	
Adjustments to Income		
Depreciation Expense	35,000	
Increase in Receivables	(35,000)	
Decrease in Inventories	25,000	
Increase in Payables	20,000	
Net Cash Inflow from Operations		$135,000
Cash Flows from Investing Activities		
Sale of Equipment	6,000	
Purchase of Land	(22,000)	
Net Cash Outflow from Investments		(16,000)
Cash Flows from Financing Activities		
Payment of Dividends	(34,000)	
Borrowing from Bank	15,000	
Net Cash Outflow from Financing		(19,000)
Net Increase in Cash		$100,000

The investigator should seek some reasonable explanation for the $15,000 loan.

The cash flow statement is particularly useful in detecting embezzlement or fraud in small businesses. The statement of cash flow, as with the other types of financial statement analysis, only suggests areas of concern. It is not, by itself, proof that embezzlement or fraud exists.

Comparisons with Other Companies or Industry Standards

Companies in similar industries should have financial statements that approximately resemble one another in terms of key ratios.[12] Some variances are inevitable because of differences in market strategy, management philosophy, and financial diversification between companies. It would be highly unlikely, however, for a steel manufacturing firm to have inventory turnovers or account receivable ratios three to four times higher than another steel manufacturer within the same geographical region. Financial analysts, investors, and company managers often compare the financial statement ratios of one company to another to assess management skill, operating performance, investment opportunities, liquidity, and solvency. Since comparisons between similar companies have become such valuable investment and management tools, many publishing companies and the United States Department of Commerce widely distribute various industry-wide statistics.

Comparing a company's ratios and performance with those of similar companies can also help identify fraud or other significant internal problems.[13] The investigator can check significant discrepancies between a firm's reported operating expenses and that which is expected, whether that expectation is based on budgets, industry statistics, or any other source. As with any other financial statement analysis, significant discrepancies do not mean that embezzlement or fraud exists, but the investigator should try to find the reason for the discrepancies.

Comparisons with Nonfinancial Data

Financial statement data are only representations of things that should exist in the real world. If a company reports cash of $10,000, that cash should be countable. If a company claims an inventory of $100,000 worth of computers, those computers should be observable. Failing to associate financial statement data with the real world assets or other items they represent is easy for a white-collar crime investigator. There must always exist analytical relationships between representations in financial statements and physical goods or movements of assets.

Examining financial statement data to see if it corresponds to nonfinancial data is one of the best ways to detect embezzlement and fraud.[14] It is unfortunate that many investigators never associate financial statements with the items they are supposed to represent. Investigators who ask themselves if reported amounts are too great, too small, too early, too late, too often or too rare, or who look at things reported at odd times, by odd people, using odd procedures are more likely to detect fraud than those who view the financial statements without any hint of skepticism.

Statistical Sampling

The purpose of an audit is to detect errors in the record keeping which would affect the fairness of a company's financial records. Often where embezzlement or fraud is present, however, a simple analysis of financial statements will not identify specific areas of concern. In such cases, it may become necessary to examine the source documents, ledgers, and journals from which the statements are derived. Often, the number of source documents to be reviewed is so large that examining every one is impossible. In these cases, auditors and investigators may use statistical sampling techniques to decide how many documents and which specific documents to sample.

To be economically feasible and justifiable, an audit can aim only to give reasonable assurance that errors will be detected.[15] It would not be cost effective to review every document produced by a business. The inherent problem with statistical sampling is that under any testing system, assurance can never be complete. Any final audit conclusion is subject to an inherent probability of error.[16] Since the investigator examines only a sample of the entire population, he can never know with absolute certainty the true characteristics of the entire population. The investigator can take certain steps, however, to increase the likelihood that a sample is representative by the way he selects a sample, designs the test, and evaluates the results.

There are two kinds of errors that may occur when using statistical sampling. The first error, known as sampling risk, is the inherent risk that the selected sample will not represent the entire population because of random chance.[17] Two ways to reduce the sampling risk are to increase the size of the sample and to use more appropriate methods of selecting a sample. The second error, known as nonsampling risk, occurs when an investigator draws a representative sample but interprets the results incorrectly.[18] Nonsampling risks occur because of an investigator's inability to recognize problems or alterations due to any number of factors: boredom, exhaustion, inexperience, lack of training, or failure to use proper examination techniques.

Statistical Versus Nonstatistical Sampling

When faced with the necessity of choosing a sample from a large population, many investigators rely on some trusted "rule of thumb," such as examining exactly 300 items, examining every 25th item, or examining every item for one given day. Such judgmental samples may work, and they may give an investigator sufficient evidence to document and prove embezzlement or fraud. Nevertheless, they are by far inferior to properly drawn statistical samples.

The use of statistical sampling qualifies the sampling risk. When using proper statistical sampling, the investigator can state with a degree of confidence that the number of problems or questionable items in an entire population does not exceed a certain percentage.[19] Knowing the degree of confidence in a sample is very useful in deciding whether additional items should be selected for review or whether it is safe to say that no documentary evidence of embezzlement or fraud exists. When using judgmental samples, it is only safe to conclude that no problems or errors existed within the sample chosen.

Sample Selection

There are two steps in statistical and nonstatistical sampling; sample selection and sample evaluation.[20] For statistical sampling to be valid, there must be a known chance for every item in the population to be selected. To satisfy such a requirement, auditors use random sampling. With random sampling, each item or combination of items in the population has an equal chance of being chosen. Investigators can ensure that each item has an equal chance of being chosen by using random number tables or a random number generator. Random numbers tables are listings of independent random digits in tabular form to simplify the selection of random numbers with multiple digits. There are many books of random number tables commercially available. Table 16 contains a small portion of a sample random number table.

Table 16. Random Number Table.

(1)	(2)	(3)	(4)	(5)	(6)
32942	95416	42339	59045	26693	49057
07410	99856	63828	21409	29094	65114
14819	12827	09574	12116	71240	81686
16389	88494	39576	53805	65912	54297
11428	25796	65856	71090	32146	00010

There are four steps in using a random number table. First, identify a number for each item in the population. If the investigator is examining prenumbered documents, such as checks or numbered invoices, the prenumbers will be sufficient. If there is no numbering system, the investigator must devise some appropriate numbering system.

Second, establish a correspondence between the random number table and the population being sampled. This is accomplished by deciding the number of digits to use in the random number table and their association with the population numbering system. For example, assume an investigator is reviewing a sample of 100 checks from a population of checks numbered 1000 through 7731. From the random number table in Table 16, the investigator would use only the last four digits of the five digit numbers. Here, the investigator would first review check 2942.

Third, select a route to follow through the table. For example, the investigator could start at the first number, going either vertically or horizontally across the table using each number, each third number, or whatever system the investigator desires. The important point to remember is to establish the route before selecting the numbers, then stick with that route throughout the sampling process.

Fourth, select the sample. If a number on the random number table lies outside the population to be sampled, disregard that number and take the next number that lies within the population.

Always document the table and route used to select the sample. Documentation allows both the investigator and others to verify the investigator's results. Additionally, should it become necessary later to enlarge the sample, the investigator should use the same table to maintain consistency. Documentation should always include the source of the random number table and the rules for establishing the route through the table. The investigator should preserve the table and rules as possible evidence.

Sample Evaluation

Once the table has been selected, the investigator must evaluate the selected sample. There are many ways to evaluate a sample, but auditors commonly use attribute sampling and variables sampling.[22]

Attribute sampling is a statistical method auditors use to estimate the proportion of items in a population that contains a certain characteristic or attribute of interest.[23] Attribute sampling allows the auditor to estimate the actual occurrence rate and the computed upper and lower deviation rates with a certain degree of confidence. Using attribute sampling, an auditor might conclude that a certain characteristic will exist in 2.5 percent of the population, but will be 95 percent certain that it will occur in not less than 1 percent (the lower deviation rate) and not more than 4 percent (the upper deviation rate). The purpose of attribute sampling is to determine the deviation rate.

Variables sampling is a statistical sampling technique that allows an auditor to determine whether the monetary amount of an account balance is materially misstated.[24] Auditors can use variables sampling to determine whether such accounts as accounts receivable, inventory balances, assets, and net income have been materially misstated.

Although attribute and variables sampling may be useful to auditors to suggest areas of additional research, they may be of little use to the white-collar crime investigator. An investigator is seldom interested in proportions of errors. Financial auditors may allow a deviation rate of 2 to 3 percent, but the investigator must produce specific documents to prove embezzlement or fraud.

A special kind of attribute sampling that may be useful to investigators trying to find whether critical errors exist is discovery sampling. Discovery sampling is a technique that allows an investigator to conclude with a certain confidence level whether any problems or critical errors exist in a population.[25] Discovery sampling is attribute sampling with an expected zero error rate. A discovery sample table is an attribute table based on a 95 percent confidence level that no errors will be found in various items of the entire population. Table 17 contains an example of a simplified discovery sampling table.

Table 17. Discovery Sampling Table.
Probability of Including at Least One Error in the Sample

Sample Size	Rate of Occurrence in the Population							
	.01	.05	.1	.2	.3	.5	1	2
50	2	5	9	14	22	39	64	
70	1	3	7	13	19	30	51	76
100	1	5	10	18	26	39	63	87
200	2	10	18	33	45	63	87	98
300	3	14	26	45	59	78	95	99+
400	4	18	33	55	70	87	98	99+
500	5	22	39	63	78	92	99	99+

Using the sampling table in Table 17, for example, an investigator reviews 300 invoices from the population and finds no errors. From this table, the investigator will conclude with only a 26 percent certainty that errors will occur in no more than 0.1 percent of the population. He will decide with a 78 percent certainty that the errors will occur in no more than 0.5 percent of the population. He will decide with 99 percent plus certainty that the errors will occur in no more than 2 percent of the population. If, however, the investigator reviews 300 invoices and finds an error, he will be 100 percent certain that a problem does exist, as he has found an example. He will know nothing about the occurrence rate or the rate of deviation, but he will know that an error exists, and that is what he wanted to know.

Discovery sampling table probabilities change, of course, depending on the size of the entire population to be sampled. The larger the population, the larger the number of samples is required to assure a constant probability. Thus the investigator can know before the audit begins how many samples he must examine to reach a certain probability that no errors exist.

The use of statistical sampling in auditing, though not universal, is growing. Its main use today is in accounts receivable and inventory. As the demands for enforcement of white-collar criminal statutes increases, statistical sampling will begin to play a greater role for the investigator.

Notes

[1] ——, *Financial Investigative Techniques* (Washington, D.C.: Department of the Treasury, Internal Revenue Service, 1986), p. 3–48.

[2] ——, "How to Read a Financial Report," *Narcotics Related Financial Investigative Techniques* (Washington, D.C.: Department of Justice, Federal Bureau of Investigation, 1992), p. 33.

[3] Joseph T. Wells, W. Steve Albrecht, Jack Bologna, Gilbert Geis, and Jack Robertson, *Fraud Examiners' Manual* (Austin, TX: National Association of Certified Fraud Examiners, 1989), Section III, p. 11.

[4] Ibid., p. 10.

[5] Ibid.

[6] Benjamin Graham and Charles McGalrick, *The Interpretation of Financial Statements* (New York: Harper & Row, 1975), pp. 79–81.

[7] Leopold A. Bernstein, *Analysis of Financial Statements* (Homewood, IL: Dow Jones-Irwin, 1984) pp. 87–108.

[8] Graham et al., op cit.

[9] Lyn M. Fraser, *Understanding Financial Statements: Through the Maze of a Corporate Annual Report* (Reston, VA: Reston Publishing Co., 1985), p. 103.

[10] Ibid.

[11] Wells et al., op cit., p. 19.

[12] Ibid., p. 16.

[13] Ibid., p. 28.

[14] Ibid., p. 19.

[15] Bernstein, op cit., pp. 79–81.

[16] Ibid., p. 349.

[17] Wells et al., op cit., p. 110.

[18] Ibid.

[19] Donald Leslie, Albert Teitlebaum, and Henry Pankratz, "Mathematics of Finance and Statistical Sampling," *Accountants Handbook, Vol. 1, 6th Edition,* Lee J. Seidler and D. R. Carmichael, eds. (New York: John Wiley & Sons, 1981), Section 15, p. 40.

[20]Wells et al., op cit., p. 111.
[21]Ibid., p. 112.
[22]Leslie et al., op cit., p. 37.
[23]Ibid., p. 38.
[24]Ibid., p. 46.
[25]Wells et al., op cit., pp. 114–115.

Chapter 6

FINANCIAL INTERVIEWING
AND INTERROGATION

There are two sides to every question.

> Diogenes Laertius
> *Lives of Eminent Philosophers,*
> *Protagoras*

Remember that in any white-collar crime investigation there may be many sides to every question and to every accusation. Issues are not always simple or easily understood. Each questionable issue may be inescapably intertwined with other ambiguous issues. Nevertheless, it remains the duty of the investigator to seek out all the facts in question. During an investigation, facts will appear from many sources, but "(t)he spoken word is potentially the largest source of the various forms of evidence available to the investigator."[1]

Few skills are as important to the white-collar crime investigator as having command of the techniques for interview and interrogation. Yet, few investigators have mastered the art. Few investigators are ever fully satisfied with their level of performance in this vital phase of the investigation.

There are many reasons for this lack of proficiency in financial investigative techniques. Among these are inadequate training in the field of financial interviewing, inadequate planning before conducting an interview, and a tendency for the investigator to underestimate the mental capabilities of the suspect.[2]

Financial interview and interrogation techniques are not much different from other interview and interrogation techniques to which investigators are accustomed. The investigator should remember, however, that in financial investigations, evidence often develops in small bits and pieces that, when viewed separately, may appear to lead nowhere. "Frustration is common, and tactics and techniques may have to be modified and carefully employed because diligence, patience, and persistence are essential to successful results."[3]

Interview Versus Interrogation

An interview is the systematic questioning of cooperative persons who have knowledge of events, persons involved, or circumstances surrounding a case under investigation, including the obtaining of documentary or physical evidence.[4] An interrogation is the systematic questioning of suspects and/or uncooperative persons to obtain evidence or proof of significant omissions, or to allow the person suspected an opportunity to volunteer facts that might have the exculpatory effect of putting the transactions under investigation in a different light.[5]

In the investigation of embezzlement and fraud, there is little difference in the two techniques. Often the line between interview and interrogation is fluid. The investigator may find while questioning a previously cooperative witness that the witness has become hostile, is withholding information, or is culpable in the crime. Additionally, even a witness who is at first cooperative may become uncooperative if he becomes aware that the investigation has centered on a friend or coworker.

On the other hand, while interrogating a suspect, the investigator may decide that the suspect is not involved in the crime, but that he is willing to discuss all he knows about it. The investigator may also find that a suspect is willing to confess and reveal evidence implicating others in the scheme.

Interviewing Victims and Cooperative Witnesses

At the outset of most investigations, the investigator possesses only limited knowledge of the facts and circumstances surrounding the allegations. In some limited instances the investigator may have access to complete information, such as when a private firm or trade association has already conducted a substantial internal inquiry and willingly conveys its findings to the criminal investigator. In white-collar crime cases, the major tool the investigator uses to close the gap between bits of information and evidence to support prosecution is the interview. It is primarily from the interview that the investigator achieves the following objectives:

1) obtain and develop information that establishes the essential elements of the crime;

2) obtain leads for developing the case and gathering other evidence;

3) obtain the cooperation of the victims and witnesses in recounting their experiences at time of trial; and

4) obtain information regarding the personal backgrounds and personal and economic motives of suspects, victims, and witnesses at trial.[6]

Little standardization of interview techniques is possible since the interview process is so strongly dependent on several factors, such as the personalities of each individual witness, victim and investigator, the complexity of the interview topic, and the respective knowledge levels of the investigator and the interviewee. Each investigator should, nevertheless, plan the interview and follow a proven set of guidelines to ensure maximum probability of achieving the objectives.

Planning the Interview

The importance of proper planning for an interview cannot be overemphasized. Proper planning enhances the probability of the investigator's success and effectiveness in the interview. The investigator will obtain the most information from the interview, and he will take less time.

Before beginning an interview, the investigator must first determine what types of information he is trying to collect. The range of information available from a victim or witness is broad, but the interview must focus on what is relevant to the investigation. Table 18 illustrates the types of information an investigator might collect, either about the person being interviewed or about a possible suspect. The table is a guideline only, and the investigator should modify it as the particular occasion demands.

Interview planning often begins with a background check of the person to be interviewed. Previously filed reports, intelligence files, and criminal history records may give the investigator an insight into the character and motives of the interviewee. Unless the interviewee is of well known and reputable stature in the community, the investigator should conduct a background check before the interview.

Before conducting an interview, the investigator should review all the information available to him, including a review of relevant documents, to refresh his memory. Rarely can the investigator follow a routine format easily committed to memory. It is therefore, advisable to prepare an outline of critical questions or areas of concern in advance. This is

Table 18. Guidelines of Information to Be Collected During a Financial Interview.

I. Identification
   A. Full name
   B. Aliases
   C. Reason for aliases
   D. Driver's license state and number
   E. Social Security number
II. Birth
   A. Date
   B. Place
   C. Citizenship
   D. Father's name
   E. Mother's name
III. Addresses during pertinent years
   A. Residence(s)
   B. Home phone number(s)
   C. Business address(es)
   D. Business phone number(s)
IV. Marital status
   A. Present status
   B. Marriage(s)
      1. Date(s) of marriage(s)
      2. Place(s) of marriage(s)
      3. Spouse's maiden name(s)
   C. Divorce
      1. Date(s) of divorce(s)
      2. Location of divorce(s)
   D. Children's names and dates of births
V. Occupation
   A. Present position
      1. Company name and address
      2. Supervisor's name
      3. Present salary
      4. Length of time employed
   B. Part time or full time
   C. Prior occupation(s)
   D. Spouse's occupation(s)
VI. General background
   A. General health
   B. Mental health
   C. Education
   D. Military service
   E. Arrest record
   F. Bankruptcy record
VII. Financial institutions
   A. Checking accounts

Table 18. (Continued)

B. Savings accounts
C. Safe deposit boxes
   1. Inventory
   2. Largest amount of cash held
   3. Contents after last visit
D. Trusts
   1. Beneficiary
   2. Donor
   3. Trustee
E. Credit union
F. Brokers
G. Currency exchanges used
H. Negotiable instruments
   1. Money orders
   2. Bank drafts
   3. Traveler's checks

VIII. Sources of income
A. Salaries, wages, business receipts
B. Interest dividends
C. Sale of securities
D. Rentals and royalties
E. Sales of assets, pensions, trusts, annuities, etc.
F. Gifts
G. Inheritances
H. Loans
I. Mortgages
J. Insurance settlements
K. Damages from legal actions

IX. Net income and expenditures
A. Assets
   1. Current cash
     a. Locations
     b. Cash on hand
   2. End of year cash balances
   3. Notes receivable
   4. Mortgages receivable
   5. Life insurance policies
   6. Automobiles
   7. Real estate
   8. Stocks, bonds, and securities
   9. Jewelry and furs
B. Liabilities
   1. Payables
   2. Loans
   3. Assets purchased by financing
   4. Mortgages

Table 18. (Continued)

C. Expenditures
  1. Debt reduction
  2. Insurance premiums
  3. Interest expenses
  4. Contributions
  5. Medical
  6. Travel
  7. Real estate and income taxes
  8. Servant's wages
  9. Casualty losses
D. Business operations
  1. Name(s) and address(es)
  2. Date(s) and nature
    a. Corporation
    b. Partnership
    c. Proprietorship
  3. Title and duties
  4. Investments
  5. Associates
E. Books and records
  1. Accounting system
  2. Period covered
  3. Location of books and records
  4. Name of person who maintains and controls the books and records
  5. Types of records available
  6. Name(s) of outside accountant(s)
F. Business receipts
  1. Forms
  2. Where are all receipts kept or deposited
  3. Business and personal receipts separated
  4. Expenses paid with undeposited receipts
  5. Checks cashed for customers.

particularly important when the investigation involves new schemes about which the investigator is not familiar.

The investigator must keep his mind open to all information. An outline should be a guide to effective interviewing, not a substitute for original or spontaneous questioning. A carefully planned outline will provide enough leeway for the investigator to cope with any unexpected leads that may arise. Without the necessary flexibility, the investigator may obtain a voluminous statement of little value.

Without proper planning the investigator may find that he does not understand the responses to his questions, that his questions are rambling or nonsensical, that he will not know what information is required to further the investigation, and that he does not recognize new leads.

The preparation varies widely from interview to interview, and the exact steps will depend on the given situation. Many interviews will not require elaborate or extensive preparation, but proper organization in advance will still reap large rewards.

To plan for the interview properly, the investigator should do several things:

1) Collect all documents to be available to the interviewee during the interview in one file. If one document is to be available to more than one interviewee during the investigation, make copies for separate files.

2) Organize the contents of each file logically. If a file is large, it may be necessary to reorganize or break down the contents. Make a summary of key points or prepare a flow chart if the facts are complicated.

3) Read the file carefully before the interview.

4) Develop a clear objective of the interview and stick to it. After having spoken with the original victim or complaining witness, the investigator should already have developed a case theory he is attempting to prove or disprove.

5) Decide the structure of the interview. Most interviews are organized by one or more of the three following methods:

   a) Chronologically—The interviewee is to relate the relevant facts and events in the order they occurred. This is the simplest and most common way to organize an interview.

   b) According to the documents—The interviewee will review and explain each document in turn. Of course, organizing the documents in some logical manner is necessary.

   c) By transaction or event—If the events or transactions have little chronological significance, the investigator may organize the interview according to each transaction.

Arranging the Interview

There are a few advantages to conducting an interview at the investigator's office, but they are mainly for the investigator's convenience. Usually, visiting the victim or cooperative witness at his home or office is advisable. This approach has several real advantages. First, the interviewee is more likely to have papers, appointment books, memoranda, or other documents available for production if it appears they are relevant to the interview. The interviewee is also able to call immediately upon family members or coworkers for additional information, should the need arise. Second, it may be more convenient for the interviewee, thus making it more likely that he will be agreeable to the meeting. Third, the investigator will usually find it more difficult to eliminate distractions at his office than will the interviewee at in his office or home. Fourth, catching a potential victim or witness off guard, before he can develop second thoughts or fears about cooperating with the investigation, may be advantageous.

Whenever an interview is to be held, the investigator should set a specific appointment for the convenience of all parties involved, unless there is a specific reason for not doing so. The investigator should always arrange to have sufficient time to conduct a complete interview. Allotting extra time for an interview is always better than creating irritations or hardships by stopping an interview before it is completed and having to schedule additional appointments. If the investigator knows he will not make a scheduled appointment on time, he should telephone the interviewee, explain, apologize, and schedule another appointment.

The investigator should never try to extend the interview beyond the scheduled time. If it appears the interview will take more than the allotted time, the investigator should stop the interview and schedule another appointment. A victim or witness may have other appointments scheduled and may not wish to cooperate if the interview becomes disruptive to his business routine.

When an investigator attempts an interview without a prior appointment, he will often find the interviewee totally unprepared. This is a particularly difficult problem when one considers the mass of paperwork and documentation often required of the interviewee to support his claims and allegations. When scheduling the appointment, the investigator should tell the interviewee what documents will be necessary for the interview and allow sufficient time for the interviewee to obtain those documents.

Unless the interviewee needs additional time to prepare adequately or obtain documents, scheduling appointments as quickly as possible after the first contact is best, usually within 24 hours if scheduling permits. The investigator should confirm the appointment a few hours before it is to begin. Forgetting an appointment can have dire consequences.

"Misunderstandings and faulty memories can cause investigators more trouble than recalcitrant witnesses in such situations since confusion easily triggers loss of confidence on the part of the victim/witness."[7]

Even the process of making an appointment can be a source of information for the investigator. The responses and mannerism of the victim or witness may alert the investigator to special problems he might encounter, such as fear, lack of awareness, or language problems. Such insights may help the investigator to plan the interview.

Setting for the Interview

Whenever possible, the investigator should select the setting for the interview to avoid or reduce distractions. Telephones, other voices, other conversations, even the presence of other people, may greatly affect the recall capabilities of a victim or witness. Interruptions will often convey to the interviewee that the investigator is not really interested in what he is saying. If the interview is at the investigator's office, he should use an interview room that is free of distractions, and is designed for pleasant but serious conversation. If the interview is at another location, the location should be convenient to the interviewee, but secluded from unnecessary interruptions.

Investigator's Demeanor

When dealing with any member of the public, whether in person or on the phone, the investigator must always be efficient, courteous, polite, and careful regarding his language and manners. The investigator represents his agency, and the impression he leaves is the impression the public will have not only of his abilities, but of the agency as a whole.

Following are some suggestions regarding an investigator's conduct during an interview:

1) Never talk down to the person being interviewed. Never assume that the subject is less intelligent than the investigator. Any hint of disrespect or condescension can quickly turn a cooperative subject into an uncooperative one.

2) Never use language that disparages the intelligence or competence of the interviewee. Never hint to the victim or witness that

he or she acted foolishly in being victimized or in failing to notify law enforcement authorities of what happened.

3) Be sensitive to the personal concerns of the victim or witness, especially when these involve perceptions of how the interviewee may be treated because of sex, race, religion or ethnic background.

4) Be businesslike. Conduct the interview professionally. The investigator should be friendly but not familiar. Do not let the interview become a social occasion.

5) Do not become authoritarian or attempt to dominate the interview.

6) Make it clear that anyone, no matter how smart or well trained, can be a victim.

7) Always be sympathetic and respectful to victims and complainants. Never damage the subject's pride in his own judgment.

8) Never belittle a victim's loss or build up false hopes of recovery or restitution.

9) Use language consistent with the victim's station and position. Avoid law enforcement jargon.

10) Compliment the victim or complaining witness for taking the time and trouble to cooperate.

11) End every cooperative interview with thankful sincere appreciation.

12) Dress appropriately for the interview; a conservative suit or blazer and tie for men, or a modest dress or suit for a woman.

Conducting an Interview

An interview has three parts: an introduction, a body, and a close. Each part has an integral role in the interview process.

The introduction to the interview is especially critical. It is here that the investigator introduces himself and sets the tone for the interview. No matter how hostile the witness may appear, the investigator should always be polite and professional. State the purpose of the contact in a general way, and ask for the interviewee's cooperation.

The key to the introduction is to get the interviewee to speak with the investigator. Do not rush into the subject matter as interviewees are often apprehensive about the encounter. Take time to allay any fears or concerns the interviewee may voice.

For a witness to agree to speak "off the record" is common during the introduction. The investigator must avoid agreeing to this. First, "off the record" information is useless unless the investigator can verify it, which often he cannot. Second, it is more likely that the investigator will give up information rather than obtain it.

Once the interviewee has agreed to cooperate with the investigator and answer questions, the body of the interview begins. The investigator should keep comments in check and stick to asking questions. He should not voice opinions. He should let the interviewee tell his story in his own words. If the interviewee rambles, be patient. The investigator can ask specific follow-up questions to get back to the topic. Be sure to separate fact from opinion.

Do not be afraid to ask questions about business procedures. When investigating embezzlement and fraud, a clear understanding of record-keeping procedures is vital. The investigator should ask the interviewee to define terms the investigator does not understand.

When closing the interview, summarize the points covered in the body. Be sure to give the interviewee the opportunity to clarify any misunderstandings or to add to his comments. Ask the interviewee if he would like to discuss anything else. Finally, ask the interviewee to keep the interview confidential. Explain that gossip could impair the investigation or ruin an innocent person's reputation.

The following guidelines are most helpful when conducting the interview:

1) Use short questions confined to one clearly and easily understood topic. Complex or broad questions usually generate complex and confusing answers with little detail.

2) Ask questions that require narrative answers. Avoid questions that require "Yes" or "No" answers.

3) Whenever possible, avoid asking questions that suggest or contain the answer.

4) Question the victims and witnesses about how they learned their facts.

5) Require victims and witnesses to give a factual basis for any conclusions they may state.

6) Stay alert to keep the victim or witness from wandering aimlessly off the topic. When possible, require direct responses.

7) Do not allow the victim or witness to lead the investigator away from the topic. Do not allow the interviewee to confuse the issue or leave basic questions unanswered.

8) Concentrate more on the answers than on the next question.

9) Avoid unrelated and incomplete chronologies. Make sure the investigator clearly understands each answer and clarifies any misunderstandings before moving to the next question.

The interviewee should completely answer all the basic questions during the interview:

1) Who? The interviewee should completely identify all known victims, witnesses and suspects.
2) What? The interviewee should give the complete details of the events from beginning to end.
3) When? Direct questioning may establish time frames, by relating the incident with known persons, places or things.
4) Where? The interviewee should provide complete details concerning where all the events took place and provide locations of documentary evidence.
5) Why? Everything is done for a reason. The interviewee could probably help explain motives.
6) How? The interviewee should explain the manner in which events took place, including the method by which the fraud or embezzlement was carried out and concealed.

It is imperative that the investigator maintains full control over the interview. He can often do this by explaining the rights, duties, and privileges to which each participant is entitled at the beginning of the interview. The investigator must immediately correct any deviation from the roles. If this cannot be done, the investigator should stop the interview until the correction can be made. A record must be made of the attempts the investigator took to correct the situation and of the reasons for stopping the interview.

Note Taking

Note taking is an important skill for the white-collar crime investigator. Since he may gather so much information from so many sources, and because the information may come in tiny bits and pieces, the ability of the investigator to note each important fact becomes essential.

There is little standardization of note taking during an interview. Whatever form the investigator chooses, the notes should accurately reflect all data and information the investigator obtained during the interview. He should write out names, places and dates with correct spellings. To ensure minimal dependence on memory, the investigator should review the notes as soon as possible after the interview, clarifying any areas that he could not detail during the interview. A follow-up phone call may clear up any confusion.

Should the interviewee permit the use of a tape recorder, the investigator should use it only as a backup to note taking. Extensive tape recordings slow the investigator's ability to review important information and prepare reports or memoranda. The investigator should always make sure that the first thing on the tape is his request for permission to tape the interview. He should make sure that the interviewee's oral consent is absolutely clear and loud enough to record.

If the interview is to be complex, technical, or very important to the case, having two interviewers may be beneficial, one to take the lead in questioning and one to take notes.

Always remember that interview notes and tapes may become evidence in a later criminal trial or civil litigation. What the investigator records on paper or tape, he may later be called upon to explain. It is important that words or abbreviations be clear and concise. Avoid extraneous words or personal abbreviations. Never editorialize on the content of the notes.

Special Considerations

The investigator must consider the emotional state of the victims or witnesses he is interviewing. The loss of all or part of their assets or wealth has been a shock to the victims. A victim may feel that government intrusion into the matter will interfere with his chances of obtaining restitution, or the victim may want the agency's assistance in recovering their losses. The investigator should explain agency policy in this regard. He should suggest that assistance might be available from private attorneys or from other public or private agencies that may have specialized enforcement or remedial jurisdiction.

Witnesses often have unsupported opinions and claims connected with the crime. These opinions may be based on rumors they have overheard, or they may be based on a bias or prejudice against an individual who is a subject of the investigation. An investigator should not discourage these opinions, but he should pursue them to their logical conclusions. What may at first seem unsupported conclusions may ultimately be proven justified. Often a person's feelings may have some logical basis even though the person cannot articulate them.

The investigator must concentrate on what the interviewee is saying. Think about one topic at a time and not about the next question. If the interviewee wanders from the question, do not stop him as the response may lead to a new line of questioning. Once the interviewee has completed an answer that strayed from the question, the investigator can bring him back to the topic with specific questions.

Remember that in an interview the investigator necessarily gives information to the interviewee regarding what kind of information the investigator wants to know. If the investigator does not want a piece of information revealed, he must be careful how he is to use it or ask questions about it in the interview.

The determination of whether an interviewee is telling the truth is always a consideration. If untruthfulness is suspected, the investigator must be prepared with facts to refute the untruthfulness. Ending an interview is always better than losing control by a confrontation based on insufficient evidence. Even an untruthful interview may be beneficial later. Witnesses and victims, who are later confronted with evidence of their untruthfulness, might be more willing to cooperate and testify truthfully.

When an investigator suspects the interviewee is untruthful or may be culpable in the incident, he should consider two options:

1) Stop the interview immediately and make a written record of the reason. This will be especially important if the investigator suspects the interviewee may become the subject of criminal prosecution; or

2) Allow the interviewee to continue to talk, on the theory that by confronting the interviewee with his own falsities, he may push the interviewee into giving valuable information.

The investigator should observe carefully the demeanor of the interviewee. They should be at ease from the beginning of the interview and remain at ease throughout.

Obstacles to Successful Interviewing

The white-collar crime investigator often faces problems and obstacles to interviewing that relate to certain characteristics of victims and witnesses.

"Somewhere in the human psyche lies an element that induces many people to hand over their savings rather than risk the possibility that some total stranger might think them stupid. If this element did not exist, neither would the fine art of swindling. . . . "[8] This element provides the greatest obstacle to the investigator, first in locating victims, and second in getting victims and witnesses to participate in a situation, such as an interview or court proceeding, in which they must admit being duped. "The guile, deception, and trickery common to frauds often silence the victim."[9]

Both privately owned and government enterprises operate based on public trust and confidence. The commission of a white collar crime involving such institutions may cause not only the initial financial loss, but the attendant publicity may also cause a loss of prestige or public trust. Consequently, the enterprise may elect to suffer the financial loss rather than risk a loss of public confidence.

The victim, whether an individual or corporation, may have already related a false or incorrect account of the incident to family, stockholders or the press and may feel a need to continue with the false account. Most victims do not welcome protracted court proceedings and appearances, especially when they feel they have nothing to gain.

A witness who is not a victim may be uncooperative for a variety of reasons such as fear of reprisal, a dislike for law enforcement, and fear of self-incrimination. Even totally innocent witnesses may feel the problem is not theirs, and it is not worth their time to help in the investigation. Technical experts, such as lawyers or accountants, may be reluctant to participate at the onset fearing the invitation of future civil liability.

Overcoming Obstacles to Interviewing

The investigator can use certain techniques to overcome obstacles to interviewing. The specific situations will determine the proper approach.

When confronting a witness who has made previous denials or given inconsistent statements, the investigator should:

1) Persist in following up every question or topic to its logical conclusion;
2) Pursue the same topic from a variety of perspectives, any of which might help to generate additional responses; and
3) Be ready to use all information obtained earlier, whether from file documents or memory, to refute denials and inconsistencies and to impart varying degrees of damaging information about the scheme and its promoters.

In all cases, especially those involving private and governmental agencies, the investigator should help the victims reduce their embarrassment. When applicable, the investigator should also show that he stands ready to give credit for a victim's or witness's assistance in the investigation. If the investigator is working for a private concern, he should tell victims or witnesses that he will note their cooperation, or lack of it, in whatever report the investigator prepares for his client, usually the victim's or witness's employer.

The investigator may find it desirable to encourage cooperation because cooperation will protect others from similar victimization. He can appeal to the victim's or witness's urge to fight back.

When attempting to gain cooperation, being sympathetic to the victim's or witness's attitudes is always advisable, even if they impede swift resolution to the obstacles. Make the interviewee feel like part of the team.

Most victims are interested in restitution. The investigator may point out that a court may order restitution. He should make sure, however, that the victim realizes restitution is not certain. He can explain to the victim that information uncovered in a criminal investigation is often admissible in a civil action for damages.

Common Mistakes in Financial Interviewing

Often, if the investigator approaches the witness too soon, he will not have developed sufficient incentives for the witness to cooperate. Always take time to analyze what could go wrong in an interview. The investigator should decide in advance what information he needs from the interview, and decide what concessions he can make to obtain it.

The investigator must avoid being overbearing. Threats and strong arm tactics rarely succeed in turning an adverse or recalcitrant witness. At the same time, however, he cannot be too lenient. Promising an interviewee favorable or lenient treatment will often lead to his giving incorrect or incomplete information.

Statements

In a general sense, a statement is nothing more than a recitation of fact. It may be in any form, but it should be signed by the investigator preparing it and by the witness from whom it is obtained. The investigator should record the statement during the interview, or as soon as possible afterwards. Statements are usually recorded in one of three forms:

1) a memorandum of interview,
2) an affidavit, or
3) a question and answer statement.

A memorandum of interview is a written record of an interview that notes what the investigator wants to remember, either as evidence or an investigatory lead. The memorandum shows the date, place, and time of the interview, and it shows the persons present. Investigators should confine the memorandum to the facts developed in the interview and should avoid stating opinions, conclusions, or other extraneous material. An investigator should prepare the memorandum of interview as soon as possible after an interview so the facts and details of the interview are still fresh in his mind.

An affidavit is a written or printed declaration of a statement of fact, made voluntarily, and confirmed by the oath or affirmation of the party making it. An affidavit should contain only facts to which a witness can testify, and should not contain hearsay or other information about which a witness cannot directly testify. The affidavit is perhaps the most commonly used form of recording witness testimony. It is often useful at trial for refreshing a witness's memory, impeaching the testimony of a witness, or for introducing evidence.

A question and answer statement is a complete transcript of questions asked of an interviewee, and of the answers and statements made by him.

The question and answer statement may be prepared from a recorder's notes or transcribed from a recording device. Additionally, the investigator may submit a list of written questions to the interviewee, and the interviewee may submit his written answers in response.

Interrogating Suspects

Clearly, the most obvious purpose of speaking with the suspect or target of an investigation is to obtain evidence or information about the matter under investigation, or to obtain admissions that could be useful at trial. The investigator must always be mindful, however, that the interrogation may also be a tool to vindicate the suspect, or to locate evidence or information that proves his innocence.

During the investigation, the suspect, his attorney, or both, may request an interview. In white-collar crime investigations, this is common. The suspect and his attorney may claim that they are concerned about false accusations that might harm the suspect's personal or business reputation. They may also claim that the allegations stem from a misunderstanding that they might resolve if given the chance to explain. The investigator must consider the possibility that such concerns are genuine.

On the other hand, the investigator must also be aware that the suspect and his attorney are attempting to obtain information on the status of the investigation. They may also be trying to stall or impede the progress of the investigation. The investigator must be careful not to divulge information to the suspect that could allow him to hinder the investigation or that could damage prosecution. The investigator should assume that the suspect and his attorney have the same motives as the investigator: they are both professionals interested in learning the status of the situation and attempting to find out what the other knows.[10]

When the investigator initiates the interrogation, the objectives of the interrogation will depend on the circumstances of the individual case. The investigator may seek to:

1) elicit information from a suspect and thereby fill any pieces missing from his investigation;
2) elicit incriminating statements from the suspect, either as an admission of guilt or as false or inconsistent statements;

3) identify the suspect's possible defenses, either real or contrived, by analyzing his responses to questions concerning the matter under investigation, and by that find ways to neutralize those defenses; or

4) confront the suspect with the evidence and allow him an opportunity to provide an explanation or exculpatory evidence.

Whether to Interrogate

The investigator must realize that interrogating the suspect in embezzlement or financial fraud is not always desirable. Obtaining a goal of an interrogation is not assured, and an interrogation is not without risk. Investigators must consider the unique aspects of each case before deciding whether to attempt an interrogation. If the chances of realizing one goal of an interrogation are negligible, the investigator only risks revealing his own information to the suspect. The investigator must consider:

1) the type of suspect, his age, education level, status in the community, experience and history, and

2) the scheme itself, the sophistication, the complexity, the scope, and the permanence.

There are many pitfalls inherent in the decision to interrogate a suspect. Such pitfalls are most pronounced when evidence of a suspect's guilt has not yet developed or if an attorney is present. Such pitfalls include:

1) the possibility that they may compromise or stymy the investigation by revealing that an investigation is underway;

2) a chance the suspect may learn something that will enable him to obscure or fabricate evidence or influence witnesses;

3) the possibility that alerting the suspect of an investigation may give him time to flee the jurisdiction before the investigator can file charges; and

4) the possibility that the investigator may waste time following fictitious leads or information the suspect gives.

The likelihood of an experienced white-collar criminal exposing information or making incriminating statements is not good. Many white-collar criminals have above average intelligence and, as a normal prerequisite for the trade, are accomplished liars. Investigators are not always immune to those skills.

The interrogation of a suspect may be totally unnecessary when the investigation reveals overwhelming evidence. It may be demoralizing for the suspect to believe that the case against him is so strong that investigators never felt it necessary to speak with him about the accusations.

When considering whether to interrogate a suspect, the investigator should also know legal consequences may imperil the case. A court may suppress evidence crucial to the investigation gathered from such an interrogation, thereby destroying the possibility of prosecution.

The investigator should also consider foregoing an interrogation when the suspect's attorney is present. While denying a suspect his Constitutional right to counsel is never proper, the risks to the case go up, and the prospective benefits go down when the attorney accompanies the suspect.

There are, of course, many arguments in favor of interrogating suspects. Confronting a suspect with overwhelming evidence already gathered during a thorough and comprehensive investigation may have such a psychological impact as to provoke admissions of guilt. Additionally, such an impact may cause the suspect to be more conducive to a later plea bargain agreement.

A meeting with a suspect, before gathering substantial evidence, rarely results in an admission of wrongdoing. Such a meeting, however, can be beneficial. The suspect is much more likely to discuss his business dealings openly when the investigator explains that someone has made a complaint, and that the investigator is merely trying to decide whether there should be a formal investigation. Such a discussion may reveal many investigative leads.

Suspects experienced in embezzlement or financial fraud often have contingency plans and explanations should the scheme be investigated. An inexperienced suspect, however, may not have developed such plans or explanations, and is, therefore, more likely to reveal information. The shock of being discovered may even result in the suspect making incriminating admissions. It is also unlikely that such inexperienced suspects can gather any useful information from the investigator during the interrogation.

Depending on the circumstances, speaking with the suspect to avoid the perception of a rush to judgment may be desirable. Juries do not look favorably on an investigation that does not allow a suspect the opportunity to explain himself, especially if he can present a viable explanation at trial. The jury is left wondering why the investigator never bothered hearing the suspect's side of the story before rushing to file a criminal complaint.

Planning the Interrogation

Once the investigator has decided that an interrogation is in order, preparations are vital. The investigator cannot be too prepared. The success of an investigation and prosecution may depend upon the investigator obtaining a confession.

In preparing for the interrogation, the investigator should use the basic steps employed in preparing for an interview:

1) collect and review all the pertinent evidence and statements already collected;
2) organize the evidence logically; and
3) determine the objectives or goals of the interrogation.

Additionally, the investigator must review the legal elements of the case and compare them with the evidence to decide whether he must cure any deficiencies in the case.

Scheduling the Interrogation

Generally, questioning of a suspect begins only after the investigator has interviewed all other known witnesses and gathered all available information and documents. Sometimes, however, interrogating the suspect early in the investigation may be advisable, especially if he already knows an inquiry is underway. This may prove helpful in developing financial information about a suspect. There should never be an attempt to question the suspect, however, before the investigator has had an opportunity to find out a few facts about the nature of the scheme. The investigator will seldom obtain an admission if he does not know to what the suspect is to admit.

In most white-collar cases such as embezzlement and fraud, the suspect is generally aware of the investigation long before the investigator is ready to approach him. He has probably heard from witnesses already interviewed. "As a general rule, it is best not to let the suspect know the interrogation has been scheduled; it will simply permit him . . . to develop exculpatory answers to the questions and make obtaining a confession more difficult."[11]

Questioning the suspect without first making an appointment may not be possible, however. Many white-collar criminals, at the first hint of an investigation, will obtain legal counsel. The attorney will advise the suspect never to talk to anyone regarding the allegations or investigation unless the attorney is present. "Unlike common crime defense work, which typically begins only after an arrest has been made, the white-collar crime attorney is intimately involved in the case from the first stages of official investigation, when there may be only the whisper of a suspicion of wrongdoing and rarely a smoking gun. Instead of being on the receiving end of a set of largely preestablished facts, the attorney is in a position to influence and shape the very pool of facts that becomes the focus of legal argument."[12] It is clear, therefore, there is little hope of developing substantial information from a suspect who has already obtained counsel.

Setting for the Interrogation

In most situations, the investigator cannot control the location of the interrogation. It is nearly impossible to arrange for a suspect to meet the investigator at some prearranged location without allowing the suspect substantial time that he might use to prepare for questioning. The investigator must usually surprise the suspect at his home or place of business to catch him unprepared for questioning. In such cases, it is imperative that the investigator attempts to reduce distractions.

The room or location established for the interrogation should be as quiet and private as possible. There must be a minimum of distractions, thus enabling the investigator to conduct the interrogation with the suspect's full attention. Unless the suspect is under arrest, the investigator should not lock the door to an interview room. The suspect should feel that he is free to leave whenever he wants. The room should be free of large objects, such as opaque drapes, that may cause the suspect to feel that someone else may be secreted in the room. The room should be adequately well lighted so that the investigator can see the suspect's facial features. The investigator should remove noise distractions such as televisions, radios, and telephones, since they impair both parties' abilities to concentrate.

The suspect should not sit behind a desk or any other physical barrier to allow the investigator full view of the suspect's body posture and language. The suspect and investigator should sit about five to six feet apart; far enough apart to allow the investigator to maintain a safe distance, but close enough to converse in a normal tone of voice.

Introduction to an Interrogation

Once all the interested parties to the interrogation arrive in the room (the investigator, suspects, attorneys, etc.), the investigator should introduce himself to the suspect, stating his name and position. If the investigator intends to record the proceedings (and he should), he must inform the suspect of that fact. The investigator should then immediately start the recorder and make a short introductory statement. This statement should identify everyone in the room and give a brief description of the nature and purpose of the investigation. It should also include the date, time of day, and location of the interview.

The investigator should then explain to the suspect why he has been asked to appear and answer questions. The investigator should not divulge specifics, but he should give the suspect a general description of the allegations under investigation. This helps define the limits for the interrogation, by assuring the suspect that the interrogation will not become an inquisition.

Constitutional Rights

The next step is to inform the suspect of his Constitutional rights. It is generally desirable to inform the suspect from a written form to ensure that no pertinent language is overlooked or confused. "It is strongly recommended that the language used to inform the target of his constitutional rights and the manner in which it is administered be cleared either with the local prosecutor, the state Attorney General, the local U.S. Attorney, or appropriate agency legal counsel in order to ensure that it conforms with local state or Federal policy, custom and/or procedure."[13]

The investigator must make sure that the suspect positively asserts that he understands his rights. The investigator should ask the suspect the following direct question: "Do you fully understand your Constitutional rights as I have just stated them to you?"

If the suspect's reply is not clearly yes, the investigator should make any necessary clarifications before proceeding. If the suspect states that he understands his rights, the investigator should then ask the suspect if he is willing to waive his rights and answer some questions. Should the suspect reply positively, the questioning may begin.

If, however, the suspect replies that he is not willing to answer any questions, the investigator should ask why. If the suspect replies that he is invoking his rights against self-incrimination, the interrogation is over. The investigator should remind the suspect, however, that his right against self-incrimination extends only to him. It does not shield him from answering questions about other suspects. While the investigator cannot compel the suspect to answer questions, a grand jury or trial court may.

When furnishing information to a suspect concerning his rights under the Constitution, the investigator should avoid using terms such as "advise" or "warn." The suspect gets advice from his attorney. The term "warn" implies a threat. As is his duty, the investigator informs the suspect of his rights.

"Perhaps the most important point to remember concerning the manner in which a criminal investigator informs a target of his constitutional rights is to never, in any way or manner, attempt to be devious, misleading, or vague."[14] This can only lead to embarrassment for the investigator, his agency, and the prosecutor, and it may result in the court refusing to admit into evidence any confession or admission made by the suspect.

Personal History

After completing the preliminary matters described above, the investigator should ask the suspect a series of questions concerning his personal history: his full name, his date of birth, his address, education, marital status, dependents, employment records, and such. Such questions relax the suspect and the investigator and aid in establishing rapport.

When questioning a suspect about his personal history, the investigator should refrain from asking about any prior criminal record. This information is readily available from other sources, and such questions may cause a suspect to become uncooperative.

Interrogation Technique

Once the investigator completes the personal history, it is time to begin questioning about the specifics of the allegations. As a rule, it is preferable to begin by asking general questions and then move to more specific questions as details emerge. Using this technique, the investigator can learn what the suspect knows before asking questions that might reveal to the suspect what the investigator knows.

The investigator should confront the suspect directly and observe his reactions. Vehement denials of the allegations are often a sign of innocence. Silence, hesitation, or a passive attitude could be an indication of guilt. This confrontation should be diplomatically made, but must still be direct and without qualification; for instance: "Mr. Smith, I have been conducting an extensive investigation that suggests that you have been embezzling funds from Widgets, Inc."

If the suspect hesitates, and neither denies nor admits the allegation, give him a morally acceptable excuse for his conduct. This may allow him to save face in admitting his guilt. For instance: "Mr. Smith, I think I understand how this happened. I know that you have been facing some serious financial problems. Faced with the same situation, many others may have done the same thing."

If the suspect tries to deny his guilt, the investigator can cut off additional denials by laying out the evidence without giving names of witnesses. He can then go back to the morally acceptable rationalization for the behavior. For example: "Mr. Smith, you may say you did not do it, but the evidence suggests that you did. I have spoken to several witnesses, and I have examined several pieces of evidence. Your denying it will not resolve this matter. I am asking you why you did it. Did you need money, or did someone coerce you into it?"

The investigator should try to get the suspect to offer an explanation for his behavior. It is common for suspects to make partial admissions but, simultaneously, try to minimize the extent of the conduct. Once this breakthrough happens, it is usually only a matter of time before the suspect is ready to make a complete admission.

Once the suspect has begun admitting his guilt, keep him talking. The more he talks, the more he will be willing to admit. The investigator should get a confession orally, and get all the details. He can assure the suspect that he is doing the right thing by telling the truth and resolving the issues at hand.

If books, records and documents are important to the investigation, as they usually are in embezzlement and fraud cases, have the suspect supply the following information:

1) a description of each pertinent record (ledger, journal, check stub, etc.),
2) the identity of individuals who maintained each record and the period they maintained the records,
3) how much responsibility each person had in maintaining or reviewing the records,
4) the present location and condition of each record, and
5) whether the suspect is willing to submit the records to the investigator for examination.

In most financial crime investigations it is necessary for the suspect to identify one or more documents related to the allegations. Remembering that the suspect should identify each document is important, particularly those that have a direct relationship to the crime. A blanket endorsement by the suspect is seldom satisfactory unless the investigator can ensure that each document and each signature, if pertinent, are clearly identified. Have the suspect acknowledge and initial each document.

The investigator should reduce the oral confession to writing, but he should try to be low key about the written confession. He should always try to include the suspect's rationale for his actions in the confession. The suspect is more likely to sign a confession that includes not only his admission of guilt, but also includes his excuses for his actions.

Conducting an Interrogation

No single characteristic separates a successful investigator from an unsuccessful one. The key point is to be professional without being distant. Under no circumstances should the investigator create the impression that he is out to "get" anyone. It is much better to show the truth, that the investigator is only seeking the facts.

The investigator's demeanor and personality will reflect his own background. The investigator should try to see himself through the suspect's eyes and try to create a favorable impression.

The investigator should always treat the suspect with respect and decency, despite the nature of the offense or the investigator's personal feelings about the matter. If the suspect lies, the investigator should not scold or berate him. It is better simply to present the facts to the suspect and let him acknowledge his falsehood.

Do not interrupt a suspect when he is answering a question. Even if he strays from the topic, the investigator may discover additional pertinent information.

Hostile questions will most often lead to a premature cancellation of the interrogation. This does not mean, of course, that the investigator should never ask hostile questions, but they should be reserved until he has exhausted all the seemingly innocuous questions.

The investigator should not ask compound questions. They require compound and confusing answers. He should ask questions that require simple answers.

Always give the suspect ample time to answer the questions. If the suspect does not answer a question immediately, allow him a few minutes of silence. Then ask him why he has not answered the question.

The investigator must understand the suspect's answers. If the answer is not clear, ask for a clarification.

Be sure to obtain all the facts about the allegations under investigation, not just those favorable to prosecution. It is far better to learn of adverse information during the interrogation than it is to be surprised at trial.

Do not be taken in by attempts to gain sympathy. The investigator can be objective and pleasant, but must remain firm.

Discourage the suspect from asking questions, keeping in mind that the purpose of the interrogation is for the investigator to ask questions. When the suspect asks a question, respond with a question: for example, "Why does that concern you, Mr. Smith?", or "What brought that question to mind, Mr. Smith?"

Do not refer to the suspect or his attorney by first names, and try to discourage them from getting too familiar. Keep the conversation professional, not social.

The investigator must control the tempo of the interrogation. Maintain order. Ensure that only one person speaks at a time.

Unless it is obviously helpful, discourage the suspect's attorney from asking questions. If it becomes necessary, remind the attorney that he is present only to advise his client.

Resist requests by the suspect or his attorney to have "off the record" discussions when recording the interrogation. Point out the advantages to both sides of having a complete and accurate record of the interrogation and of the disadvantages of interruptions in the recording. If it cannot be avoided without causing a premature termination of the interview, try to get the suspect and his attorney to allow a summary of the "off the record" discussion on the recording. If the suspect and his attorney are unwilling to allow a summary, make notes of the discussion, and preserve those notes for later use.

Listen carefully to the suspect's answers to questions. Follow up with specific questions where necessary. If an answer suggests a new course of inquiry, follow up right away or make notes of questions to ask later in the interrogation.

The investigator should always bear in mind that there may not be a second chance to interrogate a suspect. He should plan the interrogation accordingly.

Do not ask leading questions that require a yes or no answer. Ask short, concise questions and let the suspect answer.

The investigator should always ask the suspect whether he has a checking account and/or a safe deposit box. Canceled checks are a bountiful source of information in developing a net worth computation (see Chapter 9, "Proving Illicit Transactions"), and safe deposit boxes are often a source of a great deal of financial information on a suspect. Additionally, the suspect may have channeled illegally acquired funds through his checking account or secreted them in his safe deposit box.

The investigator should ask the suspect if he will allow the investigator to examine the safe deposit box and the canceled checks immediately after the interrogation. If the suspect says no, the investigator should remind the suspect that using the safe deposit box before an inventory creates the inference that the suspect has removed something, and that destroying the checks before an inspection creates the inference that the suspect has something to hide.

Once all the topics of interest to the investigation have been covered, the investigator should take the following precautions in closing the interrogation:

1) Leave the door open for further questioning. Ask the suspect whether he would be willing to answer additional questions later should the need arise. Never state or imply that the suspect will not be questioned again.

2) Have the suspect acknowledge that he has given his answers to all the questions freely and voluntarily.

3) Do not offer a transcript of the interrogation to the suspect. If the suspect or his attorney requests a copy of a transcript, explain that one will be made available if one is made.

4) Do not thank the suspect for his cooperation, but advise him that there are no more questions.

Interrogator's Demeanor

Every investigator should develop a checklist of general admonitions and should frequently review them. Some key points should include:

1) Always dress appropriately for an interrogation, such as a conservative coat or a business suit.

2) Subdue all prejudices, including racial, sexual, ethnic, and religious. Do not let contempt for a lawbreaker, no matter how serious the offense, color the tone of the interrogation.

3) Keep an open mind. Never assume that the suspect had nothing positive to add to an investigation.

4) Do not offer compromises, make misleading statements, or make promises to the suspect to obtain an admission or confession.

5) Do not get mad or sarcastic. Emotional display only reinforces the suspect's resistance to the interrogation.

6) Never ask the suspect's attorney if he wants to ask any questions. He can ask the suspect any question he wants in a private conference.

7) Do not let the suspect or his attorney see the investigator's notes or outlines. Do not give the suspect free information about the investigation.

8) When it is appropriate, ask the suspect why he committed the crime.

9) Never ridicule or belittle a suspect. A suspect who feels belittled by the investigator is not likely to cooperate with him.

10) Do not consider success a victory. The investigator must conceal his emotions and maintain a professional attitude.

11) Avoid discussing political or religious matters.

12) Avoid showing signs of nervousness.

13) Avoid asking questions that may unnecessarily antagonize or alienate the suspect.

14) The investigator must display confidence and show that he is in control. Be dominant, not domineering.

15) Be a patient listener.
16) Remember the three most important questions: Why? Why not? How do you know?

Psychology of Confessions

White-collar crime offenders can often be classified in two types: the emotional offender and the unemotional offender. The emotional offender is one who displays strong emotions such as guilt or remorse. The investigator can best deal with an emotional offender through the sympathetic approach, being sensitive to the suspect.

Sensitivity or appeals to emotion do not sway the unemotional offender. A logical and unemotional dissertation of the facts best approaches him: this means appealing to his common sense based on overwhelming evidence of guilt.

The motivation behind the deception is to avoid the consequences, both real and personal, of telling the truth. Real consequences consist of loss of freedom and income. Personal consequences include loss of pride, reputation, or integrity.

The process of the interrogation is the process of undoing deception. Lying produces certain amounts of stress in nearly everyone. One result of deception is a state of anxiety or frustration. Many suspects will confess to reduce the anxiety and frustration they feel from the stress of lying.

Even while understanding that many people deceive to avoid the consequences of telling the truth, many people confess for the mirror reason, to avoid the consequences of lying. A suspect will generally confess when he perceives that the benefits from telling the truth exceed the benefits from lying. It then becomes the goal of the investigator to decrease the suspect's perception of the consequences of telling the truth while simultaneously increasing his perceptions of the consequences of telling a lie.

There are several ways that a suspect will attempt to reduce his own level of anxiety through his behavior or through cognitive measures. Behavioral responses include verbal and nonverbal responses to questions. Verbal responses are the words used to create the deception. Nonverbal responses are manifested through body movements such as fidgeting and shaking.

Cognitive measures to reduce anxiety are sometimes known as defense mechanisms. There are two principle defense mechanisms common to embezzlers and fraud offenders: rationalization and projection.

Rationalization consists of redefining what was done to avoid the consequences of behavior. It is common for embezzlers to rationalize that they borrowed the money rather than stole it.

Projection is the shifting of the blame to another person. An example is the embezzler who acknowledges he stole money because his boss would not pay him enough.

Generally, a suspect will not confess while objecting to his guilt. Rather than object to someone denying his guilt, it may prove more effective to reduce the perceived consequences to confessing. There are many excuses acceptable to suspects that help reduce the perceived consequences of confessing:

1) denial of responsibility, placing the blame on alcohol, drugs, creditors, or stress;
2) denial of the injury, by saying no one got hurt;
3) denying the victim, saying he got what he deserved;
4) condemning the condemner, saying everyone steals; and
5) appealing to higher loyalties by saying the suspect did not steal for himself.

Using one or more of these defense mechanisms to neutralize the suspect's objections to a confession is acceptable for the investigator. Clearly the most effective technique in obtaining a confession is to give the suspect an acceptable excuse for his behavior.

Legal Aspects of an Interrogation

There are several legal aspects of the interrogation process that the investigator must know. The failure to observe proper legal procedures while obtaining a confession might render it inadmissible. In addition, a confession obtained under certain conditions may even leave the investigator subject to civil liability.

All confessions must be voluntary, and remember that the burden of proof to show that the confession is voluntary is on the prosecution. No threats, force, or intimidation is acceptable when obtaining an admission or confession. This may be evidence of misconduct by the investigator. Promises of immunity or leniency create similar problems and must be avoided.

The United States Supreme Court has held that the use of trickery and deceit to obtain confessions is Constitutional. The Court said that "(t)he fact alone that the police misrepresented the statements that (the suspected accomplice) had made is, while relevant, insufficient in our view to make this otherwise voluntary confession inadmissible. These cases must be decided by viewing the totality of the circumstances."[15]

The use of trickery and deception to obtain a confession is ill advised, however. Should the suspect realize that the investigator is relying on deceit to get information, the suspect will continue to believe that the benefits of deception highly outweigh the benefits of telling the truth. He will believe the investigator does not know what the truth really is. Additionally, the use of deception places the confession in possible jeopardy under the exclusionary rule should a trial or appeal court rule the confession was not voluntary.

Accusing the suspect of a criminal violation during the interrogation is common for the investigator, even when there is no hard evidence. The investigator may construe this as an investigative technique, but the suspect may construe it as slander or defamation of character.

Case law normally holds it is not slander or defamation when an investigator directly accuses a suspect of committing a specific offense. However, two conditions must be met. First, the investigator must make the accusation in private so that no third party is present (excluding attorneys or other parties with a legitimate common interest in the investigation). Second, there can be no publication of the remarks to others.

By understanding the psychology of offenders and the underling laws of interrogation and confessions, the white-collar crime investigator may obtain valid and admissible confessions of guilt that will greatly enhance the probability of successful prosecution.

Notes

[1]Robert F. Royal and Steven Schutt, *The Gentle Art of Interviewing and Interrogation; a Professional Manual and Guide* (Englewood Cliffs, NJ: Prentice-Hall, Inc., 1976), p. 21.

[2]Richard A. Nossen, *The Detection, Investigation and Prosecution of Financial Crimes (White Collar, Political Corruption and Racketeering)* (Richmond, VA: Richard A. Nossen and Associates, 1982), p. 91.

[3]——, *Financial Investigative Techniques* (Washington, D.C.: Department of the Treasury, Internal Revenue Service, 1986), p. 1–2.

[4]Herbert Edelhertz, ed., *The Investigation of White-Collar Crime: A Manual for Law Enforcement Agencies* (Washington, D.C.: Department of Justice, Law Enforcement Assistance Administration, 1977), p. 154.

[5]Ibid.

[6]———, *Financial Investigative Techniques,* op cit., p. 1-1.

[7]Edelhertz, op cit., p. 157.

[8]Jonathan Kwitney, *The Fountain Pen Conspiracy* (New York: Alfred A. Knopf, 1973), p. 12.

[9]Wayne K, Bennet and Karen Hess, *Criminal Investigation* (St. Paul, MN: West Publishing Co., 1981), p. 412.

[10]Edelhertz, op cit., p. 167.

[11]Joseph T. Wells, W. Steve Albrecht, Jack Bologna, Gilbert Geis, and Jack Robertson, *Fraud Examiners' Manual* (Austin, TX: National Association of Certified Fraud Examiners, 1989), Section I, p. 56.

[12]Stanton Wheeler, in the introduction to Kenneth Mann, *Defending White-Collar Crime: A Portrait of Attorneys at Work* (New Haven, CT: Yale University Press, 1985), p. ix.

[13]Nossen, op cit., p. 102.

[14]Ibid., p. 103.

[15]Frazier v. Cupp, 394 U.S. 731.

Chapter 7

PUBLIC INFORMATION, SUBPOENAS, AND SEARCH WARRANTS

Knowledge is of two kinds. We know a subject ourselves, or we know where we can find information upon it.

Samuel Johnson
From James Boswell, Life of Johnson

It is not possible for the white-collar crime investigator to know everything about embezzlers and fraud violators, or the multifarious types of businesses, business transactions and financial matters. Learning where to obtain necessary information on practically all those subjects is possible, however. Most criminal investigators have had academic training and considerable practical experience in cultivating a broad variety of information sources.

The investigator should view financial sources as any other information sources. The primary purpose of these sources is to aid in tracing financial transactions as they relate to white-collar crime, to identify or find suspects or conspirators in embezzlement and fraud, or to locate hidden assets. Some of these sources of information are well known, others may be less known. Some of these are primary sources of financial information. Some can only lead the investigator to other potential sources and identify the names of associated businesses. Many are interrelated. The discovery of one source may require the investigator to pursue another. Some are readily available and easily obtainable. Others are only available through the appropriate legal process such as a subpoena or search warrant.

The major violator with large amounts of cash available for spending or for investment often has the assistance of a cadre of professionals such as attorneys, accountants, bankers, and realtors. Such professionals may hide behind a range of associates and corporate "straws" or "fronts." Such associates range from secretaries to family members, from criminal cronies to the legitimate business community seeking new and lucrative investments.

As major violators begin to use such professionals and associates, law enforcement officials face major barriers in proving fraudulent transactions, identifying the real ownership of assets, and revealing sources of investment. There are, however, many methods and sources of information that, when applied diligently and explored fully, can help reveal these assets and investments and help remove the veil of secrecy guarding these transactions.

Much information is available to the investigator from public records. Public agencies maintain information according to the laws. Private organizations, such as trade associations and credit bureaus, maintain information as their business.

The importance of financial information available from public records or from private information sources cannot be overemphasized. The important point, of course, is to know where to look. Many publications list sources of financial information on individuals or businesses. Appendix D is a brief Guide to Sources of Financial Information. Whether the information from these many sources is available for review by the investigator depends on the laws governing the distribution of information and the internal policies of each agency or organization possessing the information.

A myriad of laws governs the distribution of personal and financial information. This chapter does not address whether information from a particular source will be available without a subpoena or search warrant. The individual agency or organization controlling that information must decide. Three federal laws, however, are of particular concern to the white-collar crime investigator: The Privacy/Freedom of Information Act, The Fair Credit Reporting Act, and The Right to Financial Privacy Act.

Privacy/Freedom of Information Act
(Title 5, United States Code, Section 552, et seq.)

The Privacy/Freedom of Information Act is a complicated statute. The provisions of the Privacy/Freedom of Information Act regulate, among other things, the types of records that a federal agency may maintain about a person, the conditions under which the agency may disclose or disseminate the information to another governmental agency, and the circumstances and methods under which an individual may obtain copies of agency records that may pertain to him.[1]

Generally, the law prohibits disclosure of government records that would constitute an invasion of an individual's privacy, except in compliance with a subpoena or court order. An individual may obtain copies of his own records by requesting them, in writing, from the agency that maintains them. However, because of heavy demands for Freedom of Information material, requests to some federal agencies are backlogged for years.[2]

Fair Credit Reporting Act
(Title 15, United States Code, Section 1681)

The Fair Credit Reporting Act regulates the activities and record keeping of mercantile credit, insurance, and employment investigation agencies and bureaus. In its broadest sense, this act requires that consumer reporting agencies inform persons who are subjected to investigations of their background, character, habits, and associates. "A consumer reporting agency is generally an organization like a credit bureau; however, it can include any organization that provides such information to third parties."[3]

The key to being included as a "consumer reporting agency" is whether financial, credit, or personal information obtained by a company or individual is to be reported to a third party. If so, the information probably falls under the Fair Credit Reporting Act.

"If adverse action is taken against an employee as the result of a third party inquiry, the employee must be given notice thereof. However, the employer is not obligated to tell the employee what specific information was contained in the third party report; the employee may obtain that information directly from the third party agency."[4]

For an internal investigation, the law does not require notification by the employer. If the employer falls under the definition of a consumer reporting agency, however, the employer may be compelled to release information in its files to the effected individual. The employer can eliminate such exposure by not releasing any information obtained from a third party source which regards a suspected employee. Consequently, a white-collar crime investigator must use caution when using information obtained from a consumer reporting agency since its use may be illegal.

Following are some provisions of the Fair Credit Reporting Act that may be of the greatest interest to white-collar crimes investigators:

1681b. Permissible purposes of consumer reports

A consumer reporting agency may furnish a consumer report under the following circumstances and no other:

(1) In response to the order of a court having jurisdiction to issue such an order.

(2) In accordance with the written instructions of the consumer to whom it relates.

(3) To a person which it has reason to believe—

   (A) intends to use the information in connection with a credit transaction involving the consumer on whom the information is to be furnished and involving the extension of credit to, or review or collection of an account of, the consumer; or

   (B) intends to use the information for employment purposes; or

   (C) intends to use the information in connection with the underwriting of insurance involving the customer; or

   (D) intends to use the information in connection with a determination of the consumer's eligibility for a license or benefit granted by a governmental instrumentality required by law to consider an applicant's financial responsibility or status; or

   (E) otherwise has a legitimate business need for the information in connection with a business transaction involving the consumer.

Section 1681(d) provides that a person may not obtain an "investigative consumer report" on any consumer, which includes information as to the consumer's character, general reputation, personal characteristics, and mode of living, without first notifying the consumer of the request. The consumer may then demand additional information about the nature and scope of the requested report.[5]

There are civil penalties for willful or negligent noncompliance with the act. Any person who attempts to obtain information from a consumer reporting agency on false pretenses commits a criminal offense and may be fined up to $5,000 or imprisoned up to one year, or both.[6]

Right to Financial Privacy Act
(Title 12, United States Code. Section 3401, et seq.)

The Right to Financial Privacy Act (RFPA) protects certain customer accounts at certain financial institutions from informal federal access, and it specifies the formal methods by which federal officers may access protected account information. The RFPA applies to banks, savings and loans, credit unions, consumer finance institutions, and credit card issuers. For the RFPA to apply, the account must be in the true name of the customer, and the customer must be an individual or a partnership with five or fewer partners.[7]

The RFPA does not protect the following records and information;

1) accounts in fictitious names,
2) accounts of corporations and partnerships with six or more partners,
3) forged or counterfeited financial instruments,
4) checks and money orders cashed for noncustomers of a financial institution,
5) bank surveillance photographs, and
6) records of functions not related to the account relationship (e.g., the exchange of cash for a cashier's check).[8]

Information and records from protected accounts are available under the RFPA under one or more of the following processes;

1) customer authorization,
2) a search warrant,
3) a judicial subpoena issued by a trial judge,
4) formal written request,
5) an administrative subpoena (where otherwise authorized by law), and
6) a Federal Grand Jury subpoena.[9]

When seeking information or records from a protected account through the issuance of a judicial subpoena, a formal written request or an administrative subpoena, the RFPA requires the investigating agency to notify the customer that it is seeking information from his account. The agency can comply by giving the customer a copy of the process, a statement about why it is seeking the information, and an explanation of the customer's rights to contest the financial institution's compliance with the process. The agency can mail the necessary information to the customer at least 14 days before accessing the information, or it can physically serve the customer at least 10 days before the access.[10]

Obviously, when RFPA protected information is obtained through customer authorization, no customer notification is necessary.[11] When an investigator executes a search warrant for RFPA protected information, he must notify the customer within 90 days after the execution of the warrant.[12]

Under the above processes, avoiding the customer notification required under the RFPA is not possible. Obtaining a delay in the notification by articulating in an affidavit certain exigent circumstances is possible, however. A court order known as a nondisclosure may effect such a delay. A magistrate or district court judge may issue a nondisclosure. The investigator can and should present the nondisclosure to the financial institution to prevent its independent notification to the customer.

The customer notification requirements of the RFPA do not apply to Federal Grand Jury subpoenas.[13] A financial institution, however, may have a policy of automatically notifying the customer when it receives a Federal Grand Jury subpoena, or state laws may compel it to do so. In such instances, when it is necessary to delay or avoid notification, the investigator should obtain a court order that prohibits the financial institution from disclosing the investigative interest in the customer's account.

In 1989, the Financial Institutions Reform, Recovery, and Enforcement Act (Title 18, United States Code, Section 1510) added a new obstruction of justice provision. 18 U.S.C. 1510 prohibits an officer, employee, agent or attorney of a financial institution from notifying any other person about the existence or content of a Federal Grand Jury subpoena for customer records with the intent to obstruct justice. A violation is punishable by five years imprisonment.[14]

The RFPA applies only to federal government agencies attempting to access protected customer account information at designated financial institutions. Therefore, financial institutions can voluntarily provide customer account information to state and local law enforcement agencies, unless a state or local law applies. As a practical matter, however, because of some misunderstanding about RFPA provisions and the liability concerns of financial institutions, most financial institutions will require legal process from any law enforcement agency for any access to customer account information. The investigator must recognize that, to access information from a financial institution, using a method prescribed under the RFPA will be necessary. Financial institutions are under no obligation to allow access to any records without legal process.

The RFPA and consequent civil liability concerns stifled much of the information sharing between law enforcement officials and financial institution employees that had previously existed when financial institutions suspected criminal activity. It is difficult to estimate or measure the subsequent detrimental effect: not only on law enforcement, but also upon the surge of financial institution failures of the 1980s. In recognition of this, certain provisions of the Money Laundering Act of 1986 and the Anti-Drug Abuse Act of 1988 provided limited relief from the restrictive provisions of the RFPA.[15]

The Money Laundering Act authorized employees of financial institutions to give appropriate governmental authorities sufficient information concerning the nature of suspected criminal violations and the parties concerned to allow the authorities to obtain process for additional information and records. The Act also provided for a "good faith" exemption from civil liability for the disclosure of information.

The Anti-Drug Abuse Act amended the RFPA in two very important ways:

1) It provided that bank supervisory agencies may transfer to the Attorney General financial records obtained during examinations, if there is reason to believe that the records may relate to the violation of federal criminal law; and

2) The amendment allowed financial institutions and their supervisory agencies to transfer to the Attorney General the records of financial institution insiders who are suspected of violating any law relating to crimes against financial institutions, or of violating the Bank Secrecy Act.

Obtaining Documentary Evidence

The investigator may obtain the leads needed to investigate embezzlement or financial fraud from a variety of sources, from victims and witnesses, to suspects, to governmental records, to business records, to newspapers. Often, however, the information will be available only through the legal processes of a subpoena or a search warrant. Many witnesses may refuse to cooperate and speak with an investigator, but will respond to a subpoena to testify before an appropriate investigative body, such as a grand jury. Certain laws prohibit the distribution of some information and documents, except according to legal processes. Some companies and corporations, citing privacy concerns of their customers or clients, or out of concern for civil liability, will refuse to release information or documents absent legal process, though nothing legally prevents them from simply revealing the requested information.

White-collar crime investigators should not construe such concerns and limitations as impediments to an investigation. As Justice Felix Frankfurter noted in *U.S. v. Rabinowitz*, "It makes all the difference in the world whether one recognizes . . . the Fourth Amendment search requirement . . . [as] a safeguard against recurrence of abuses so deeply felt by the colonies as to be one of the potent causes of the Revolution, or one thinks of it as merely a requirement for a piece of paper." The laws of the United States still allow an investigator to pursue investigative leads into areas of private concern, but only after meeting certain stringent requirements. When an investigator takes the time to obtain a subpoena or search warrant, it displays his willingness to be fair and objective in his efforts and in his intent to protect the rights of the suspect.

There are, in essence, four ways an investigator can obtain documentary evidence:

1) voluntary consent,
2) public records,
3) subpoena, or
4) search warrant.

The investigator can obtain documents through voluntary consent, and this is the preferred method whenever circumstances suggest that the person possessing the documents will be cooperative. The suspect can give his consent orally or in writing. When obtaining voluntary consent from adverse witnesses or possible targets of an investigation, obtaining written consent is preferable. Appendix F contains an example of a Customer Consent and Authorization for Access to Financial Records form. The investigator should edit the form to fit specific needs.

It is important to remember that even after a suspect has given consent to authorize access to information or documents he can withdraw it. Should the witness or suspect withdraw consent before the investigator obtains the information or documents, the consent is no longer valid, and legal process becomes necessary.

For those public records that are available without legal process, such as real estate records or records of court proceedings in divorces and bankruptcies, it is a simple matter to make or purchase copies of those documents. Some documents, however, because of the Privacy/Freedom of Information Act, the Fair Credit Reporting Act, and the Right to Financial Privacy Act, are only available to the criminal investigator through legal process.

Subpoenas, ordinarily issued by a court or a grand jury, can either summon a witness to testify before a grand jury, a court, or an administrative body, or can compel a witness to produce records or documents for inspection.

A judge of competent jurisdiction issues a search warrant upon presentation of probable cause to believe the records sought constitute evidence of a crime. The investigator may also conduct searches pursuant to consent from the person whose property is to be searched or seized. Appendix E provides an example of a Consent to Search form and a supplemental Receipt for Property.

Subpoenas

A subpoena is "a process to cause a witness to appear and give testimony, commanding him to lay aside all pretenses and excuses, and appear before a court or magistrate therein named at a time therein mentioned to testify for the party named under a penalty therein mentioned."[16] This type of subpoena is distinctively called a subpoena ad testificandum.

All fifty states and the federal government have laws authorizing subpoenas to compel witnesses to appear before investigative bodies, such as grand juries, trial courts and administrative boards. Faced with a noncooperative or recalcitrant witness, the investigator can apply, through an appropriate prosecuting attorney, to a judge or grand jury to have the witness subpoenaed to testify. A judge or grand jury may compel such testimony, provided the witness is not compelled to testify against himself. Therefore, the power of a subpoena is very important to the white-collar crime investigator.

A subpoena duces tecum is "a process by which the court, at the instances of a suitor, commands a witness who has in his possession or control some document or paper that is pertinent to the issues of a pending controversy, to produce it at the trial."[17] The subpoena duces tecum is the legal process by which an investigator can compel a witness, a business, or a governmental entity to produce for examination original documents, copies, reproductions, or transcripts.

The principal advantage of the subpoena and the subpoena duces tecum is that it can compel a person legally to submit the information sought without the showing of probable cause that a crime has been committed and that evidence of the crime will be found at the place to be searched, as is required when a search warrant is used.[18]

Regulatory agencies are extremely valuable sources of information to the white-collar crime investigator, and the investigator should fully use them, especially when following a trail of financial transactions. However, the investigator must keep some important facts in mind when he develops evidence from such sources. When obtaining information by using a subpoena or subpoena duces tecum, the investigator should evaluate the admissibility of this evidence considering the following factors:

1) Was the investigator acting within the scope of his delegated authority?
2) Was the action taken for the purpose for which the authority was granted?
3) Did the investigator comply with the regulations or other rules relating to the procedures for exercising the authority?
4) Does the exercise of such authority abuse a right protected by the U.S. Constitution?

In applying these principles, the investigator must also remember that various communications are privileged and protected from use as evidence. The subpoena power cannot compel a person to reveal such privileged communications. In addition, a judge or grand jury may not use a subpoena to compel a person to produce information, records, or documents in violation of his Fifth Amendment right against self-incrimination.

Individuals cannot be compelled to incriminate themselves. However, the Fifth Amendment privilege does not protect the records of certain entities, including corporations, large impersonal organizations such as labor unions, associations, and limited partnerships. Though a subpoena may compel a responsible official or company officer to produce the records of such entities, the official or company officer may still refuse to testify against himself.[19]

The investigator should also note that the subpoena must be served on the person who is in care, custody or control of the records. That is not always the chief operating officer of a corporation. The investigator needs to learn in advance who the custodian of the records is.

Depending on the nature of the investigation, the type of information necessary to conduct the investigation, and the type of business being subpoenaed, the information requested on a subpoena duces tecum will widely vary. Tables 19, 20, 21, and 22 contain samples of language to include in a subpoena for records. The investigator should edit the language to meet the specific needs of individual investigations, since not all records will be needed in every case.

Table 19. Attachment to Subpoena.
(Proprietorship)

Any and all original documents in your custody or subject to your control, whether owned by you or by anyone else, for ___(Name of Company)___ , for the calendar years beginning 19__ and ending 19__, including, but not limited to, the following:

1. General Journal(s) and Chart of Accounts
2. General Ledger(s) and Subsidiary Ledger(s)
3. Cash Receipts Journal(s) and Cash Disbursements Journal(s)
4. Sales Journal(s) and Purchase Journal(s)
5. Balance Sheet(s), Income Statement(s), Profit/Loss Statement(s)
6. Records pertaining to customer accounts, Account Receivables, Notes Receivables, etc.
7. Records pertaining to Allowances for Bad Debts and Bad Debt expenses
8. Records pertaining to Accounts Payable, Notes Payable, Loans Payable, Mortgages Payable, etc.
9. Cash Receipt Book(s)
10. Bank Statements, Deposit Slips, Cancelled Checks, Withdrawal Slips, Debit Memos, and Credit Memos for all checking and/or savings accounts
11. Assets and/or Investments, such as Certificates of Deposits, Stocks, Bonds, Real Estate, Vehicles, Aircraft, Boats, etc.
12. Itemized Inventory Record(s)
13. Purchase Orders, Vouchers, Invoices, Receipts, etc.
14. Payroll Records, Payroll Journals, W-2's, 1099's
15. Copies of all certified audits along with accountant's confidential file
16. All work sheets, accountant work papers, adjusting entries, etc.
17. Copies of all federal and state income tax, and/or employment tax returns for the identified period
18. Any and all reconciliations of books to tax returns for the identified period
19. Any other financial records which were created for, by, or on behalf of the proprietorship, such as Loan Applications, Deeds to Real Estate, schedules of loan payments, etc.

The interstate subpoena is another useful investigative tool. It allows the investigator to reach beyond his own state lines to obtain testimony and documentary evidence. This process is normally used to obtain financial records from out of state sources. When interstate subpoena papers are used in an investigation, it is prudent for the investigator to contact the person to be subpoenaed, usually the attorney or law department of a bank, corporation, or financial institution, to work out the details of the service and waivers beforehand.

The details of obtaining and serving an interstate subpoena may vary from state to state, so it is important for the investigator to coordinate the efforts of the state's prosecuting attorney and the parties to be subpoenaed to ease the service and return process.

Table 20. Attachment for Subpoena.
(Partnership)

Any and all original documents in your custody or subject to your control, whether owned by you or by anyone else, for ___(Name of Company___, for the calendar years beginning 19__ and ending 19__, including, but not limited to, the following:

1. Partnership Agreement
2. Partnership Minute Book(s)
3. Partnership Capital Account Record(s)
4. General Journal(s) and Chart of Accounts
5. General Ledger(s) and Subsidiary Ledger(s)
6. Cash Receipts Journal(s) and Cash Disbursements Journal(s)
7. Sales Journal(s) and Purchase Journal(s)
8. Balance Sheet(s), Income Statement(s), Profit/Loss Statement(s)
9. Records pertaining to customer accounts, Account Receivables, Notes Receivables, etc.
10. Records pertaining to Allowances for Bad Debts and Bad Debt expenses
11. Records pertaining to Accounts Payable, Notes Payable, Loans Payable, Mortgages Payable, etc.
12. Cash Receipt Book(s)
13. Bank Statements, Deposit Slips, Cancelled Checks, Withdrawal Slips, Debit Memos, and Credit Memos for all checking and/or savings accounts
14. Assets and/or Investments owned by the partnership, such as Certificates of Deposits, Stocks, Bonds, Real Estate, Vehicles, Aircraft, Boats, etc.
15. Itemized Inventory Record(s)
16. Purchase Orders, Vouchers, Invoices, Receipts, etc.
17. Payroll Records, Payroll Journals, W-2's, 1099's
18. Expense Vouchers submitted by the Partners
19. Copies of all certified audits along with accountant's confidential file
20. All work sheets, accountant work papers, adjusting entries, etc.
21. Copies of all federal and state income tax, and/or employment tax returns for the identified period
22. Any and all reconciliations of books to tax returns for the identified period
23. Any other financial records which were created for, by, or on behalf of the partnership, such as Loan Applications, Deeds to Real Estate, schedules of loan payments, etc.

It is also important to remember that a person cannot refuse to furnish information pursuant to a subpoena because that information may incriminate someone else. Thus, if an investigator serves a subpoena on a business owner for records that may prove another person committed a crime, the owner must claim that the production of such records would incriminate the owner, not that it would incriminate another person, should the owner try to quash the subpoena.

Table 21. Attachment for Subpoena.
(Corporation)

Any and all original documents in your custody or subject to your control, whether owned by you or by anyone else, for ___(Name of Company)___ , for the calendar years beginning 19__, and ending 19__, including, but not limited to, the following:

1. Articles of Incorporation
2. Corporate Minute Book(s)
3. Stock Record Book(s)
4. General Journal(s) and Chart of Accounts
5. General Ledger(s) and Subsidiary Ledger(s)
6. Cash Receipts Journal(s) and Cash Disbursements Journal(s)
7. Sales Journal(s) and Purchase Journal(s)
8. Balance Sheet(s), Income Statement(s), Profit/Loss Statement(s)
9. Records pertaining to customer accounts, Account Receivables, Notes Receivables, etc.
10. Records pertaining to Allowances for Bad Debts and Bad Debt expenses
11. Records pertaining to Accounts Payable, Notes Payable, Loans Payable, Mortgages Payable, etc.
12. Cash Receipt Book(s)
13. Bank Statements, Deposit Slips, Cancelled Checks, Withdrawal Slips, Debit Memos, and Credit Memos for all checking and/or savings accounts
14. Assets and/or Investments owned by the corporation, such as Certificates of Deposits, Stocks, Bonds, Real Estate, Vehicles, Aircraft, Boats, etc.
15. Itemized Inventory Record(s)
16. Purchase Orders, Vouchers, Invoices, Receipts, etc.
17. Payroll Records, Payroll Journals, W-2's, 1099's
18. Expense Vouchers submitted by Officers and Employees
19. Copies of all certified audits along with accountant's confidential file
20. All work sheets, accountant work papers, adjusting entries, etc.
21. Copies of all federal and state income tax, and/or employment tax returns for the identified period
22. Any and all reconciliations of books to tax returns for the identified period
23. Any other financial records which were created for, by, or on behalf of the corporation, such as Loan Applications, Deeds to Real Estate, schedules of loan payments, etc.

Search Warrants

In any instance when an investigator feels that the records or documents he seeks may be compromised or destroyed if subpoenaed, such as when they are in the possession of the embezzler, or when a realtor or banker is conspiring with the operator of a fraudulent enterprise, then the investigator should seize the documents and records pursuant to a search warrant.

The financial search warrant is a very formidable weapon for the

Table 22. Attachment to Subpoena.
(Bank)

Any and all bank documents, either original, copies of originals, reproductions or transcripts, in your custody or subject to your control, whether owned by you or by anyone else, for __(Name of Company or Individual)__ , for the calendar years beginning 19__ and ending 19__, including, but not limited to, the following:

1. All open or closed checking, savings, and NOW accounts, including:
   A. Signature cards
   B. Bank statements
   C. Cancelled checks
   D. Deposit tickets
   E. Credit and debit memos
   F. Wire transfer records
   G. Forms 1099 of back-up withholding statements
2. Retained copies of all open or closed bank loan or mortgage documents, including:
   A. Loan application
   B. Loan ledger sheet
   C. Copy of loan disbursement document
   D. Copy of loan repayment document
   E. Loan correspondence file
   F. Collateral agreements
   G. Credit reports
   H. Copies of notes or other instruments reflecting the obligation to pay
   I. Copies of real estate mortgages, chattel mortgages or other security for bank loans
   J. Copies of annual interest paid statements
   K. Copies of loan amortization statements
3. Certificated of Deposit (purchased or redeemed), including:
   A. Copies of certificates
   B. Records pertaining to interest earned, withdrawn or reinvested
   C. Forms 1099 or back-up withholding statements records
4. Open or closed investment or security custodian accounts, including:
   A. Documents reflecting purchase of security
   B. Documents reflecting negotiation of security
   C. Safekeeping records and logs
   D. Receipts for receipt or delivery of securities
   E. Copies of annual interest paid statements
5. All open or closed IRA, Keogh, and Other Retirement Plans, including:
   A. Statements
   B. Investment, transfer and redemption confirmation slips
   C. Documents reflecting purchase of investment
   D. Documents reflecting redemption of investment
   E. Copies of annual interest earned statements
6. Customer correspondence files
7. Retained copies of all Cashier's, Manager's, Bank, or Traveler's checks and money orders, including:
   A. Copies of documents used to purchase check/money order
   B. Copies of documents reflecting negotiation of check/money order

Table 22. (Continued)

    C. Retained copy of application
    D. Retained copy of negotiated check/money order
  8. Wire transfer files, including:
    A. Federal Wire, Swift or other documents reflecting wire transfer of funds to, from or on behalf of (Name of Business or Individual)
    B. Documents reflecting source of funds for wire out
    C. Documents reflecting disposition of wire transfer in
  9. Retained copies of all open or closed safe deposit box rental and entry records
  10. Open or closed credit card files, including:
    A. Application for credit card
    B. Monthly statements
    C. Copies of charges
    D. Copies of documents used to make payments on account
  11. Retained copies of Currency Transaction Reports (Forms 4789)
  12. Retained copies of bank's CTR Exempt List (if subject is exempt) and documents reflecting justification for exemption.

investigator of white-collar crime. Most investigators are knowledgeable of the requirements for a search warrant—probable cause, affidavits, the detached magistrate. Just as the search warrant is widely used to produce physical evidence such as stolen property or narcotics, it may also be used to obtain financial information about an embezzler or operator of a fraud.

It has become a common tactic of defense attorneys to argue about the historic abuse of search warrants to detract attention from the facts of a case. It is important, therefore, to remember that the founding fathers never intended to forbid searches, only to ensure that they first be approved by a judicial officer after full disclosure of the circumstances by the investigating officer.

The Fourth Amendment provides that "no Warrant shall issue, but upon probable cause." Over the years, probable cause has become a threefold test:

    1) probable cause to believe a crime has been committed,
    2) probable cause to believe that specific items constitute evidence of a crime, and
    3) probable cause to believe that such evidence is at the place specified in the search warrant.

Probable cause means that the investigator must show "a fair probability," not a certainty or near-certainty, of the three elements described above.[20]

Exceptions to the Search Warrant Requirement

A judicially authorized search warrant is required in all cases except where exigent circumstances exist.[21] Some examples of such exigent circumstances that require no search warrant include:

1) Search incident to an arrest—but the warrantless search must be no broader than is necessary to protect the arresting officer's safety or to prevent the individual being arrested from concealing or destroying evidence. The scope of the search is therefore limited to the area within the individual's immediate control.[22]

2) Consent search—the burden, however, is on the government to prove that the consent was knowingly and voluntarily given. Voluntariness is determined from the circumstances viewed in their entirety.[23] The courts have consistently refused to imply voluntary consent from mere "acquiescence to lawful authority."[24]

3) Automobile searches—The two justifications for warrantless searches of an automobile are their mobility and the lesser expectation of privacy in an automobile as compared to a home.[25] It is important to note, however, that locked or sealed containers within a vehicle require a search warrant since the exigent circumstances cease to exist once the vehicle is stopped and the container seized.

4) Plain view—if probable cause exists, a law enforcement officer may seize evidence of a crime or contraband within plain view of a place the officer had a right to be.[26]

5) Certain administrative searches—when a regulatory scheme provides for periodic searches, such as fire marshal searches for safety and fire code violations.

6) Border searches—No warrant is required to search an individual, luggage, packages, or mail crossing a national border or its functional equivalent, such as an international airport.[27]

7) Abandoned or discarded property—Property abandoned or otherwise disposed of as the result of a stop without probable cause cannot be seized, but property abandoned without prior unlawful intrusion on a person's privacy may be seized without a warrant or probable cause.[28]

8) Investigative stops—An individual may be detained for an investigatory stop for as long as is reasonably necessary for the police to "confirm or dispel their suspicions quickly. . . ."[29] Reasonable cause is a less demanding standard than probable cause.

In any event, particularly in marginal situations when, arguably, a search warrant may not be needed, the investigator should still, when time permits, obtain a warrant before conducting any search. When deciding the constitutionality of a search, the courts have shown a strong preference for searches based on a warrant.[30]

Preparing the Financial Search Warrant Affidavit

Table 23 contains an example of a blank probable cause affidavit. It contains the major points to be covered in an affidavit for a search warrant, but the investigator should be aware of details necessary for a well-drafted affidavit.

Detailed Description of the Places or Things to Be Searched

The first paragraph of the probable cause affidavit calls for a detailed description of the place or thing to be searched. If the place to be searched is a home or business, it should be described fully so that anyone could read the search warrant, locate and specifically identify the home or business, e.g., "a two-story red brick house with beige trim and a beige two-car overhead garage door, at 123 Anywhere Street, Austin, Travis County, Texas. The house has 123 in gold numbers on the porch post to the right of the front door," or "a white frame farmhouse with green trim and shutters, a large wraparound porch, and no garage. The house is 1.2 miles north of U.S. Highway 71 on the west side of Ranch Road 620 in Travis County, Texas. At the driveway leading to the house from Ranch Road 620 is a black mailbox with the route number 'St.Rt.1, Box 350' in white letters. The house is surrounded by a white rail fence in front." If necessary, attach a map to the affidavit to show the location of the house.

Some examples of descriptions held to be constitutionally sufficient include a description of the location without reference to county and state,[31] and a description without a street address, but with a reference to a mailbox that had the suspect's name on it.[32]

Conversely, some examples of descriptions held to be insufficient to be constitutionally valid include listing the wrong address with no other description of the premises to be searched,[33] and listing a description of the premises, but listing the wrong address and the officers knew before executing the warrant that the address was wrong.[34]

If the place to be searched is a business, it may be necessary to identify

Table 23.

THE STATE OF TEXAS	§	IN THE _____
	§	
COUNTY OF TRAVIS	§	JUDICIAL DISTRICT COURT

AFFIDAVIT FOR SEARCH WARRANT

The undersigned affiant, being a peace officer under the laws of Texas and being duly sworn, on oath makes the following statements and accusations:

1) There is in Travis County, Texas, a suspected place and premises described and located as follows:
2) There is at said suspected place and premises personal property concealed and kept and subject to seizure under the laws of Texas and described as follows:
3) Said suspected place and premises and personal property are in charge of and controlled by each of the following persons:
4) It is the belief of affiant, and he hereby charges and accuses that said personal property aforedescribed constitutes evidence of a theft by (embezzlement) (fraud) and/or was obtained as the consequences of a theft by (embezzlement) (fraud) and is subject to seizure under Article 18.02, Code of Criminal Procedure.
5) The affiant has probable cause for said belief by reason of the following facts:

Wherefore, affiant asks for issuance of a warrant that will authorize him to search said suspected place and premise for said personal property and seize the same pursuant to the Texas Code of Criminal Procedure.

_____
Affiant

Subscribed and sworn to before me by said affiant on this _____ day of _____, 19__.

_____
Judge Presiding

---

which parts of the business are to be searched, unless the whole business is involved in a fraudulent enterprise. In embezzlement, it may be necessary to particularly describe one office or desk, e.g., "one office within the offices of ABC Company, located in Suite 100, of the Bank Office Building, 3456 Somewhere Street, Houston, Harris County, Texas. The office to be searched is the third door right of the hallway left of the front entrance to the business. The name 'Ima Faux' is on the door. This is the office of the chief accountant for ABC Company."

If the place to be searched is a vehicle, include the make, model, color, body style, license plate number, vehicle identification number, and usual location, e.g., "a white over red 1994 Ford Mustang Convertible, bearing Texas license plates FOX-92Q, parked on the second floor of the parking garage of the Fortune Office Building, 987 Lost Avenue, Beaumont, Jefferson County, Texas." As with premises descriptions, minor unintentional errors in the description will not render the warrant invalid for want of particularity since the affidavit adequately describes the vehicle and eliminates the possibility that the wrong vehicle may be searched by mistake.

If a specific person is to be searched along with the premises, the investigator should specifically identify him by name, race, sex, age or date of birth, height and weight, hair color and eye color. A warrant can authorize the search of a "John Doe," if the investigating officer can identify with reasonable certainty the person to be searched. Blanket search warrants authorizing the search of "any and all persons present" on the search premises are unconstitutional.[35] A person may not be searched just because he is present on the premises to be searched.[36]

Detailed Description of the Property to Be Seized

The second paragraph of the search warrant affidavit calls for a description of the property to be seized. The list should be as specific as possible about the nature of each item and its appearance. The investigator must specify the property to be seized either by a specific description of the property or in relation to the underlying violations cited in the affidavit and search warrant.

"Perhaps the highest standard of particularity under the Fourth Amendment applies to documents, since by their nature documents require analysis to see whether they do or do not fit under the description contained in a search warrant. But the 'analysis' can be described equally as a general search through a person's private papers. Thus, with documents it is important to be specific about not only the kinds of documents sought but also the location and other physical descriptions that may be available."[37]

Examples of search warrants authorizing the search and seizure of documentary evidence held valid under the Fourth Amendment include:

1) documents and records that are evidence and fruits of certain specified commodities fraud statutes, sought from an operation that was completely "permeated with fraud,"[38]
2) representative handwriting samples,[39] and
3) "All checkbooks, canceled checks, deposit slips, bank statements,

trust account receipts, check stubs, books and papers, etc., which would tend to show a fraudulent intent or any elements of the crime of false pretense or embezzlement."[40]

For financial search warrants, it is particularly important to explain in the probable cause narrative what types of documents and records the investigator is seeking, and why he is seeking them.

Table 24 contains an example of a description of business records to be seized pursuant to the search warrant. Table 25 contains an example of a description of financial records to be seized pursuant to the search warrant. The investigator should edit the lists to include only those items necessary to further a specific investigation since not all documents will be necessary in every case.

Table 24. List of Business Records Items to Be Seized.

All business records for _____ of _____, including, but not limited to:

1) financial reports showing current and fixed assets, notes receivable, marketable securities, accounts receivables, merchandise inventory, accounts payable, accrued expenses payable, long-term liabilities, mortgages payable, income statements, balance sheets, work sheets, and trial balance sheets:
2) general ledgers, subsidiary ledgers, general journals, sales journals, purchases journals, cash receipts journals, cash payments journals;
3) vouchers, voucher jackets, voucher registers, check registers, cash register receipts, purchase receipts, merchandise return receipts, cash register summary sheets;
4) employee lists, employee time records;
5) partnership agreements, trust agreements, power of attorneys, corporation records including corporation charters, corporate minutes, annual reports;
6) tax records, local, state and federal;
7) indicia of ownership or occupancy, including utility and phone bills;
8) address/telephone books or phone files reflecting names, addresses, and phone numbers of customers and conspirators;
9) licensing records, health certificates, insurance records, annuity records, all regulatory licenses.

When naming the owner of the premises to be searched and the owner of the property to be seized, it is important to remember that they may not be the same person. If necessary, separate the names and specify which names own or control the place or premises to be searched and which names own the property to be seized.

Table 25. List of Financial Records Items to Be Seized.

1) All records including but not limited to copies of the contents of the "Customer Information Files" under the name of _____, for the period of time beginning _____ to _____;
2) All records of savings accounts, trust or custodian accounts, NOW or Keogh accounts;
3) All records of loan and credit accounts;
4) All safe deposit box records;
5) All records of certificates of deposits, Treasury bills, commercial paper, stocks, bonds or other securities;
6) All records of wire transfers of funds, to and from or on behalf of the customer;
7) All bank checks, official checks, cashier's checks, treasurer's checks, money orders or traveler's checks;
8) All credit card monthly statements;
9) All Treasury currency reports, exempt currency transaction lists and foreign currency transaction reports;
10) All correspondence;
11) All domestic or international letters of credit issued to or on behalf of, or presented by, listed account holders;
12) All foreign currency exchange documents;
13) All accounts receivable financing documents;
14) All lease agreements, discounted notes or contracts;
15) All documents relative to any litigation involving the listed account holders, including any subpoenas previously served upon the bank or financial institution;
16) All internal memoranda, whether formal or informal, pertaining to any and all of the above;
17) All auditor's reports and bank examiner reports relating to transactions of or with the listed account holders;
18) Insurance documents including riders;
19) Mortgages and associated financing documents;
20) Tax returns and associated documents for federal, state, or local taxes;
21) All accountant's work sheets, audit reports, and financial statements.

Accusation and Charge

The accusation and charge must allege what specific crime has been committed, and it must specifically designate under what legal authority the investigator intends to seize the property. Various state statutes list the specific categories of authorities under which property may be seized. Examples include:

1) property acquired by theft or in any other manner that makes its acquisition a penal offense;
2) property specially designed, made, or adapted for or commonly used in the commission of an offense;
3) any property the possession of which is prohibited by law;

4) implements or instruments used in the commission of a crime;
5) property or items, except the personal writings of the accused, constituting evidence of an offense or constituting evidence tending to show that a particular person committed an offense; or
6) persons.[41]

In financial search warrants, the documents or records the investigator is seeking are usually "mere evidence," paperwork to document the existence of embezzlement or fraud, or to identify additional victims and witnesses. Occasionally, however, the property to be seized constitutes the "fruits of the crime," such as the stolen money. The investigator must support the allegations with probable cause in the narrative section of the affidavit.

Probable Cause Narrative

The facts regarding the investigation should be set forth in sufficient detail for the magistrate to make a finding of probable cause. Especially in white-collar crime cases, where documentary evidence is being sought, great detail is needed to satisfy the three probable cause elements needed to obtain a constitutionally valid search warrant:

1) probable cause to believe that a crime has been committed;
2) probable cause to believe that the documents and records sought constitute evidence of that crime; and
3) probable cause to believe that the documents and records sought are at the place and premises to be searched.

"The magistrate is entitled, and should be encouraged, to consider the background of the experienced officer. The warrant application should indicate the officer's current employment, how long the position has been held, and other similar investigations with which he or she has been involved."[42]

"Any specialized training should be listed with specific references to the titles and dates of . . . specialized courses. Any conversations the officer may have had with other law enforcement personnel about the investigation should be detailed as well, since hearsay evidence can be used in the application for a search warrant."[43]

Federal courts have held that the magistrate should consider the affiant's expertise in deciding probable cause and objective good faith. Always remember, however, that an investigator's training and experience are not substitutes for the articulable facts and circumstance that constitute probable cause.

The facts of the investigation should be presented in detail, and in a logical and easily understood format, and should include:

1) a synopsis of victims' statements;
2) a synopsis of witnesses' statements;
3) corroborative information provided by governmental or private business sources;
4) the nature and results of a physical surveillance;
5) observations of affiant and/or other investigators, including a synopsis of the results of the investigation to date;
6) a synopsis of statements made by the target of the investigation; and
7) information regarding the suspect's bank accounts and tax records, identifying the source of the information;

When information obtained early in an investigation is significant to the finding of probable cause, it is usually helpful to update that information just before presenting the affidavit to the magistrate. The question about when information becomes stale is simply a matter of the opinion of the magistrate. In deciding when probable cause becomes stale, the courts look to the nature of the property to be seized. Financial documents are far more likely to remain at a location for longer periods than other types of property such as narcotics.

In white-collar crime cases such as embezzlement and fraud, it is crucial for the investigator to demonstrate to the magistrate that assets to be found and seized represent the unlawful fruits of a crime. Also, if the investigation involves a net worth compilation, it is important to demonstrate in the probable cause affidavit an absence of evidence of legitimate income. Even though the old adage, "You can't prove a negative" is still true, the investigator should have no trouble convincing a magistrate that the subjects lacks legitimate income when a thorough investigation has failed to turn up any indication of legitimate employment or other sources of legitimate income.

Executing the Financial Search Warrant

To avoid negating the effectiveness of a constitutionally valid search warrant, the investigator should consider several factors.

Timeliness

In virtually every state, statutes set the maximum period following the issuance of a search warrant during which time the warrant must be executed. Once the statutory limit has expired, the warrant is no longer valid, and any property seized under an expired warrant is subject to suppression.[44] Even when the statutory limit has not passed, the warrant may, nonetheless, be stale, meaning that the probable cause upon which the warrant was based did not continue to exist at the time the warrant was executed.[45]

Presence of the Search Warrant at the Scene

In a federal case, the court ruled that "(w)hile it may be foolhardy to proceed in the absence of the physical presence of the warrant, it is not unconstitutional."[46] Clearly, with search warrants executed in embezzlement and fraud cases, there is seldom an emergency requiring an investigator to begin a search before the warrant arrives. When such exigent circumstances exist, it is best to secure the premises to be searched and await the arrival of the search warrant before beginning the search.

Items Located in Plain View

It is important for an investigator to remember he must connect evidence seized pursuant to a search warrant, or found in plain view during the execution of a warrant, to the commission of the crime.[47] Only when the incriminating nature of evidence is "immediately apparent" to the executing officers who have lawfully seen it in plain view, and there is probable cause to seize the evidence is the seizure constitutional, unless officers knew of the evidence in advance, planned to seize it, but purposely left it out of the affidavit.[48]

Conversely, during the execution of a search warrant for specifically named documents, the seizure of tape recordings, paper bags, and cash register tapes was held unconstitutional, absent proof of "some specific and articulable fact from which a rational link between the item seized and criminal behavior can be inferred."[49]

Personal Papers and Fifth Amendment Considerations

The question has arisen about whether there is a Fifth Amendment privilege against self-incrimination when law enforcement officers seize private papers pursuant to a valid search warrant. According to the

United States Supreme Court, there is not. The Court held that if Fourth Amendment requirements have been met, seizure of private papers does not contravene Fifth Amendment protection against self-incrimination if the author or possessor of the papers had not been asked to say or do anything, and the search for and the seizure of private records is conducted by law enforcement personnel.[50]

Computer Records

Computerized information may include financial records, personal notes, trade secrets, games, and so forth, and many questions have been raised regarding a law enforcement officer's authority to search the files. There has been little law on this subject. What decisions there are essentially treat computer records as any other kind of record.[51]

When the investigator expects to seize computerized records, he should include in the affidavit and warrant the computer software containing the incriminating information, the program software, computer manuals, and the computer itself. Such items and information may be necessary for an expert to extract the information from the computer.

Attorney-Client Privilege and Law Office Searches

During white-collar crime investigations, it may become necessary to search the offices of an attorney. Many high level embezzlers and operators of fraudulent enterprises employ lawyers to protect themselves, and to help them disguise the nature of their activity. Unfortunately, law enforcement officers searching through file cabinets might invade the attorney-client privilege. This privilege extends to communications between attorney and client concerning the motivation for creating the relationship, possible litigation strategy, and even bills, ledgers, statements, and time records if those particular items contain a communication. Possibly even the identity of a client may be privileged, and the attorney-client privilege may be breached by simply viewing names on file folders. One federal court granted an injunction against searching a lawyer's office but refused to hold that searches of law offices were illegal in general.[52]

Notes

[1]Joseph T. Wells, W. Steve Albrecht, Jack Bologna, Gilbert Geis, and Jack Robertson, *Fraud Examiners' Manual* (Austin, TX: National Association of Certified Fraud Examiners, 1989), Section II, p. 82.

[2]Ibid.

[3]Ibid., Section I, p. 102.

[4]Ibid., p. 103.

[5]Ibid., Section II, p. 81.

[6]Ibid.

[7]——, *Narcotics Related Financial Investigative Techniques* (Quantico, VA: U.S. Department of Justice, Federal Bureau of Investigation, Bureau of Justice Assistance, 1991) p. 36.

[8]Ibid., p. 36–37.

[9]Ibid., p. 37.

[10]Ibid.

[11]Ibid., p. 38.

[12]Ibid.

[13]Ibid.

[14]Ibid., p. 40–41.

[15]Ibid., p. 40.

[16]Alexander v. Harrison, 28 N.E. 119, 121.

[17]Ex parte Hart, 240 Ala. 642.

[18]——, *Financial Investigative Techniques* (Washington, D.C.: Internal Revenue Service, Department of the Treasury, 1986), p. 4–20.

[19]Ibid., p. 4–23.

[20]Illinois v. Gates, 462 U.S. 213.

[21]New York v. Belton, 453 U.S. 545.

[22]Chimel v. California, 395 U.S. 752.

[23]Schneckloth v. Bustamonte, 412 U.S. 218, 248–249.

[24]Bumper v. North Carolina, 391 U.S. 543.

[25]U.S. v. Ross, 456 U.S. 798, 809.

[26]Texas v. Brown, 460 U.S. 730.

[27]U.S. v. Ramsey, 431 U.S. 606.

[28]State v. Fleming, 457 So.2nd 1232 (La.)

[29]U.S. v. Sharpe, 470 U.S. 675.

[30]U.S. v. Leon, 468 U.S. 897, 913–914.

[31]Conn v. State, 496 N.E.2d 604 (Ind. App.)

[32]Luster v. State, 443 So.2d 481 (Ala.App.)

[33]Commonwealth v. Douglas, 503 N.E.2d 28, 30 (Mass.)

[34]People v. Royse, 477 P.2d 32 (Wash.)

[35]Beeler, v. State, 677 P.2d 653, 656 (Okla.)

[36]Ybarra v. Illinois, 444 U.S. 90, 92.

[37]Richard S. Stolker, *Asset Forfeiture: Financial Search Warrants* (Washington, D.C.: The Bureau of Justice Assistance, 1989), p. 12.

[38]U.S. v. Sawyer, 799 F.2d 332.

[39]U.S. v. Gomez-Soto, 723 F.2d 649.

[40]State v. Kornegay, 326 S.E.2d 881 (N.C.)

[41]Texas Code of Criminal Procedure, Article 18.02.

[42]Stolker, op cit., p. 13.

[43]Ibid.

[44]Sgro v. U.S., 287 U.S. 206.

[45]U.S. v. Bedford, 519 F.2d 650.

[46]U.S. v. Hepperle, 810 F.2d 836.

[47]Warden v. Hayden, 387 U.S. 294.

[48]Texas v. Brown, 460 U.S. 730.

[49]People v. Hill, 528 P.2d 1 (Cal.)

[50]Andresen v. Maryland, 427 U.S. 463.

[51]Ling v. IRS, 596 F.2d 362.

[52]Klitzman, Litsman, & Gallagher v. Krut, 591 F. Supp. 258 (N.J.)

Chapter 8

EVIDENCE AND DOCUMENTATION

People in general have no notion of the sort and amount of evidence often needed to prove the simplest matter of fact.

Peter Mere Latham
Collected Works, Book II

The principal goal of applying financial investigative techniques is to gather information that will be admissible in court. Most investigators will recognize that some of these techniques can be tedious and require substantial time and patience. As more investigators become involved in white-collar criminal cases, and as they bring more white-collar cases to trial, the need for investigators to become familiar with the sort and amount of admissible documentary evidence needed to prove embezzlement or financial fraud becomes obvious. A brief review of the basic legal principles relating to the preservation and use of evidence in white-collar criminal cases could alleviate some problems and misunderstandings in this critical area of investigation.

One problem investigators encounter is a lack of knowledge concerning the admissibility of financial documents. Too often, investigators spend countless hours gathering a vast array of documents relating to pertinent transactions necessary to prove embezzlement or financial fraud, only to find at the time of trial, or at a pretrial hearing, that he failed to obtain or to preserve the necessary evidence in admissible form.

Such frustrations, born out of the complexities of the rules of evidence, often inhibit investigators from gaining expertise in the fundamentals governing the admissibility of evidence. The investigator's effectiveness is thus severely impaired. To solve such problems, the investigator must become familiar with the rules of evidence. He must ensure that whatever evidence he obtains during the investigation will be admissible in court.* Investigators must consult with local prosecutors to ensure that

---

*Throughout the chapter references are made to the Federal Rules of Evidence (F.R.E.). These rules are contained in Public Law 93-595 and became effective January 2, 1975. All fifty states have based their rules of evidence on the Federal Rules.[1] The Federal Rules in this chapter illustrate key principles of law that are uniformly applicable throughout the United States.

they follow the prosecutor's interpretations of the local rules of evidence in each specific case.

Evidence

Evidence is "any species of proof, or probative matter, legally presented at the trial of an issue by the act of the parties and through the medium of witnesses, records, documents, concrete objects, etc., for the purpose of inducing belief in the minds of the court or jury as to their contention."[2] Evidence is all means by which any alleged matter or fact, the truth of which is submitted to inquiry, is established or disproved.

Investigators attempt to obtain evidence that proves or disproves the ultimate, main or principal fact. For example, in an investigation of embezzlement the investigator obtains documents and oral testimony to prove that a suspect's bank balance has increased substantially over a short period, coinciding with the loss of funds from the suspect's employer. The increase in the suspect's bank account is a fact from which some inference may be drawn concerning the ultimate, main or principal fact, that the suspect was involved in a profitable venture, specifically embezzlement. "Evidence is distinguished from proof in that the latter is the result or effect of evidence."[3]

In legal terms, evidence has various classifications. Evidence may be classified by its proof results (direct or circumstantial evidence), by its source (oral evidence), or according to its nature (real or documentary evidence).

Direct Evidence

Direct evidence is "that means of proof which tends to show the existence of a fact in question, without the intervention of the proof of any other fact. . . . "[4] Direct evidence is that which, if believed, proves the existence of the ultimate, main, or principal fact without any inference or presumption. It is direct evidence when those who have actual knowledge of the facts by means of their senses swear to them. It is evidence to the precise point at issue.

For example, for an agreement involved in a financial fraud, the testimony of a witness who was present, who saw or heard the agreement being made, is direct evidence. Direct evidence may also take the form of an admission or confession made by a suspect in or out of court.

Circumstantial Evidence

Circumstantial evidence, also known as indirect evidence, is "evidence of facts or circumstances from which the existence or nonexistence of (a) fact in issue may be inferred."[5] This is the type of evidence normally discovered in white-collar crimes investigations. Circumstantial evidence is that which tends to prove the existence of the ultimate, main, or principal fact by inference. A conviction based on circumstantial evidence requires proving several material facts that, when considered in their relationship to each other, establish the existence of the ultimate, main, or principal fact.

In the investigation and prosecution of embezzlement and financial fraud cases, circumstantial evidence is the principal means of proof. Embezzlers and perpetrators of fraud take great care to hide the fact that a crime has been committed. Even when the victim uncovers discrepancies, the suspect will often claim that such discrepancies were not intentional, or that they were simply the products of mistake or misunderstanding. The enormous complexity of business transactions makes proof of intent most challenging. Consequently, the systematic and logical presentation of the various bits and pieces of circumstantial evidence becomes the only means of proving the crime.

Oral Evidence

Oral evidence is "evidence given by word of mouth; the oral testimony of a witness."[6] Oral evidence consists of statements made by living witnesses under oath or affirmation. Especially in fraud cases, where the representations and misrepresentations relating to an agreement were made verbally, oral testimony is the only way to prove the ultimate, main or principal fact, or to establish the intent of the suspect. Even in embezzlement, when proving the case relies heavily on proving falsified books and records, the court requires oral testimony from a witness to introduce the records, to guarantee their authenticity, and to explain the content of the documents.

Real Evidence

Real evidence is "evidence furnished by things themselves, on view or inspection, as distinguished from a description of them by the mouth of a witness. . . . "[7] Real evidence is also called physical evidence or demonstrative evidence. It relates to tangible objects or properties admitted in court or inspected by the trier of facts, such as large amounts of currency recovered in embezzlement cases.

Documentary Evidence

Documentary evidence is "evidence supplied by writings and documents of every kind in the widest sense of the term; evidence derived from conventional symbols (such as letters) by which ideas are represented on material substances. Such evidence as is furnished by written instruments, inscriptions, documents of all kinds and also any inanimate objects admissible for the purpose, as distinguished from 'oral' evidence or that delivered by human beings viva voce."[8] Documentary evidence consists of any type of written or printed matter such as formal or informal writings, maps, diagrams, photographs, and computer printouts.

Admissibility of Evidence

Once an investigator has obtained documents related to the investigation, either by voluntary consent or through appropriate legal process, the decision must be made whether those documents will be admissible at trial. To be admissible, evidence must be both relevant and competent.

Frequently, evidence is admissible against one party only, such as a confession, or for a specific purpose, such as impeaching the credibility of a witness. This is known as limited admissibility. In any case, the admissibility of evidence and the determination of relevancy and competency are questions of law for the trial judge to determine.

Relevancy

Any fact, offered into evidence, must relate in some way to the ultimate, main or principal fact to be relevant. Relevancy is "that quality of evidence which renders it properly applicable in determining the truth and falsity of the matters in issue between the parties to a suit."[9] "Relevancy of evidence does not depend upon the conclusiveness of the testimony offered, but upon its legitimate tendency to establish a controverted fact."[10] A fact need not bear directly on the principal fact, but it must have a traceable and significant connection.

One fact is logically relevant to another if, when taken by itself or concerning other facts, it proves or disproves, or tends to prove or disprove the existence of another fact. Therefore, relevant evidence is "evidence having any tendency to make the existence of any fact that is of consequence to the determination of the action more probable or less probable than it would be without the evidence."[11] "Evidence which is not relevant is not admissible."[12]

There are no absolute standards for relevancy because the facts vary from case to case. Consequently, judges have broad discretion in determining what evidence is relevant. Investigators should, therefore, obtain and report all the facts logically relating to the subject of an investigation and not omit significant facts because of doubts regarding their relevance.

Under the Federal Rules of Evidence, materiality is no longer a criterion of admissibility. Materiality is now included under relevance.

Competency

Competency is "the presence of those characteristics, or the absence of those disabilities, which render a witness legally fit and qualified to give testimony in a court of justice; applied, in the same sense, to documents or other written evidence."[13] Evidence must not only be logically relevant, but must also be legally admissible. Relevant evidence may be incompetent because of the hearsay rule, the best evidence rule, or because an investigator obtained it in violation of statute or Constitutional requirements.

As applied to documents, evidence is competent if the investigator obtained it in a way, in a form, and from a source deemed proper under law. Examples of incompetent evidence include a confession involuntarily obtained, documents obtained in violation of the Bank Secrecy Act or the Right to Financial Privacy Act, or a copy of a document offered into evidence absent a reasonable explanation for the failure to produce the original.

Although competency may relate to documentary evidence, it also relates to oral evidence. A witness may be under some disability that prevents him from testifying in a particular case.

Limited Admissibility

Some evidence may have limited admissibility. Evidence that may not be admissible for one purpose may be admissible for another. An evidentiary fact that may not be admissible in the presentation of a case in chief may be admissible later to corroborate other testimony or to impeach the testimony of a witness.

Hearsay

Hearsay is "evidence not proceeding from the personal knowledge of the witness, but from the mere repetition of what he has heard others say."[14] Hearsay is not limited to strictly oral evidence. It also relates to the offering by a witness of a document that someone else prepared.

The hearsay rule concerns the reliability of evidence offered to prove the truth of what was said or written. In hearsay situations, the person making the original statement or preparing the document is not the person offering the evidence. Therefore, the major tool for testing the reliability and truthfulness of the evidence, cross-examination, is not available.

Certain utterances, variously called verbal acts, original or operative facts, or utterances circumstantially relevant, are not hearsay. Under the verbal act doctrine, "utterances accompanying some act or conduct to which it is desired to give legal effect are admissible where conduct to be characterized by words is material to (the) issue and equivocal in its nature, and words accompany (the) conduct and aid in giving it legal significance."[15] Such statements are appropriately described as verbal acts because of their identity with relevant transactions. Examples include the words of bribery or of an illegal sale. In the verbal act situation, the witness is not testifying about what someone told him earlier, he is testifying about the words that explain an ongoing and independently admissible act.

Admissions and confessions are not hearsay. An admission is a statement or act of a party offered in evidence against him.[16] An admission is "the avowal of a fact or of circumstances from which guilt may be inferred, but only tending to prove the offense charged, and not amounting to a confession of guilt."[17] Additionally, it may be a prior oral or written statement or act of a party that is inconsistent with his or her position at trial. A prosecutor may use an admission either as evidence of facts or to impeach or discredit a party as a witness. An admission may be oral, written, or inferred by conduct. Admissions are either judicial or extrajudicial.

Judicial admissions are pleadings, stipulations, affidavits, depositions, or statements a defendant makes in open court during a judicial proceeding. Such admissions may be admissible against a party in a subsequent action where there is a different adversary. A plea of guilty is an admission. A plea of no contest is not an admission.

Extrajudicial admission is anything said outside court by a party to litigation that is inconsistent with facts asserted in the pleadings or testimony in court. It is not limited to facts that are against the party's interest when made, although the weight of an admission increases if it is against his interest at the time.

Competent and relevant statements of fact made by a person before his alleged commission of a crime may be admissible against that person to prove such facts without the need for corroborations. Admissions made as part of the act of committing an offense may also be admissible without corroboration. For example, in a criminal prosecution for tax evasion based upon understated receipts from a business, the costs of goods sold and other deductions shown on a tax return are admissions that do not need corroboration.

Unlike admissions made before or during the commission of an offense, extrajudicial admissions made by a person after the alleged commission of a crime require corroboration. Evidence corroborating admissions made after the offense need not prove the offense beyond a reasonable doubt, or even by a preponderance of the evidence. The evidence, however, must be substantial enough, when considered as a whole and in connection with the admission, to prove the person's guilt beyond a reasonable doubt.

A confession is "a voluntary statement made by a person charged with the commission of a crime or misdemeanor, communicated to another person, wherein he acknowledges himself to be guilty of the offense charged, and discloses the circumstances of the act or the share and participation he had in it."[18] It is the comprehensive statement of one person that he is guilty of a crime. It embraces all the necessary elements of the offense, and is related, either verbally or in writing, to another person.

A confession, as with an admission, may be judicial or extrajudicial. All confessions must be corroborated.

Exceptions to the Hearsay Rule

The courts, in the interest of justice, have made certain exceptions to the hearsay rule. The exceptions are based on two general principles:

1) the person who made the statement or the written document is not available to testify, and
2) the nature of the statement or writing is such that its truthfulness appears logical.

Evidence meeting the above standards is admissible under the necessity rule as an exemption to the hearsay rule. Following are some important exceptions to the hearsay rule.

Testimony by Experts

Expert opinions are the conclusions of a person, qualified by his knowledge, skill, experience, training, and education, or any combination, as an expert in his field.[19] They are admitted to aid the jury or the court in its deliberations. The basis for allowing this opinion testimony is that the witness, who has examined the evidence, has specialized experience beyond that of the ordinary person. That experience would qualify him to give an opinion on the matter.

Recorded Recollection

Often, a witness cannot remember every detail of the relevant events, and he requires the use of some type of written material to refresh his memory. A record or memorandum is admissible as an exception to the hearsay rule if the proponent can show that the witness once had personal knowledge of the matter, that the record or memorandum was prepared or adopted by him when it was fresh in his memory, that it accurately reflected his knowledge at the time, and that the witness currently has insufficient recollection to enable him to testify fully and accurately.[20]

Often, an investigator will not remember the details of an interview or investigation and must view his report or a memorandum of interview to refresh his memory. If the investigator can then remember, his testimony can proceed. When an investigator or witness uses such a writing for refreshing his memory, either before or during his testimony, opposing counsel is entitled to see the writing and use it to try to impeach the individual's credibility.

Occasionally, even after viewing the writing, the investigator or witness is still unable to remember the relevant matter. For example, an investigator may not remember a list of more than a hundred checks he seized in an embezzlement scheme. If the witness can testify positively that he prepared the writing at or near the time he seized the checks, and that the writing was a correct reflection of what occurred, the record itself may be admissible as an exception to the hearsay rule.

Records of Regularly Conducted Activity; Business Records

This exception to the hearsay rule is the most important for the white-collar crime investigator. "A memorandum, report, record, or data compilation in any form, of acts, events, conditions, opinions, or diagnoses, made at or near the time by, or from information transmitted by, a person with knowledge, if kept in the course of a regularly conducted business activity, and if the regular practice of that business activity was to make the memorandum, report, record, or data compilation, all as shown by the testimony of the custodian or other qualified witness, is admissible as an exception to the hearsay rule, unless the source of the information or method or the circumstances of preparation indicate a lack of trustworthiness."[21]

Under the common law this exception was known as the "shop book rule." Records made in the ordinary course of business, or transmitted by someone with personal knowledge and the duty to make an accurate record, are admissible although the maker of the record does not testify. Business records are considered trustworthy principally because those with personal knowledge are under strict and continuing duty to make accurate records.

The Federal Rules of Evidence require that such documents meet two tests before they fall within the exception:

1) the records were kept during a regularly conducted business activity, and

2) it was the regular practice of that business activity to make the record.

Absence of Entry in Records of Regularly Conducted Activity

The failure to record or include a matter that would ordinarily be included in a record of a regularly conducted business activity, offered to prove the nonoccurrence or nonexistence of the matter, is a hearsay exception.[22] This is the logical extension of the "shop book rule." If business records are trustworthy accounts of what happened, they must also be trustworthy accounts of what did not happen.

Other Records

Records containing entries made in the regular course of conduct, such as marriage and baptismal certificates, are admissible without the testimony of the person who made the entries, if some witness can properly identify the documents. Public records made by a public officer, in the performance of his duties, are admissible after proper authentication. Some examples include public records and reports;[23] records of vital statistics;[24] records of religious organizations;[25] marriage, baptism, and similar certificates;[26] family records, such as family Bibles and engravings on rings, urns, or crypts;[27] market reports; commercial publications and mortality tables;[28] and learned treatises.[29]

Records of public agencies that set forth the activities of the agency, or matters observed pursuant to a duty imposed by law about which there was a duty to report, are admissible. Matters observed and reported by law enforcement officers in criminal cases are not, however, within the scope of this exception to the hearsay rule.

Absence of Public Record or Entry

The Federal Rules of Evidence also provide for an exception to the hearsay rule regarding the absence of a public record or entry. If the public office would ordinarily have made and preserved a record of an event, the absence of a regular entry may be offered to prove that such does not exist.[30] It must be shown that a diligent search failed to discover any record or entry.

Records of Documents Affecting Interest in Property

If a document affecting an interest in property (e.g., a deed) is recorded in a public office, and an applicable statute authorizes the recording of documents of that kind in that office, the record of such document may be admissible as proof of the original recorded document. It may also be admissible as proof of the document's execution and delivery by each person by whom it purports to have been executed.[31]

Former Testimony

Former testimony given by a witness may be admissible as an exception to the hearsay rule.[32] The witness may have given the testimony:

1) at another hearing of the same proceeding,
2) at a hearing of a different proceeding, or

3) in a deposition taken according to law during the same or another proceeding.

To be admissible in a criminal proceeding, the party against whom the previous testimony is to be offered must have had an opportunity and similar motive to develop the testimony by direct, cross or redirect examination.

Statements Against Interest, Declarant Unavailable

A statement against interest relates to an oral or written declaration by someone not a party to the action and not available to testify. The proponent must show that the statement was, at the time of the making, so far contrary to the declarant's pecuniary or proprietary interest, or so far tended to make invalid a claim by him against another, that a reasonable person in his position would not have made the statement, unless he believed it to be true.[33] The Federal Rules and some courts have extended the rule to statements against penal interest.

Nonexpert Opinion on Handwriting

A witness who is not an expert can give his opinion authenticating a writing or signature if he is sufficiently familiar with the handwriting of the putative writer. However, the witness must not have acquired the familiarity for purposes of the litigation.[34]

Documentary Evidence

Documentary evidence is evidence supplied by writings and documents of every kind in the widest sense of the term. All of the rules discussed above bearing on the admissibility of evidence generally are applicable to the admissibility of documentary evidence.

Best Evidence Rule

The best evidence rule, which applies only to documentary evidence, is that the best proof of the contents of a document is the original document itself. This rule, requiring the production of the original document, is confined to cases where one party seeks to prove the contents of the document. Production consists of either making the writing available to the judge or counsel for the adversary or reading the writing aloud in open court. Facts about a document other than its contents are provable without its production. For example, the fact that a sales contract was made is a fact issue separate from the actual terms of the contract, and is provable through testimony alone.

In the traditional sense, the best evidence rule applied to written documents. However, current techniques of data storage have mandated expansion of the rule to include "letters, words or numbers, or their equivalent, set down by handwriting, typewriting, printing, photostating, photographing, magnetic impulse, mechanical or electrical recording, or other form of data compilation."[35]

The original of a writing or recording is "the writing or recording itself or any counterpart intended to have the same effect by a person executing or issuing it."[36] Certain documents such as leases, contracts, and letters signed or executed in more than one copy are all originals, and any copy may be produced as an original. An original of a photograph includes the negative or any print from it. If data is stored on a computer or similar device, any printout or other output readable by sight, shown to reflect the data accurately, is an original.

A duplicate of an original is admissible to the same extent as an original unless:

1) a genuine question is raised as to the authenticity of the original, or
2) under the circumstances, it would be unfair to admit the duplicate instead of the original.

A duplicate is a counterpart produced:

1) from the same impression as the original,
2) from the same matrix as the original,
3) by means of photograph, including enlargements and miniatures,
4) by mechanical or electronic rerecording, or
5) by other equivalent-techniques that accurately reproduce the original.

The definition describes copies produced by methods possessing an accuracy that virtually eliminates the possibility of error. Photocopies of documents are duplicates.

The reason for the best evidence rule is to prevent fraud, mistake, or error. Since the best evidence applies only to documentary evidence, the court cannot use it to exclude oral testimony of one witness merely because another witness could give more conclusive testimony.

Secondary Evidence

When an original document is not available and the absence is explainable, the court may admit secondary evidence to prove the contents of the missing writing. Secondary evidence may consist of either the testimony of a witness or a copy of the writing. There is no settled rule stating which of these is a higher degree of secondary evidence.

Evidence of the content of a document, other than the original document, is secondary evidence. The Federal Rules of Evidence allow the court to admit secondary evidence under certain conditions. First, there must be a satisfactory showing of the present or former existence of an original document, properly documented and genuine. Second, there must be a showing of one of three prerequisite conditions:

1) All originals have been lost or destroyed, unless the loss or destruction was deliberately caused by the party offering the evidence to prevent the production of the original. If the original is lost, there must be testimony that a diligent search was made for the original, and that it could not be found. The sufficiency of the search is a matter to be decided by the court.

2) The original is not obtainable by judicial process. This would require a showing that the original writing has not been produced in answer to a subpoena, or that it is beyond the jurisdiction of the court.

3) The original is in the possession of the defendant. In a criminal case not involving corporate records, it is sufficient for the government to introduce secondary evidence of the defendant's records by showing that the originals are in the possession of the defendant and, at the time the original was under the control of the defendant, against whom it is offered, he was put on notice by the pleadings or otherwise that the contents would be subject to proof at the hearing, and he does not produce the original at the hearing. The defendant cannot be compelled to incriminate himself by producing the document.[37]

Admissibility of Specific Forms of Documentary Evidence

Records of Regularly Conducted Business Activity

As stated above, The Federal Rules of Evidence permits showing that an entry was made in a book maintained in the regular course of business without requiring the person who made the entry having to identify it. The essence of the "regular course of business" rule is the reliance on records made under circumstances showing no reason or motive to misrepresent the facts.

The fact that a record has been kept in the regular course of business is not of itself sufficient to make it admissible. The rules of relevancy and competency still apply. If a party offers as evidence a ledger to prove entries posted from a journal, then he should also produce the journal as the book of original entry.

When the regular course of business is to photograph, photostat or microfilm the business records, such reproductions, when satisfactorily identified, are as admissible as the original. Similarly, enlargements of the original reproductions are admissible if the original reproduction is in existence and available for inspection.

Photographs, Photostats, and Microfilmed Copies

Photographs, photostats, and microfilmed copies of writings not made in the regular course of business are secondary evidence of the contents, generally inadmissible if the original is available, and no acceptable reason exists for failure to produce it. A photographic or photostatic reproduction of a document may be admissible upon producing evidence that the original cannot be obtained, and that the reproduction is an exact and accurate copy. Such copies may be admissible when the original is in the hands of the defendant, and the government cannot compel production of the original.

When an investigator obtains photostats of documents during an investigation, he should initial the back of the photostat, noting the date and time he made the copy. He should note on the reverse side of the photostat, or on an initialed attachment, the source of the original document. This procedure will ensure proper authentication at trial.

Transcripts

Transcripts are copies of writings and are admissible as secondary evidence under the same principles governing all secondary evidence. An investigator must take certain precautions in preparing transcripts to ensure proper authentication for admission at trial. He must carefully compare the transcript with the original and certify that it is a correct transcript. The certification should show the date the transcription was made, by whom and where it was made, and the source from which it was taken. The investigator should identify each page to show that it forms part of the whole.

Charts, Schedules, and Summaries

Charts, schedules, and summaries prepared by investigators may be placed in evidence at the discretion of the court if they are summaries of evidence already presented. The rules of evidence allow this as a matter of convenience for the court and the jury. The investigator must be careful in preparing the items to avoid using prejudicial headings or titles.

Notes, Diaries, Work Papers, and Memoranda

Notes, diaries, work papers, and memoranda prepared by auditors and investigators are not normally considered evidence. If, however, a witness uses them to refresh his memory before or during his testimony, the adverse party may have them admitted to impeach the testimony. Any documents a witness uses while on the stand are subject to inspection.

Official Records

As a condition precedent to the admissibility of official records as documentary evidence, the party offering the evidence must establish that the item produced is what it purports to be. For example, the proponent must show that a certain document he seeks to introduce as a governmental record is an official record of a particular government entity. The Federal Rules of Evidence provide: "the contents of an official record, or of a document authorized to be recorded or filed and actually recorded or filed, including data compilations in any form, if otherwise admissible, may be proven by copy, certified as correct in accordance with Rule 902 or testified to be correct by a witness who has compared it with the original. If a copy which complies with the foregoing cannot be obtained by the exercise of reasonable diligence, then other evidence of the contents may be given. Under this rule, there is no requirement that the original be introduced."[38]

The Federal Rules of Evidence also provide that extrinsic evidence of authenticity as a condition precedent to admissibility is not required for certain types of documents. These exceptions include:

1) public documents under seal,
2) certified copies of public records,

3) newspapers and periodicals,
4) trade inscriptions, and
5) commercial paper and related documents to the extent provided by general commercial law.

The United States Code provides for the admissibility of copies of legislative acts of any state or territory of the United States and of court records and judicial proceedings. "Such acts, records and judicial proceedings or copies thereof, so authenticated, shall have the same full faith and credit in every court within the United States and its territories and possessions as they have by law in the courts of such state, territory or possession from which they are taken."[39]

The United States Code makes admissible nonjudicial records or books kept in any public office of any state, territory or possession of the United States, or copies thereof. The United States Code gives them full faith and credit upon proper authentication.[40]

Authentication of Copies, Reproductions, and Transcripts

The investigator should authenticate any copy, reproduction, or transcript of an original document. If the original document is lost or destroyed, the court will more readily accept the authenticated copy, reproduction, or transcript into evidence. No statute defines proper authentication. Evidence sufficient to support a finding that the matter in question is what its proponent claims it to be satisfies the requirement for authentication.

Copies of Original Documents

The person who handles or supervises the process should authenticate documents reproduced by photocopy equipment. He should compare each copy with the original. The back of each copy should include a statement that he compared the copy with the original, and that it is a true and correct copy. The person making the comparison should also date and sign it. The date of certification should be the date the copy was made and compared with the original.

Under no circumstances should anyone make a certification without first making the comparison. To preserve the document's authenticity, the investigator should make no marks or alterations on the face of the copy. If many copies are involved, and the witness is reluctant to authenticate the back of each copy, a cover letter or affidavit may accomplish the same purpose. The letter or affidavit should describe the records in question and include a statement that they are true and correct copies of the originals. The copies should be numbered so the witness can refer to the number of copies in the letter or affidavit, and to make the copies easier to identify.

Sometimes, particularly in large firms, the witness will have employees under his supervision handle the copying of the records. The investigator should figure out what specific instructions supervisory personnel gave the employees when obtaining the copies. If the investigator obtains an affidavit in such a situation, it should include a statement to the effect that employees maintained and controlled the copied records under the supervisor's direction and control.

Reproductions

With the increase in automated data processing systems, particularly by financial institutions, obtaining a copy of a record exclusively reflecting a specific account is often not possible. The account activity may be on a computer-generated transcript along with thousands of other accounts. Financial institutions are often reluctant to allow an investigator to examine the entire transcript. It will, instead, reconstruct the subject's account activity on a separate document.

If the investigator obtains a reproduction of the original record, he should request the person making the reproduction to include a statement on the back of the document describing the records from which it was reconstructed, and certifying that the person carefully compared the entries on the reproduction with the original records. The person and the investigator should also date and sign the document. A cover letter or affidavit may accomplish the authentication.

Transcripts

The investigator must be especially careful when preparing transcripts of records, particularly those of the suspect. The investigator preparing the transcription should number, date, and sign or initial each page of the document he is preparing. The last page of the transcript should fully describe the original records from which the transcript was prepared, the place where it was prepared, and the identity of the person who submitted the original records. The investigator should identify each page to show that it forms part of the whole. The investigator should show the page number and the total number of pages involved, as "page 2 of 7 pages." When making a partial transcript, the investigator should note that also, for example, "excerpt from page 94 of the cash disbursements ledger."

Ideally, the person submitting the original records should review the records and the transcript. If he is satisfied that the transcript accurately reflects the contents of the original records, he should then initial and date each page of the transcript. A cover letter or affidavit can accomplish the authentication. The affidavit should fully describe the original records from which the transcript was prepared. It should also include statements that the witness examined and approved the transcript, and that the witness certifies that the transcript accurately reflects the contents of the original records.

ᛝ Chain of Custody

Chain of custody is the expression applied to the preservation, by successive custodians, of the instrument of a crime or of any relevant writing in its original condition. Before a judge can allow documentary evidence to be admitted at trial, he must be assured that the writing is in the same condition as when law enforcement officers seized it. Consequently, the investigator must ensure that all documentary evidence seized is readily identifiable, and that he preserves it in its original form.

Several people may handle a document or writing before a prosecutor offers it into evidence in court: investigators, handwriting experts, forensic technicians, and prosecutors. Any time an investigator seizes or subsequently handles any document or writing, he must mark each item for later identification. He must also be prepared to show where or from whom he received the document, and into whose custody he released the document or writing. He must show this chain of custody from the time of seizure until the time the document or writing is introduced in court.

The investigator may place his initials and the date and time the document came into his possession on some inconspicuous place on the document, either in a margin, on the corner, or on the back. If circumstances suggest that such marking may render the document subject to attack on the grounds that it has been defaced, the investigator should make a photostatic copy of the original for working purposes. He may then place the original in an envelope, seal the envelope, and place his initials across the seal. In every event, the investigator must record in his report of the events the complete chain of custody for each writing or document.

Privileged Communications

The common law held that certain types of verbal and written communications were the results of certain types of relationships meant to be private, and that the importance to society of maintaining this privacy outweighed the importance of revealing the evidence to a jury. Such communications were deemed confidential, and thus privileged, between the parties to the communication. Three relationships recognized as privileged are important to the white-collar crime investigator:

1) attorney-client,
2) government-informant, and
3) husband-wife.

Attorney-Client Privilege

The attorney-client privilege is strictly interpreted. Not every communication between an attorney and his client falls under the privilege. It applies only to those communications meant to be confidential and made to the attorney in his capacity as an attorney, such as a consultation for legal advice or representation in a legal proceeding. The privilege, when it does apply, covers corporate and individual clients, but it does not normally include a right by the attorney to withhold the name of a client.

The privilege does not apply when an attorney serves in a strictly fiduciary capacity, such as handling contracts and money in a real estate transaction, stock sales, and various other actions where the principal function is to handle the transfer of funds from one party to another. When the advice an attorney gives concerns business instead of legal matters, the communication is not privileged. This is especially important where an attorney acts as both attorney and accountant in embezzlement or fraud cases. When acting as the accountant in this dual relationship, there is no attorney-client relationship. The federal courts have never recognized an accountant-client privilege.

There is one situation in giving legal advice where the courts do not recognize the attorney-client privilege: when the attorney gives advice or renders assistance in planning, perpetrating, or concealing a crime or fraud. By taking part in a crime or fraud, the attorney destroys any privilege that would otherwise have attached to confidential communications.

As with most privileges, the presence of a third party during the communication between an attorney and his client will usually annul the privilege. The exception to this is when the presence of the third party is necessary for the attorney to accomplish his task as legal advisor.

Government-Informant Privilege

The government-informant privilege allows law enforcement agencies to withhold from disclosure the identity of people who furnish information of violations of law to officers charged with the enforcement of the law. The purpose of the privilege is the furtherance and protection of the public interest in effective law enforcement.

Unlike other privileges, it is the identity of the informant that is privileged and not the communication. This privilege differs from all others in that it is waivable only by the government, whereas the others are essentially for the benefit of the individual and waivable by him. Since the privilege exists for the government, it is deemed waived if the government puts the informant on the witness stand.

To provide maximum security regarding the identity and existence of an informant, the investigator should not use confidential informants as witnesses unnecessarily, place them in a position where they might become witnesses, or position them to be identified in court without their consent. Where the disclosure of an informant's identity is essential to the defense of an accused, the trial court may order disclosure. If the government then withholds the identity of the informant, the court may dismiss the indictment.

Husband-Wife Privilege

Communications between a husband and wife, when privately made, are assumed to be of a confidential nature, and are therefore privileged. It is essential, however, that the communications must be, from their nature, fairly intended to be of a confidential nature. If it is obvious from the nature of the communication that they intended no confidence, there is no privilege. Communications made between a husband and wife in the presence of children, who are old enough to understand the communication, and other family members are not considered confidential and are therefore not privileged. Similarly, communications made in the presence of third parties are not privileged.

The courts do not extend privilege to communications made before the marriage or after a divorce. Further, the privilege applies to communications, not acts. Doing an act in the presence of a spouse is not a communication. Communications made during the marriage remain privileged even after the end of the marriage, despite whether the marriage ends by death of a spouse or by divorce.

Beyond the privilege of a husband and wife to prevent the other from revealing confidential communications that occurred during the marriage, there exists an independent privilege of one spouse to refuse to testify adversely against the other. With respect to this privilege, the testifying spouse alone has the choice of whether to refuse to testify adversely against his or her spouse on any act observed before or during the marriage and on any nonconfidential communications. The courts may not compel the spouse to testify nor foreclose the spouse from testifying.

The attorney-client and husband-wife privileges relate only to testimony. There is nothing to prevent the development of evidence based on leads provided by a spouse or by an attorney. The fact that such testimony may be inadmissible does not affect the admissibility of the testimony of another witness not within the privileged relationship.

Questioned Documents

A questioned document is one that someone has questioned in part or in whole with respect to its authenticity, identity, or origin. Since concealment is especially important to the white-collar criminal, the tools or methods for perpetrating such crimes are not the obvious sort used by common criminals. White-collar criminals use tools and methods common to legitimate day-to-day activities. Consequently, the white-collar crime investigator has added burdens in proving that a crime has been committed, in identifying the responsible person, and in finding the elements of intent.

The ability to detect and prove that a suspect has falsified documents in some manner may allow the investigator to provide:

1) the ultimate proof of the suspect's guilt, such as a forged document or instrument,
2) one link in the chain of circumstantial evidence, such as the

alteration or erasure of booking entries to conceal embezzlement, or

3) the element needed to prove the suspect acted with criminal intent, such as alterations in a document the suspect claims were merely a product of mistake.

To detect a questionable document, the investigator must first have some indication of the particular criminal activity suspected. He must then have some reason to believe the perpetrator of the particular criminal activity would benefit from the use of such a document.

If he questions the authenticity of a document, the investigator can obtain known legitimate similar documents, known as exemplars, and compare them with the questioned document. Differences in paper quality, style of print, color of ink, or the water mark may be readily apparent on the documents. The investigator may then submit the known exemplar and the questioned document to experts for scientific analysis to determine the authenticity of the questioned document.

If he questions the identity of a document, the investigator can examine the document for signs of alterations or erasures. Individuals prepare documents to attest to a transaction that should be the same for all parties involved. The investigator can compare the document with its counterpart copy or duplicate original, if the document has a copy or duplicate original, to decide whether the two documents are identical. If a copy or duplicate original of the questioned document cannot be found, the investigator can interview other parties to the transaction to find whether the questioned document accurately reflects the transaction, and whether it is what it purports to be.

If he questions the origin of the document, the investigator can interview the purported maker of the document to see whether he can attest to making the writing. Sometimes, where the maker is not available for an interview or is unwilling or unable to cooperate, the investigator can submit the questioned documents, known samples of the purported maker's handwriting, and known samples of any suspect's handwriting, to an expert who might then identify the maker of the document.

Exemplars

Exemplars are simply samples of the matter at issue to use as a comparison with the questioned document, such as the ink, the type, the handwriting, the paper, or another copy of the document. Since the exemplars may be critical to the evidentiary results, the investigator must be careful in obtaining them.

The investigator should obtain and submit as many known samples as needed for comparison purposes. This will naturally depend on the item at issue.

Handwriting Exemplars

Handwriting exemplars may consist of previous writings the subject has admitted making, or that are proven to be the suspect's. Securing such samples during interviews with the subject may be possible. The more numerous and lengthy the specimens, the better the opportunity for accurate comparison, and the less likely the possibility the suspect may successfully disguise the handwriting, should he be so inclined.

For the best effect, the exemplar should duplicate the questioned document. The suspect should make it with a similar writing instrument, on similar paper, and should include, as nearly as possible, the full content or text of the questioned document.

The investigator should remain alert to the possibility of disguises in handwriting. The most common forms of disguise include: writing extremely fast or painstakingly slowly, writing unusually large or small, backhand or other extreme changes in the slant, complicated embellishments, or a simplified disconnected printing style. If the questioned document contains disguised handwriting, however, specimens of a disguised hand may be most useful.

The taking of handwriting exemplars does not violate a person's constitutional rights against self-incrimination. The Fifth Amendment privilege extends to communications, but a mere handwriting exemplar, in contrast to the content of the writing, is an identifying physical characteristic outside its protection.[41]

Typewriting Exemplars

When a questioned document is typewritten, the investigator should obtain sets of impressions of all the characters on the keyboard. To bring out the technical irregularities, the investigator should type sets with light, medium, and heavy touch, and at varying rates of speed. In the ordinary course of use, typewriters undergo deterioration: type bars lose vertical and horizontal relationships to each other; spacing mechanisms develop irregularities; type faces deform and wear. Such factors impart to each typewriter an individuality that serves to distinguish it from all others and makes positive identification of an individual machine possible.

When possible, the investigator should make exemplars with the ribbon found in the machine. The exemplar should repeat the complete text of the questioned document. If the text is too extensive for one ribbon, the investigator should prepare enough of it to give all the important letters and figures.

To get the sharpest impressions, roll the paper and carbon into the machine and set the ribbon adjustment on stencil. The presence of type scars in ribbon specimens should be confirmed by carbon specimens.

If it is believed the ribbon in the machine was used to type a questioned document, the investigator should remove the ribbon and preserve it as evidence, if possible, since the original keystroke impressions may be recreated or duplicated.

The rise of computers and word processors, along with the use of daisy wheel, dot matrix, bubble jet and laser printers, has added additional difficulties for the investigator. Nevertheless, abnormalities in the mechanics and performance of such printing devices may be singularly identifiable. Of course, if the questioned document is stored in the computer or word processor, a copy of that document may be obtainable through proper legal process. If not, the investigator may duplicate the questioned document in the computer or word processor and print it on the suspected printing devices. The investigator should treat such exemplars just as a typewritten exemplar.

Other Exemplars

In proving erasures, alterations, overwriting, or blotter impressions, or in determining the age of a questioned document, exemplars are not normally used. Through infrared light technique, microscopes, ultraviolet light, and chemicals, the laboratory can resolve many questions about a document. Occasionally, exemplars have aided in determining the age of certain documents. Standards of comparison consisted of documents allegedly existing at the time of the questioned document. Comparison of inks, water marks, condition of paper, and other characteristics provide clues to the age of the questioned document.

Identifying, Proving, or Disproving Questioned Documents

Having obtained the necessary numbers and kinds of exemplars, the investigator should initial and date them on the back so that they are readily identifiable in court. The investigator should take the original questioned document, along with the exemplars, to a questioned document examiner. It is, of course, necessary to preserve and record the chain of evidence.

Questioned document experts examine and analyze documents to assure their authenticity; to detect evidence of erasure, alteration, addition, interpolation, and forgery; to identify handwriting and typewriting; and to develop information concerning ink, paper, writing instrument, and other materials. In some areas, experts from the U.S. Postal Service, the Federal Bureau of Investigation, and the Bureau of Alcohol, Tobacco, and Firearms may be available to help state and local investigators.

The investigator, himself, can probably prove or disprove the authenticity of a questioned document with simple tools at his disposal, such as a magnifying glass or an enlarged photograph. Even so, expert assistance is still advisable if the suspect will not admit to the falsity of the document. In court, expert testimony is more impressive, and, usually, opinion testimony is only admissible through an expert.

Notes

[1]Richard A. Nossen, *The Detection, Investigation and Prosecution of Financial Crimes* (Richmond, VA: Richard A. Nossen & Associates, 1982), pp. 68–69.

[2]Hotchkiss v. Newton, 10 Ga. 567.

[3]Nossen, op cit., p. 69.

[4]State v. Calder, 23 Mont. 504.

[5]People v. Steele, 37 N.Y.S.2d 199, 200.

[6]Bates' Ann.St.Ohio, 1904.

[7]Reggie v. Grand Trunk Ry. Co., 93 Vt. 282.

[8]People v. Purcell, 70 P.2d 706.

[9]1 Greenl.Ev. 49.

[10]State v. Upson, 162 Minn. 9.

[11]F.R.E. Rule 401.

[12]F.R.E. Rule 402.

[13]Henry Campbell Black, ed. *Black's Law Dictionary: Revised Fourth Edition* (St. Paul, MN: West Publishing Co., 1968), p. 355.

[14]State v. Ah Lee, 18 Or. 540.

[15]Keefe v. State, 50 Ariz. 295.

[16]F.R.E. Rule 801.

[17]Theis v. State, Ga., 164 S.E. 456, 457.

[18]Spicer v. Commonwealth, 21 Ky.L.Rep. 528.
[19]F.R.E. Rule 702.
[20]F.R.E. Rule 803(5).
[21]F.R.E. Rule 803(6).
[22]F.R.E. Rule 803(7).
[23]F.R.E. Rule 803(8).
[24]F.R.E. Rule 803(9).
[25]F.R.E. Rule 803(11).
[26]F.R.E. Rule 803(12).
[27]F.R.E. Rule 803(13).
[28]F.R.E. Rule 803(17).
[29]F.R.E. Rule 803(18).
[30]F.R.E. Rule 803(10).
[31]F.R.E. Rule 803(14).
[32]F.R.E. Rule 804(b)(1).
[33]F.R.E. Rule 804(b)(3).
[34]F.R.E. Rule 901(b)(2).
[35]F.R.E. Rule 1001.
[36]F.R.E. Rule 1001.
[37]F.R.E. Rule 1004.
[38]F.R.E. Rule 1005.
[39]28 U.S.C. 1738.
[40]28 U.S.C. 1739.
[41]Gilbert v. California, 388 U.S. 263.

Chapter 9

PROVING ILLICIT TRANSACTIONS

There is always something to upset the most careful of human calculations.

Ihara Saikaku
The Japanese Family Storehouse

The white-collar criminal, due to the nature of his activities, must operate in the open. His identity is already known to his victims. Consequently, he must carefully calculate and plan his activities for his schemes to be successful. In white-collar criminal cases, however, there is no perfect crime, no matter how carefully the suspect planned. To embezzle money, there must be at least one witness to the crime—the victim. To defraud money, there must be at least one witness to the crime—the victim. No matter how painstakingly the white-collar criminal tries to disguise his activities, there are witnesses to testify about the facts, or there are documents concerning the crime that are outside the criminal's scope of control. Once the suspect obtains money or other property, he must then do something with it. He must spend or invest the money, or he must use or dispose of the property. No matter how carefully the white-collar criminal planned his scheme, leads exist for the investigator to pursue.

Proper and thorough documentation is imperative in any financial investigation. Incorrect witnesses, inadequate documentation, or inadmissible evidence will severely weaken or destroy a case. Whether the investigation is based on direct or indirect methods of proof, the investigator must obtain each detail of each transaction of the scheme. He must correctly obtain and accurately document each item of evidence.

In proving specific transactions, such as the sale and purchase of real estate or similar events, it is not enough for the investigator merely to obtain the written record of those transactions. Documents and recorded entries, regardless how carefully and honestly made, are not facts. They are written descriptions of events, but they are not in themselves proof of the entire events. It is important for the investigator to locate and interview witnesses who can testify about the transactions, and who can

179

attest to the authenticity of the documents. The investigator must learn whether the documents or entries truthfully relate all the facts or circumstances, some of which may not have been recorded.

It is now that the investigator begins to piece together the various disciplines of the financial investigation process:

1) deciding whether the initial complaint suggests elements of an offense that can be proven, either embezzlement or fraud,
2) figuring out which, if any, applicable federal or state laws may have been violated,
3) interviewing victims and witnesses to gather information and leads to further the investigation,
4) obtaining the records and documents to support claims of embezzlement and fraud, and
5) examining and auditing the financial and accounting records and data.

If, for example, proving fraud requires proving sales by the suspect, the investigator must interview the vendees to decide whether the checks and invoices obtained represent all the transactions between the vendees and the suspect. He must also decide whether the documents truthfully recorded the events, whether additional sums might have been paid or refunded, whether there were any other methods of payment, whether there were other parties to the transactions, and whether there is any other relevant information.

If, for example, proving embezzlement requires proving a real estate transaction, it is important to remember that a contract for sale, a settlement sheet, a closing statement, and a recorded deed do not necessarily reflect all the facts involved in a real estate transaction. Cash payments besides those shown in the documents or "straw parties" may become evident when questioning the parties to the transaction. Mortgages and other encumbrances may not exist, although recorded documents seem to show they do.

There is no problem with admissibility when different items of documentary evidence may be used to prove a fact. The only matter involved in such a case is the weight the jury attaches to the evidence. If the investigator is trying to prove a purchase from a suspect, the court will not exclude from evidence a canceled check from the purchaser made payable to the suspect simply because invoices, purchase journals, or cash disbursement books of the purchaser have not been produced, even if they are available. The fact that the check may not be the best proof of the purchase is a factual question for the jury. To make a better case, the investigator should attempt to produce the purchasing invoice, purchase journals, and cash disbursement books of the purchaser. Additionally, basic items of documentation coupled with reliable testimony from a credible witness, are generally necessary to establish certain financial facts.

Making Illegal Payments and Transfers

There are various audit and examination techniques to identify and trace the secret movements of funds in embezzlement and fraud. The techniques vary because the methods of taking and disposing of the property vary. Company funds can be used to purchase expensive personal gifts as a form of embezzlement, or they may be used as corrupt gifts. An embezzler may siphon money from a company or trust account by cash or by check as a benefit for the taker or to bribe another. The promoter of a fraud may take hidden interests in related transactions to earn fraudulent profits, or he may use them to make illicit payoffs. The illegal objectives may differ, but the means are the same.

There are certain traditional methods of making and concealing illegal payments and transfers. These methods fall into a surprising few but commonly repeated patterns, including:

1) corrupt gifts and favors,
2) cash payments,
3) checks and other financial instruments,
4) hidden interests,
5) fictitious loans,
6) transfers at other than fair market value,
7) promises of subsequent employment, favorable separation payments, employment of spouse or relatives,
8) floating,
9) lapping, and
10) cooking.

Corrupt Gifts and Favors

Gifts given with corrupt intent include everything from a box of cigars to houses and large tracts of land. Favored items include expensive wines and liquors, clothes, and jewelry. Savings bonds are also popular, probably because they are available at a discount off face value. Also popular are lavish paid vacations, free transportation, and the free use of resort facilities such as beachfront condos or ski lodges. Businesses often make gifts out of their own inventory or services, such as a building contractor providing free home improvements or materials, since it is less costly.

Gifts and other favors provide an easy and safe way to initiate the corrupt relationship. Parties can test each other without becoming too obvious. They are impractical, however, if the relationship flourishes over a long period. In such cases, the parties normally turn to currency.

Cash Payments

Cash is the favored method of making corrupt payments. When given in small amounts, cash is difficult to trace directly. The utility of cash payments decreases as the amount increases and larger sums are required. Large amounts of cash are often difficult to generate without drawing attention to the transactions. Large cash transactions are difficult to conceal when deposited with a financial institution or spent on consumer or durable goods. Even the use of currency in major transactions may be incriminating.

Checks and Other Financial Instruments

Because large cash payments are easy to detect and difficult to explain, and for convenience and security, illegal payments are often made via normal business checks, cashiers' checks or wire transfers. Such payments may exist on the books of the payer as a legitimate business expense. Fraudulent promoters may send those payments through a shell business, an intermediary, or through a series of such persons, business entities or accounts.

Hidden Interests

Rather than simply hand over cash or make payments through intermediaries, the payer may suggest that he and the recipient invest the illicit funds into some joint venture. The recipient keeps an undisclosed interest. The recipient's interests may be concealed through a nominee, hidden in a trust or other business entity, or included as an undocumented verbal agreement. These arrangements are difficult to detect. Even when detected, proof of corrupt intent is difficult to show, especially if the recipient can produce some evidence of payment for his interest.

Loans

There are three types of loans, actual or purported, which frequently arise in fraud cases. The first is an outright payment described as a loan. The investigator can easily test such claims by finding whether:

1) the lender documented the loan at the time he made it;
2) the recipient signed a promissory note;
3) a schedule on which to repay the loan exists;
4) the lender charged a normal interest rate;
5) the recipient had a legitimate purpose or need for the loan;
6) the lender filed a mortgage or financing statement in relation to the loan;
7) the parties involved included the loan on their financial statements, and;
8) the lender deducted the loan as a bad debt, if the loan was not repaid.

The second type loan is structured so that the recipient receives a legitimate loan, made by a third party bank or financial institution, with the illicit payer guaranteeing or making the payments.

The third type loan is payable to the recipient under favorable circumstances, such as an interest free loan, or any other circumstance that shows the loan was given and received with corrupt intent.

Transfers at Other than Fair Market Value

The corrupt payer agrees to sell or lease property to the recipient at less than its fair market value, or he agrees to purchase or rent property at an inflated price. A variation of this technique is the phantom sale in which the recipient sells the asset to the payer, but retains use and control of the property.

Promises of Subsequent Employment; Favorable Separation Payments; Employment of Spouse or Relatives

Another subtle method of making corrupt payments is for the payer to promise the intended recipient lucrative employment, or, on the other hand, giving a retiring executive inflated retirement and separation benefits. The payer's company may also employ the spouse or another relative of the recipient at an inflated salary and with little or no job duties.

Floating

Floating is an embezzlement scheme by which the embezzler appropriates a day's receipts, or part of them, and substitutes the following day's receipts, or part of them, to satisfy the accounting. Consequently, deposits of the receipts are a day late. As the scheme develops and grows, the day's deposits are made later and later.

Lapping

Lapping is the substitution of checks for cash received in a business. The business receives cash, and the cashier or clerk records the receipt in the books. The business receives checks, but the cashier or clerk does not record the receipt in the books. When the cashier or clerk makes the deposits for the day's receipts, he substitutes the checks for an equivalent amount of cash. The records of the business will show cash receipts, but limited or no cash deposits.

Cooking

Cooking the books is a reference to altering the journals and ledgers of a business, or in manufacturing a completely fictitious set of books, to disguise embezzlement. Examples include writing off the amount of a theft to advertising expenses, inventory returns, and even such noncash expenses as depreciation.

Concealing Illegal Payments and Transfers

Typically, schemes to conceal embezzlement and fraud fall into two categories: on-book and off-book schemes.

On-Book Schemes

On-book schemes occur only after the receipt of the funds in question. The fraudulent promoter draws illicit funds, in the normal manner, from regular bank accounts and through regular channels, but disguises the withdrawal in the accounting as some legitimate expense. Such illicit payments occur through regular business checks payable to some sham business established by the payee or some intermediary. Occasionally, the payer will cash the check and tender cash to the recipient. Direct withdrawals of significant amounts of cash may be difficult to explain, but the payer can easily charge small amounts to travel or entertainment expenses.

On-book schemes are simple to use, convenient, and offer protection for the payer, especially in those areas where such payments are not normally suspected. When there may be severe tax consequences, or when the only source of funds available to make such payments are the regular receipts of the payer's business, the on-book method of disguising illicit payments is necessary.

There are, of course, many disadvantages to on-book schemes: they create an audit trail and leave evidence within the company's own accounts and records. The parties get careless about covering the transactions, especially when the scheme has succeeded for a time. Backup documentation, such as receipts and invoices, is often incomplete or missing. Often parties fail to coordinate their accounting, the payer showing an expense for advertising, for example, while the recipient shows a receipt for a commission from the sale of real estate.

The payer in an on-book scheme is usually reluctant to make his books and records available to an investigator because he recognizes his vulnerability. The investigator should notice the possible existence of such a scheme when a previously cooperative witness or victim balks at making his records available for inspection.

One common variation of the on-book schemes described above requires the assistance of a third party contractor or supplier. The payer adds the illicit payment to an otherwise legitimate expense and forwards it to the cooperative third party. The third party then forwards the excess payment to the intended recipient or returns it to the payer to distribute.

Such overbilling schemes are more difficult to detect and prove than regular on-book direct pay schemes because the payer's records will reflect only the apparently routine payables and expenses that can be documented. The investigator who uncovers an overbilling scheme must identify not only which of the hundreds of suppliers is providing such cooperation, but must then obtain and examine the books and records of the supplier to find what may be small additions to legitimate charges.

Suspects employing overbilling schemes are generally very confident that the scheme will avoid detection, and they are often willing to make their accounts and books available for inspection. There are drawbacks to this approach, however. Such schemes require the assistance of a third party, who may become another potential witness against the payer and recipient. Additionally, the scheme may be more expensive than a direct pay scheme since the third party may require part of the illicit payment as a fee for his services.

Off-Book Schemes

Off-book schemes are those in which funds for the illicit payments or transfers do not come from regular sources and do not appear on the accounts and records. In small amounts, such payments may come from the payer's pockets, from his personal accounts, or may be borrowed from other ventures. In larger amounts, unrecorded sales generate the funds. Off-book schemes are popular in businesses with large cash sales.

The principal advantage of off-book schemes is secrecy. Even a complete audit of the suspect's accounts and records may reveal nothing abnormal. Consequently, suspects who use off-book schemes will normally be willing, even eager, to open their accounts and records for inspection, fully believing there is nothing for the investigator to find. It is possible to detect such off-book payments, but the method is different from on-book payment schemes.

The major disadvantage of off-book schemes for most businesses is the difficulty in generating large amounts of off-book funds. Larger schemes often require access to offshore or foreign cash sources that most domestic companies lack.

Use of On-Book and Off-Book Schemes

The type of scheme employed, whether on-book or off-book, depends primarily on the source and type of funds available to the payer. When funds are limited to normal business receipts that, as a rule, are deposited into regular accounts used to pay normal business expenses, the illicit payments most likely will come from those same accounts. A payer who has the potential to generate cash or other unrecorded income will usually opt for an off-book scheme, especially if he is making extremely sensitive payments, is operating in a heavily regulated industry, or is otherwise concerned about intense audits.

Methods of Proving Illicit Transfers

"There are but two ways to identify and trace illicit funds: from the point of payment, or from the point of receipt."[1] The choice of which method to use depends on the circumstances, such as whether records are available, whether one person is taking payments from many sources, whether several people are receiving payments from one source, and the size or complexity of the organization involved. Generally, on-book schemes are easier to investigate and prove from the point of payment, while off-book schemes are easier to investigate and prove from the point of receipt.

Normally, there is some sort of business organization involved in originating on-book illicit payments. Depending on the size and complexity of the organization, the search for witnesses, documents and records may become complex. Many financial investigators are unsure how to proceed, what to ask of whom, what documents and records to find, and what to do with them once found.

The Business Profile

The investigator, normally pressed for time because of the number of cases assigned to him, must learn to make the most efficient use of his time and resources. A Business Profile has been developed to help the investigator to overcome these difficulties when beginning an investigation.[2] The Business Profile helps the investigator identify prospective witnesses and suspects, and locate relevant documents and transactions. It also helps the investigator decide whether to look for an on-book or off-book scheme.

Using the Business Profile, the investigator will:

1) determine how the business is organized, legally and structurally,
2) identify key personnel associated with the enterprise,
3) identify the money flow pattern involved in the suspected transactions,
4) determine the location of the suspect's bank accounts,
5) determine the financial condition of the suspect, and
6) determine the suspect's record keeping system.

Determine How the Business is Organized, Legally and Structurally

This information helps to determine what records are available and what steps are necessary to obtain them. The records of sole proprietorships may be available only through a search warrant as such records will be protected from the subpoena process through the Fifth Amendment. The records of partnerships, corporations, and mutual companies are normally obtainable through the subpoena process.

Identify Key Personnel Associated with the Enterprise

This information helps locate potential witnesses, informants and suspects. Key positions include:

1) the owner or owners of the business,
2) the person or persons directly involved in the suspect transactions, including the secretarial and clerical staff, present and former,
3) the bookkeeper, outside accountants, and tax preparers,
4) outside consultants, sales representatives, and independent contractors, and
5) competitors.

Identify the Money Flow Pattern Involved in the Suspected Transactions

It is very important to identify the source of the enterprise's funds and expenditures, especially those related to the suspect transactions. Information regarding the source of funds should provide leads about whether a suspect is using an on-book or off-book scheme, and the location of off-book accounts.

To determine the sources of funds find:

1) what goods or services the business provides,
2) who the customers or clients are,
3) how the business receives payment, and
4) what other sources of funds are available to the business, such as rebates from suppliers, insurance claims, sales of assets, loans, etc.

To determine the expenditures associated with the suspected transactions find:

1) what disbursements are made to third parties, such as sales commissions, consultant expenses, shipping, contractors, etc.,
2) any extraordinary expenses incurred by the business, such as extra commissions, inventory losses, etc.,
3) how the expenses and disbursements are paid,
4) whether the business maintains an account or fund to pay miscellaneous expenses, where such accounts are located, and who maintains those records,
5) how travel and entertainment expenses are reimbursed and from what account, and
6) the business's policy and practice with respect to business gifts.

Determine the Location of the Suspect's Bank Accounts

Find out where the suspect deposits his receipts. This information is available from the bank stamp on deposited checks. Each bank has a unique identifier that they stamp on every check. The number identifies the Federal Reserve District, state and city of each bank. Bank records may contain a wealth of information about the suspect, including how he spent the illicit funds (see Appendix A—The Numerical System of the American Bankers Association).

Determine the Financial Condition of the Suspect

Knowing the suspect's financial condition may provide evidence of a motive for the crime. It may also help the investigator locate fruits of the crime. If a suspect is behind on payments to a creditor, the investigator knows where to look first for the stolen funds (see Appendix B—Affidavit of Financial Information).

Determine the Suspect's Record Keeping System

The investigator should find how the suspect documents receipts, expenses, and disbursements. He should also find out who keeps the suspect's records, and where the documents are kept. This information allows the investigator to prepare the proper subpoena requests and search warrant affidavits.

Examination from the Point of Payment

Proving On-Book Payments

There are three categories of on-book payment schemes: fictitious payables, payments to ghost employees, and overbilling schemes.[3] Following are outlines of steps to identify and trace illicit payments involved in such on-book schemes.

Fictitious Payable Schemes. Whenever possible, the investigator should obtain the following records from the business or organization suspected of making illicit payments.

1) Bank Account Information
   a) All records of payments, canceled checks, wire transfer receipts, receipts for the purchase of cashiers' checks and money orders, and cash withdrawal slips
   b) Check registers

c) Account statements
2) Sales Backup Documentation
   a) Purchase orders
   b) Invoices
   c) Documents showing receipt of goods or services
3) Accounting Books and Records
   a) Cash disbursement journals
   b) Cash receipts journals
   c) Ledgers

Most important is the bank account information. The investigation should begin by examining the checks, check registers, and cash disbursement journal for payments that fall into the following categories:

1) Payables and expenses charged to the account on which the illicit payments are suspected. If it is suspected that kickbacks were paid to XYZ Corporation, the investigator should examine the payables and expenses charged to the XYZ accounts.

2) Payments for services. The investigator should carefully examine such accounts as sales commissions or consulting fees that require relatively little documentation to obtain payment, and that do not require the actual delivery of goods.

3) Anomalous charges for the business. The investigator should question payments for expenses a business would not normally incur. After the preliminary investigation, the investigator should focus on the suspect payments, noting:

   a) The endorsement on the check. The endorsement on the check may be a signature, but more commonly, is a stamp in the name of the payee. The investigator should note the identity of the endorser. Frequently, the corrupt recipient has endorsed the check in his own name.

   b) The location where the check was negotiated. If it is not obvious from the endorsement, the investigator needs to identify the bank at which the suspect negotiated the check. The bank's stamp will appear on the back of the check. The location of the bank may be a vital lead to uncovering the suspect's identity and additional financial information about the suspect.

   c) Checks with a second endorsement. Checks payable to a business that are endorsed by that business and then endorsed personally, thereby permitting an individual to cash them or deposit them into a personal account, are typical of a fictitious payable scheme. Also typical is a check payable to a third party that was then endorsed back to the issuer of the check.

d) Checks payable to a business cashed and not deposited. In most business situations a "For Deposit Only" stamp appears on the back of a negotiated check. It is common for businesses to deposit checks into a bank account instead of cashing them. Converting checks to cash, so the cash can be given to corrupt recipients, is typical of businesses engaged in illicit payments. Most banks have a coded stamp that indicates whether a check was cashed or deposited. Additionally, banks stamp most cashed checks on the face and deposited checks on the back.

e) Checks that fall into an unexplained pattern. Checks drawn on a regular schedule, equal to a percentage of sales or for a flat fee, and which are not otherwise explained, may suggest a kickback or other illicit payment.

If the examination of the checks does not yield clear and obvious results, the investigator should compare the various records of payment with the backup documentation. The investigator should be particularly aware of the following situations:

1) The absence of documentation to support a particular payment. The investigator should question transactions when no invoice appears in the files for a payment to a supplier or contractor, when there is no receipt to indicate that materials paid for were delivered, or no consultant's report exists to substantiate consulting fees paid.

2) Discrepancies between the payment information and the backup documentation. The investigator should question checks payable to suppliers in amounts different than the supplier's invoice, or checks payable to a person or entity different from that identified on the invoice.

3) Anomalies in the backup documentation. The investigator should be alert to invoices from several suppliers in different names that have the same address or post office box number, or that are signed by the same person.

4) Unnumbered or sequentially numbered invoices. Investigators should question sequentially numbered invoices that are dated several days apart. It is unreasonable to believe that a legitimate

business is not generating invoices to other concerns during the same period.

5) Alterations on or photocopies of the backup documents. Alterations on documents are obvious clues to potential fraudulent transactions. Photocopies are often made to conceal alterations to the originals.

6) Location and other information on the invoices which may tie it to the suspected recipient.

When the above steps do not yield suspect payments, the investigator should return to the check registers and cash disbursement journals to find any discrepancies between those entries and the checks or backup documents.

Once he has isolated the suspect, the investigator begins the tracing process. Remember that illicit payments may go directly to the recipient or through an intermediary account, person or entity. The payer may convert the check to cash, himself, and pay the recipient in cash. In instances where the individual recipient is not apparent from the face of the check, as in checks payable to a business entity, the investigator should:

1) Examine the check to see where the check was deposited. If the account number is not noted on the endorsement, the bank can determine the account from its internal documents.

2) Obtain the bank's records of the account where the check was deposited. The signature card will show the nominal account holder and any other persons authorized to sign on the account. For business accounts, the bank should also have a copy of the corporate resolution or partnership agreement authorizing the account.

3) If the identity of the individual recipient is still not apparent, check public filings required of business entities to determine ownership. Corporate documents and limited partnership agreements are usually filed with the Secretary of State. The fictitious name index, business license files, and public utility records can also show the identity of the principals.

4) If the original check is missing or has been destroyed, obtain a microfilm copy of the check from the bank upon which it was drawn.

5) Look for payments by wire transfer or cashier's check that may

also be traceable to the recipient. Records of a wire transfer are traceable to the sender and recipient, provided that the origin or destination of the wire is first identified. Cashier's checks are endorsed and stamped in the same manner as any regular check. It is important to remember, however, that such instruments are available from any bank, not only the one where the payer's account is located.

6) If the trail described above leads to an intermediary, repeat the entire process. The investigator must attempt to obtain the intermediary's bank records, particularly his checks and other disbursements.

Ghost Employee Schemes. Illicit funds may be generated or funneled through fictitious salary payments to nonexistent or former employees, or by making extra payments to current employees. These payments are then returned to the payer or passed on to the corrupt recipient. In such instances the investigator must obtain the following records from the suspect company:

1) payroll and employee lists,
2) personnel files, employment records, tax withholding forms, and
3) payroll checks.

The investigator can attempt to identify the ghosts through the following procedure:

1) Compare a list of all current and former employees from the personnel office to the payroll list, noting any discrepancies. Determine whether any employees have failed to execute tax withholding forms, or have not elected any health benefits or other elective withdrawals. The absence of such elections is often an indicator that the employee does not exist.
2) Verify the employee's social security administration numbers. A fictitious employee may have a number that does not exist.
3) A regular employee's normal salary may also be inflated. Commonly, travel and expense reimbursements may be padded, to generate illicit funds. The investigator should look for unusual disbursements from the accounts where such checks are deposited.

Once the investigator identifies a ghost employee's paychecks, the process of tracing the funds to their final destination is the same as any other fictitious payable. The investigator should determine whether the check was cashed or deposited, noting the endorsements, the banks and accounts affected, and whether there are any secondary endorsements. Cashed checks usually contain identification information under the endorsement, such as a driver's license number, that may aid in identifying the recipient.

If the ultimate recipient is not apparent from the above analysis, and ghost employee checks were deposited, the investigator can obtain the account signature cards and monthly account statements from the depository bank, and any other documents concerning the account holder.

Overbilling Schemes. A corrupt payer may add illicit funds to legitimate payments for the delivery of goods and services with the supplier distributing the additional amounts or returning them to the corrupt payer for distribution. These schemes differ from legitimate rebate programs because of the secrecy involved.

The same kinds of records and documents required to trace fictitious payables are necessary to trace overbilling schemes; bank account information, backup documentation, and the accounting records. It is necessary for the investigator to obtain these records from the original payer, the intermediary and the recipient. The investigator should be observant for indicators of suspect payments to intermediaries, such as:

1) Notations on invoices or other billing instruments showing extra or special charges, particularly those that require no delivery of goods for payment;
2) Discrepancies between the purchase order or invoice amounts and the amount of payment, noting especially those invoices that have been altered or copied;
3) Unusually large amounts appearing on particular bills, or bills that break a consistent pattern of amounts, schedule or purpose.

Disbursements from an intermediary are investigated in the same way as any other on-book scheme, and the tracing process remains the same. The investigator should remember, however, that the overbilling entity or individual will usually add a fee of its own to compensate for its involvement in the scheme. The amounts of the overpayments, therefore, may not equal the amounts of the payments made to the ultimate recipient.

Proving Off-Book Payments

Identifying and tracing off-book payments is usually much more difficult than on-book schemes. Investigative success depends on identifying the source of the funds or accounts from which funds can be traced. Such success usually requires cooperation from an inside witness or an examination based on the point of receipt of the funds.

The source of off-book schemes may be located through:

1) Indirect evidence of unrecorded sales on the suspect company's books and records. A suspect company's books and records may reflect unusual costs and expenses that are not associated with the enterprise's known sales or business, such as rental payments for an undisclosed warehouse or a warehouse that shows to contain no inventory, shipping documents showing delivery of goods to a customer not listed in the journals, or commissions paid to a sales agent in a region where no sales are reported. This principle applies to service companies as well.

2) Unbalanced ratios of costs of sales. The costs of producing and selling particular items usually bear some fixed relationship to the revenue the items generate. The amounts of raw material, labor, and administrative costs required to produce an item are usually fairly constant. Any sudden, significant and unexplained imbalance in such ratios may suggest unrecorded transactions. This technique is frequently used to gather circumstantial evidence of off-book funds in cash related businesses.

3) Investigation in the marketplace. Customers of a suspect business, whose payments may have been diverted to off-book accounts, may possess records or documents, including canceled checks, which would reflect such sales and identify the bank and account to which the funds were deposited. Additionally, competitors may identify previously undisclosed customers.

Proving Payments in Cash

Proving payments in cash is very difficult. Even eyewitness testimony can be suspect. There are, however, techniques to prove cash payments circumstantially, and to corroborate testimony from witnesses.

The investigator should look for evidence of cash withdrawals or disbursements by the payer, matching the dates and amounts of those withdrawals or disbursements with corresponding cash deposits and expenditures by the recipient. Additionally, the investigator should note whether the recipient made trips to a safe deposit box that correspond with cash withdrawals by the payer.

The investigator should look for evidence of the purchase of cashiers' checks, travelers' checks or wire transfers payable to the recipient at or shortly after cash withdrawals or disbursements by the payer. There may also be a direct correlation between cash withdrawals and packages sent by Express Mail or private mail delivery services such as Federal Express or United Parcel Service.

If the scheme is ongoing, and payments are made hand-to-hand, visual or electronic surveillance may be in order. Such techniques require extraordinary intelligence as to the time and location of the exchange, however, and considerable advance planning is necessary to make such surveillances effective.

The investigator should be aware, also, of unexplained or unusual cash disbursements from a business that does not ordinarily conduct cash transactions. Such transactions in and of themselves may suggest illicit transactions. The investigator must be mindful, however, that he will be required to identify and rebut any legitimate explanations for the cash payments.

Examination from the Point of Receipt

It is often the case when investigating embezzlements and frauds that the only reasonable approach to identifying and tracing illicit funds is to focus the investigation on the recipient of the funds. This is especially true when the person making the payments is unknown, the payments are in cash and from off-book sources, or one person is suspected of taking cash from many sources.

An investigator may establish proof of illicit income by direct or indirect methods. The direct approach relies on specific transactions, such as sales receipts and expense records, to establish income. The indirect method relies on circumstantial proof of income by using such methods as net worth analysis.

Almost all individuals and business entities engaged in legitimate pursuits maintain books and records in which they record various transactions. In financial investigations, the investigator can usually establish income with less difficulty and with greater certainty by the direct method. Therefore, the investigator should use the direct method whenever possible.

In many investigations of financial crimes, however, the suspect's books and records are not available to the investigator, or they may be nonexistent. Therefore, it is necessary for the investigator to take an indirect approach to prove illicit or unreported income. The courts have approved the use of indirect methods in determining income for both civil and criminal cases on the theory that proof of unexplained funds or property in the hands of a suspect may establish a prima facie understatement of income.[4]

The primary indirect methods of proving income are:

1) net worth analysis,
2) source and application of funds analysis,
3) bank deposit analysis,
4) disbursement analysis,
5) percentage analysis, and
6) unit and volume analysis

Net Worth Analysis

The net worth analysis is a frequently used indirect method of proving income from an unknown or illegal source. The analysis is presented in the familiar balance sheet format which is readily recognizable in the business world and which presents a complete financial picture of the suspect. It is based on the theory that increases or decreases in a person's net worth during a period, adjusted for living expenses, result in a determination of income.

By comparing the suspect's net worth at the beginning and end of a specific period, usually a calendar year, the investigator can determine the suspect's increase or decrease in net worth during the period. The investigator can make adjustments for living expenses to arrive at income. Income determined by this method includes receipts derived from all sources. Thus, by subtracting funds from known legitimate sources, such as salaries, wages, interest and dividends, the investigator will determine the funds derived from unknown or illicit sources.

The courts have approved the use of the net worth method in numerous cases.[5] These cases outlined the broad principles governing the trial and review of cases based upon the net worth method of proving income.

The formula for computing funds from unknown or illicit sources using the net worth method is:

	Assets
Less:	*Liabilities*
Equals:	Net Worth
Less:	*Prior Year's Net Worth*

Equals:	Net Worth Increase (Decrease)
Plus:	*Living Expenses*
Equals:	Income
Less:	*Funds from Known or Legitimate Sources*
Equals:	Funds from Unknown or Illicit Sources

Table 26 contains a sample of a simplified net worth computation.

Table 26. Net Worth Analysis.

Assets	12/31/x1	12/31/x2	12/31/x3
Cash on hand	$ 1,000	$ 0	$ 0
Checking account	4,000	9,000	2,000
Jewelry	0	25,100	25,100
Mink coat	0	0	15,900
Car	25,000	25,000	25,000
Boat	0	0	24,000
Residence	130,000	130,000	130,000
Pool	0	20,000	20,000
Total assets	$160,000	$209,100	$242,000
Liabilities			
Loan—pool	$ 0	$ 7,000	$ 1,000
Mortgage—residence	98,000	96,500	94,500
Loan—finance company	5,000	5,000	5,000
Total liabilities	$103,000	$108,500	$100,500
Net worth	$ 57,000	$100,600	$141,500
Less: prior year's net worth		57,000	100,600
Change in net worth		$ 43,600	$ 40,900
Plus: personal living expenses:			
Mortgage interest		10,500	10,000
Real estate taxes		1,500	1,500
Apartment rental		18,000	18,000
Lease payments—auto		3,600	3,600
Vacation		0	12,000
Total income		$ 77,200	$ 86,000
Less: funds from known sources		40,000	45,000
Funds from unreported or illicit sources		$ 37,200	$ 41,000

The net worth method is most useful when several of the suspect's assets and/or liabilities have changed during the period under investigation, and one of the following conditions exist:

1) the suspect maintains no books or records,
2) the suspect's books and records are not available,
3) the suspect's books and records are inadequate, or
4) the suspect withholds his books and records from the investigator.

Besides being used as a primary method of proving income in civil and criminal financial cases, the net worth can also be used:

1) to corroborate other methods of proving income, and
2) to test-check the accuracy of known or reported income.

The investigator can figure an individual's assets, liabilities, and living expenses from a variety of sources such as:

1) the subject of the investigation (see Chapter 6—Financial Interviewing and Interrogation and Appendix B—Affidavit of Financial Information); or
2) public and business records (see Chapter 7—Public Information, Subpoenas, and Search Warrants).

In using the net worth analysis, the investigator should use the same accounting method, cash or accrual, that the suspect uses. Accordingly, if the suspect is on the accrual basis, trade accounts receivable and payable will be shown.

Assets must be valued at cost. The use of fair market value will cause distortions of income if appreciation or depreciation occurs between periods. However, if the suspect values inventories with another method (lower of cost or market, LIFO, FIFO, etc.) and he consistently applies the method according to standard accounting procedures, the investigator should use the same valuation technique in the net worth computation.

In preparing the net worth statement, the question arises why the investigator should include items that do not change in the net worth statement, especially since these items have no bearing on the result. It is important to remember that a net worth statement gives a complete financial picture of the suspect. The statement should, therefore, be as complete as possible so that the subject will not have grounds to contest the credibility of the statement because items are omitted. Additionally, the correct net worth statement may be the foundation for a future investigation of the suspect, and a complete statement may prove extremely valuable to the investigator then.

Cash on Hand. Cash on hand is coin and currency in the suspect's actual possession, be it in his pocket, under his mattress, or in a safe deposit box. It does not include any money the suspect has on deposit in any account with any type of financial institution.

When using the net worth analysis, the item most difficult to prove is cash on hand. A defendant may claim a sufficient amount of cash on hand to account for all or part of the unknown sources of income. To establish a firm starting net worth, it is necessary to show that the suspect had no large sum of cash for which he was not given credit. The investigator can accomplish this by offering evidence that negates the existence of a cash hoard, such as:

1) written or oral admissions of the subject to the investigator concerning net worth, including affidavits of financial information or oral admissions,
2) low earnings in preprosecution years as shown by records of former employers and/or tax returns filed by a suspect,
3) net worth as established by books and records of the suspect,
4) financial statements presented for credit or other purposes at a time before or during the period under investigation,
5) bankruptcy before prosecution periods,
6) prior indebtedness, compromise of overdue debts, and avoidance of bankruptcy,
7) installment buying;
8) history of low earnings and expenditures, and checks returned for insufficient funds, and
9) receipt of public assistance.

Proof of Continued Ownership of Assets. In using the net worth analysis, it is not only necessary to prove that a suspect acquired an asset, but that he either disposed of it during the years involved in the computation, or retained it throughout the years in question. If a suspect sold an asset during any of the years included in the net worth computation, he would have funds available to make other expenditures. If the investigator finds evidence of the other expenditures and adds them to the expenditures previously determined, the result would incorrectly show that the suspect spent the same funds twice. The need to determine whether a suspect maintained or sold an asset is obvious.

Proof of continued ownership of assets is not difficult to obtain. Inquiries through corporation stock transfer agents can confirm continued ownership of stocks. Proof of continued ownership of real property can be determined through county records. Automobile registration records or evidence of retention of insurance coverage can establish the continued ownership of an automobile. An insurance rider can be an excellent means of determining whether the suspect has retained possession of valuable jewelry or furs.

Living Expenses. Living expenses are expenditures made by a subject that are neither assets nor liabilities. Living expenses include, but are not limited to, household expenses, food, auto repairs, insurance premiums, medical expenses, personal taxes, entertainment expenses, and gifts. Losses on the sale of personal assets are also included in living expenses to prevent distortion of income.

Personal living expenses can be a critical factor in the net worth computation if the total expenditures above known sources of income are nominal. If, on the other hand, the excess of expenditures is clearly well beyond the suspect's legitimate income, there is little need to expend investigative time and energy to prove personal living expenses.

Even if personal living expenses are not available, the investigator should still include the line in the net worth schedule and show the amount as zero. The argument then follows that even if the suspect incurred no living expenses throughout the period under investigation, he still spent more money than he legitimately made. The suspect is precluded from arguing that the computation is inaccurate or incomplete because of the lack of personal living expenses, since every dollar he then claims to have spent on living expenses is an additional dollar he must have received from illegal or illicit sources.

Funds from Known Sources. Funds from known sources include, but are not limited to, salaries, wages, business profits, insurance proceeds, interest, dividends, inheritances, public assistance payments, tax refunds, and gifts. Do not include loans received in this section if the loan was included in the liabilities section of the net worth computation; otherwise, the amount would be included twice.

The known sources of funds are subtracted from the income determined to arrive at funds from unknown or illicit sources.

Defenses. It is the investigator's duty to anticipate the defenses a suspect may raise to a net worth analysis and to prepare for those defenses during the investigation. The investigator must check all reasonable leads to ensure that he has not understated the opening net worth, that he has accounted for all legitimate sources of income, and that the net worth statement is as complete and accurate as possible.

The defenses a suspect may raise to a net worth analysis are innumerable, but some common defenses include:

1) ***Cash on hand*** —Commonly the suspect alleges that he had a large amount of cash on hand that the investigator had not considered in the initial net worth computation. The suspect may also allege that the cash balances for years following the base years are incorrect. In cases where the net worth is the primary method of proving illegal or illicit income, the investigator must anticipate this defense and attempt to obtain evidence to negate it during the investigation. Establishing and documenting a firm cash on hand starting point is perhaps the most important and most difficult phase of a net worth investigation. Admissions of the subject are very effective in pinning down the amount of cash on hand and should be obtained at the initial interview or early in the investigation. The line of questioning should be directed toward developing:

a) the source and amount of cash on hand at the starting point and at the end of each year under investigation,

b) the source and amount of cash on hand at the date of the interview;

c) where the cash was kept,

d) why the cash was not kept in a financial institution or invested,

e) who knew about the cash,

f) whether anyone other than the suspect counted the cash,

g) whether any record of the alleged cash on hand was made,

h) the denominations of the cash on hand,

i) when and for what the cash was spent, and

j) whether the suspect would consent to an inventory of the cash during the interview. The investigator should conduct the inventory in the presence of another investigator for witness purposes, and the amount should be recorded in a memorandum of interview.

In most cases, an attempt should be made to question the spouse about cash on hand, and any other important financial matter. The suspect and spouse also should be questioned regarding their financial history from the time they were first gainfully employed concerning employers, positions, and salary. Besides admissions, evidence used to establish the starting point, such as a financial statement submitted to a lending institution, usually will be sufficient to refute the defense of cash on hand.

2) *False loans, gifts, and inheritances* — The objective of this defense is to suggest a legitimate source of funds by claiming nonexistent loans, gifts, and inheritances, usually from the subject's relatives, friends or other decedents. Often the investigator can overcome this defense by showing that the alleged lender or decedent was financially unable to lend or make gifts of the amounts claimed.

3) *Holding funds or other assets as a nominee* — In a few cases, the suspect will falsely claim that he was holding funds or assets as nominee for someone else. Such defenses can be overcome by interviewing all parties to the transaction transferring the asset. Additionally, the suspect may be unable or unwilling to name the allegedly true owner of the asset for fear of subjecting a confederate to investigation.

4) *Jointly held assets of the suspect and a spouse* — Sometimes the suspect and spouse may have separate sources of income or funds, but the assets they acquire are held in joint title. If the jointly held assets are included in the net worth computation, the suspect could claim that they were acquired with the funds of the spouse. Normally, the investigator can overcome this defense by tracing the invested funds to the suspect and by showing the disposition of the spouse's funds. In other cases, the suspect and spouse may have intermingled their funds so that it is not possible to trace the invested or applied funds to either party. In such cases, the net worth analysis must include the assets, liabilities and income of both subjects.

5) *Overstated inventories* — Occasionally the investigator must rely upon inventory figures provided by the suspect as prima facie evidence to establish the values of this asset in the net worth computation. In a few cases, the suspect will argue that, because of ignorance or other reasons, he reported inventory at retail value instead of at cost. This would cause distortions of income in the net worth statement. The investigator can resolve these issues by corroborating inventory figures by admission of the suspect, by obtaining statements of employees who took the inventory, and by reviewing copies of inventory records.

6) *Failure to account for other sources of funds* — The investigator has the responsibility to investigate all leads furnished by the suspect or generated by the investigation which are reasonably susceptible to being checked.[6] Besides loans, gifts, and inheritances, the inves-

tigator must watch for funds that the suspect may have received from pensions and annuities, accident settlements, insurance policies, public assistance, the Veteran's Administration, worker's compensation, or any other legitimate source of funds.

Source and Application of Funds Analysis

Investigators often use source and application of funds analysis because it is an easy method to understand and use. The method is based on the theory that if expenditures for a given period exceed the subject's known sources of funds for that same period, it may be inferred that the excess expenditures represent unknown or illegal income.

The source and application of funds method is simply a comparison of all known expenditures with all known receipts during a particular period, usually a calendar year. When using this method, the investigator determines from where the suspect's funds came and how the suspect spent, invested, or applied the money. This method has been known by various names; the expenditures method, flow of funds method, and the statement of application of funds. Whatever the name applied to the method, the courts have accepted the use of source and application of funds analysis.[7]

In theory, this method is closely related to, if not identical with, the net worth analysis. The two computations are merely accounting variations of the same basic method, the source and applications of funds method being an outgrowth of the net worth method.[8] The similarity is further indicated by the fact that the same items of accounts employed in the net worth analysis are considered in the source and application of funds analysis. In source and application of funds analysis, however, only the increases and decreases in assets are considered along with living expenses. When a suspect has assets and liabilities that remain unchanged during the period, those assets and liabilities are not listed on the source and application of funds statement.

The formula for computing funds from illegal or illicit sources using the source and application of funds methods is quite simple:

> Application of funds (expenditures)
> Less: *Known sources of funds*
> Equals: Funds from unknown or illicit sources

Just as in the net worth analysis, the source and application of funds analysis is useful when one of the following conditions exist:

1) the suspect maintains no books or records,
2) the suspect's books and records are not available,
3) the suspect's books and records are inadequate, or
4) the suspect withholds his books and records from the investigator.

In cases where the suspect has several assets and liabilities whose cost basis remains the same throughout the period under investigation, the source and application of funds method may be preferable to the net worth method since a simpler and more brief presentation can be made in the computation. The source and application of funds method is preferable to the net worth method in those cases where the suspect spends his income on a lavish life style, and there is no appreciable increase in his net worth. The investigator can also use this method to compute cash on hand for the base year when a cash on hand starting point is found in a prior year.

For the source and application of funds analysis, the investigator should consider these items in the computation:

1) Application (expenditures)
   a) Increases in cash on hand or in accounts at financial institutions,
   b) Increases in other assets (both personal and business),
   c) Decrease in liability balances, and
   d) Personal living expenses.
2) Known sources
   a) Decrease of cash on hand or in accounts at financial institutions,
   b) Sale or exchange of assets,
   c) Salaries or business profits,
   d) Tax refunds, interest, dividends, or insurance proceeds,
   e) Loans, gifts, or inheritances received, and
   f) Unemployment or public assistance receipts.

Any excess of the application of funds over known sources of funds is a result of funds from unknown or illicit sources. The format of the source and applications of funds statement is found in Table 27.

Cash on Hand. It is imperative for the investigator to be able to prove the suspect's cash on hand available at the beginning of the period under investigation. Otherwise, the suspect can contend that an accumulation of cash from previous periods was the source of the funds expended during the periods under investigation.

In many instances, the cash on hand figure will be most difficult to determine. The investigator may have to calculate that information from financial information for previous years. If the investigator has informa-

Table 27. Source and Application of Funds Analysis.

Application of Funds	19x2	19x3
Increase of bank account	$ 5,000	$ 0
Purchase of jewelry	25,100	0
Purchase of mink coat	0	15,900
Purchase of boat	0	24,000
Down payment—pool	10,000	0
Pool loan repayments	3,000	6,000
Mortgage repayments	12,000	12,000
Real estate taxes	1,500	1,500
Apartment rental payments	18,000	18,000
Lease payments—auto	3,600	3,600
Vacation	0	12,000
Total application of funds	$78,200	$93,000
Less: known sources of funds		
Cash on hand	1,000	0
Bank account decrease	0	7,000
Reported income	40,000	45,000
Total known sources of funds	$41,000	$52,000
Funds from unknown or illicit sources	$37,200	$41,000

tion which documents the suspect's cash on hand on a previous date, he may be able to compute the suspect's cash on hand for the beginning of the period under investigation by showing all sources of funds and their applications during the interim. Such analysis would yield the maximum amount of cash on hand that the subject could claim as a defense to either a net worth analysis or a source and applications of funds computation.

Accrual Method. By including the increase or decrease of the accounts receivable and accounts payable in the source and application of funds computation, no separate adjustments are necessary when the subject uses the accrual method of accounting.

Defenses. The defenses regarding the net worth method of determining income are equally applicable to the source and application of funds method. Frequently, it may be desirable to prepare a net worth statement to rebut a defense that the funds used for the expenditures were derived from the conversion of some asset that was not considered in the expenditures computations.

Bank Deposits Analysis

Bank deposit analysis is another means of proving unknown sources of funds by indirect or circumstantial evidence. Similar to other indirect methods of proof, the bank deposit method allows the investigator to compute the suspect's income by showing what happened to the funds. This method is based on the theory that when a suspect receives a payment as, he must spend it as cash or deposit it into a financial institution.

By the bank deposit method, the investigator proves the suspect's income through analysis of bank deposits, canceled checks, and currency transactions of the suspect. Adjustments for nonincome items are made to arrive at income. The courts have allowed bank deposit analysis as a means to determine income in numerous cases.[9]

The basic formula for bank deposit analysis is:

	Total deposits to all accounts
Less:	*Transfers and redeposits*
Equals:	Net deposits to all accounts
Plus:	*Cash expenditures*
Equals:	Total receipts from all sources
Less:	*Receipts from known sources*
Equals:	Finds from unknown or illicit sources

The bank deposit method is the primary method of proof when the suspect deposits most of his income and his books and records are unavailable, withheld from the investigator, or incomplete. Even when the suspect's books and records are available and appear to be accurate, the method is still useful. There is no requirement for the investigator to disprove the accuracy of the books and records for the bank deposit analysis to apply.

An example of a simplified bank deposits analysis is shown in Table 28.

Total Deposits. Total deposits consist not only of amounts the suspect deposited to all bank accounts he maintained or controlled, but also of deposits made to accounts in savings and loan companies, investment trusts, brokerage houses, and credit unions. It also includes an accumulation of cash on hand. Since some suspects have bank accounts in fictitious names or under special titles, such as "Special Services Account," "Trustee Account," or "Trading Account," the investigator should inquire about these types of accounts during the investigation.

If a suspect lists checks on a deposit ticket and deducts an amount paid

Table 28. Bank Deposits Analysis.

	12/31/x4	12/31/x5
Total deposits	$22,160	$19,585
Less: redeposits	660	100
Net deposits	$21,500	$19,485
Outlays:		
Purchase of jewelry	$ 5,000	$ 6,000
Down payment on residence	50,000	0
Purchase of automobile	0	18,250
Monthly mortgage payments	6,000	6,000
Credit card payments	1,460	3,000
Loan repayments	600	1,200
Other personal living expenses	11,000	10,000
Total outlays	$74,060	$44,450
Less: net bank disbursements	$18,250	$19,010
Cash expenditures	55,810	25,440
Total receipts	$77,310	$44,925
Less: funds from known sources		
Cash on hand	$ 1,000	$ 0
Interest on bank accounts	250	475
Loans	3,000	0
Wages	25,200	22,200
Total	$29,450	$22,675
Funds from unknown or illicit sources	$47,860	$22,250

to him in cash, the investigator should use only the net amount of the deposit in computing total deposits.

Additional items the investigator must include in a deposit analysis are property and notes that the suspect received in payment for services rendered, inasmuch as property and notes received in payment are income and must be accounted for in some manner. The accepted accounting practice is to consider these items as forms of depositories into which funds have been placed for future use.

Net Deposits. All transfers or exchanges between bank accounts and funds that are redeposited are nonincome items, and the investigator must subtract them from total deposits to arrive at net deposits. Failure to eliminate these items would result in an overstatement of income.

Cash Expenditures. Cash expenditures consist of the total outlay of funds less net bank disbursements and is expressed as follows:

	Total outlay of funds
Less:	*Net bank disbursements*
Equals:	Cash disbursements

The total outlay of funds include all payments made by cash or check. There is no need for the investigator to determine which part was paid by cash and which part was paid by check. Total outlays include:

1) purchase of capital assets or investment,
2) loan repayments,
3) living expenses,
4) purchases, and
5) business expenses, rental expenses, etc.

The investigator can determine the net bank disbursements by using the following formula:

	Net deposits to all accounts
Plus:	*Beginning balances*
Equals:	Net bank funds available
Less:	*Ending balances*
Equals:	Net bank disbursements

Funds from Known Sources. Funds from known sources include salaries, business profits, insurance proceeds, gifts received, and inheritances. To arrive at funds from unknown or illicit sources, subtract funds from known sources from total receipts.

Requirements of Proof. The evidentiary facts an investigator can use to establish a prima facie bank deposits case are:

1) the suspect had a probable source of income, such as a business, profession, or other income producing activity,
2) the suspect made periodic deposits indicating a pattern of receipts from an ongoing income producing activity (occasional or irregular deposits are not necessarily ruled out and may, if properly analyzed, be considered income), and
3) the deposits reflect current income.

Defenses. The common defenses in a bank deposit case include:

1) the deposits are nonincome items, such as loans, inheritances, or insurance proceeds,
2) the deposits are not current income,
3) the deposits are a duplication of current income, or
4) the deposits belong to a person or entity other than the suspect.

Deposit Analysis. A deposit analysis is exactly what the name implies—an analysis of all deposits into an account at a financial institution. The purpose of the deposit analysis is to identify deposits as income or nonincome and to develop leads for third-party contacts. Source items for the deposit analysis include bank statements and deposit slips.

There are two sections to a deposit analysis, the transcription section and the classification section. In the transcription section, the investigator should schedule all the deposits made to an account. He should list the deposits as they appear on the bank statement for easy verification. Worksheet headings should include:

Item	Source
1) Date cleared	Bank statement
2) Amount	Bank statement
3) Deposit date	Deposit slip
4) Coins	Deposit slip
5) Currency	Deposit slip
6) Checks	Deposit slip
7) Cash withheld	Deposit slip
8) Total deposit	Deposit slip

The classification section should have the following categories:

1) business income or total sales,
2) wages and salaries,
3) other income,
4) loans,
5) transfers,
6) redeposits,
7) other non-income,
8) unidentified, and
9) notations.

The investigator may identify individual deposits through the suspect's admissions, the suspect's books and records, deposit slips, bank ledger sheets, transfer letters, and bank microfilm. After preparing the deposit analysis worksheet, the investigator must classify each deposit as income or nonincome items.

Disbursement Analysis. A disbursement analysis, also known as a check spread, is simply a scheduling of all withdrawals from an account. The purpose of a disbursement analysis is:

1) to identify withdrawals for operating expenses, purchases of inventory, etc.,
2) to identify checks written for cash or transfers to other accounts,
3) to identify assets purchased or payments of liabilities, and
4) to develop leads for third party contacts.

Source items for the disbursement analysis include bank statements and canceled checks.

As with the deposit analysis, there are two main sections to a disbursement analysis, the transcription section and the classification section. In the transcription section, the investigator should schedule all the withdrawals from the bank account. For easy verification, he should list the withdrawals as they appear on the bank statement. Work sheet headings should include:

Item	Source
1) Date cleared	Bank statement
2) Amount	Bank statement
3) Check number	Canceled check
4) Date written	Canceled check
5) Payee	Canceled check
6) Notation/Endorsement	Canceled check

The classification section of the disbursement analysis will vary depending upon the nature of the account. A personal account should include classifications such as:

1) personal living expenses,
2) loan repayments,
3) checks to cash
4) transfers to other accounts,
5) other, and
6) unidentified.

A business or corporate account should include classifications such as:

1) operational expenses,
2) purchases of inventory,
3) payments to the suspect,
4) payments on behalf of the suspect,
5) loan repayments,
6) checks to cash,
7) transfers to other accounts,
8) other, and
9) unidentified.

Occasionally, there will be missing checks that the investigator cannot obtain from the suspect or the bank. In such cases, the investigator should classify the check as unidentified. It may be possible to reclassify those checks later through third party contacts.

If the suspect is uncooperative and will not identify or classify the checks, the investigator may not classify the checks himself. The investigator's analysis would constitute hearsay, and, consequently, would not be admissible in court. The investigator must contact the appropriate third party to obtain a classification on each check.

Percentage Analysis

The percentage method of proving unknown or illicit sources of income relies upon a computation of percentages or ratios considered typical of the business under investigation. By referencing similar businesses, percentage computations are secured to determine sales, cost of sales, gross profits, or even net profits. Similarly, by using some known base and typical applicable percentages, the investigator can determine individual items of income.

Such percentages may be available from such sources as trade associations, or government and industrial publications. The investigator may also derive these percentages from the suspect's accounts from other periods or from an examination of the suspect's records, even though only a portion of the records is available.

The investigator can determine gross profit percentages by comparing purchase invoices with sales invoices, price lists, and similar data. Additionally, examination of records pertaining to previous years under investigation may indicate typical percentages applicable to the entire period under investigation.

Percentage analysis is not a primary method of proving illegal or unreported income. However, there have been cases in which the courts have allowed the use of this method for limited purposes. The percentage method is useful for test checking other data.

Following are examples illustrating percentage analysis. The percentages are purely arbitrary, for the sake of illustration only, and are not necessarily applicable to the businesses mentioned.

1) Computation of sales based upon cost of goods sold for a tavern:

Cost of liquor	$20,000
Cost of beer	15,000
Cost of food	5,000
Total cost of goods sold	$40,000

Cost of liquor = 33⅓% of sales
Cost of beer = 66⅔% of sales
Cost of food = 50% of sales

Therefore:

Revenues from liquor	$60,000
Revenues from beer	22,500
Revenues from food	10,000
Total estimated revenues	$92,500

2) Computation of net profit on sales for a service station:

Net sales	$30,000
Net profit percentage	× 8%
Net estimated profit	$ 2,400

Comparison Factors. Although percentage analysis may be useful in determining or verifying income, especially when the books and records are incomplete or inadequate, the investigator must make comparisons with situations similar to those under investigation. The investigator must consider:

1) the type of merchandise involved,
2) size of operations,
3) locality, '
4) time period covered, and
5) general merchandising policy.

Unit and Volume Analysis

Often, the investigator can determine or verify gross receipts by applying price and profit figures to the known or ascertainable quantity of the suspect's business. This method is feasible when the investigator can determine the number of units handled by the suspect, and when the price or profit margin per unit is known. The investigator may determine the number of units sold or quantity of the suspect's business in some instances from the suspect's books, since the records may be adequate regarding the cost of goods sold or expenses, but inadequate regarding sales. Additionally, there may be a regulatory body to which the subject reports units of production or service.

The use of unit and volume analysis lends itself to those businesses in which only a few types of items are handled or there is little variation in the type of service performed.

The following example illustrates the unit and volume method of computing income:

	Number of units manufactured	92
	Average sales price per unit	× 1,000
Equals:	Estimated total sales	$92,000
Less:	Reported sales	80,000
Equals:	Omitted sales	$12,000

Notes

[1] Joseph T. Wells, W. Steve Albrecht, Jack Bologna, Gilbert Geis, and Jack Robertson, *Fraud Examiners Manual* (Austin, TX: National Association of Certified Fraud Examiners, 1989), Section III, p. 34.

[2] Ibid., Section III, p. 35.

[3] Ibid., Section III, p. 38.

[4] ——, *Financial Investigative Techniques* (Washington, D.C.: Internal Revenue Service, Department of the Treasury, 1986), p. 6-1.

[5] See Holland v. U.S., 348 U.S. 121.; Friedberg v. U.S., 348 U.S. 142; Smith v. U.S., 348 U.S. 147; and U.S. v. Calderon, 348 U.S. 160.

[6] Holland v. U.S., 348 U.S. 121.

[7] U.S. v. Johnson, 319 U.S. 503.

[8] McFee v. U.S., 206 F.2d 872.

[9] See Gleckman v. U.S., 80 F.2d 394; Stinnett v. U.S., 173 F.2d 129; Oliver v. U.S., 54 F.2d 48; and Capone v. U.S., 51 F.2d 609.

Chapter 10

INVESTIGATIVE REPORT
AND CASE PREPARATION

Explanation separates us from astonishment which is the only gateway to the incomprehensible.

Eugene Ionesco
Decouvertes

The result of all work an investigator does is expressed in a report. The report suitably presents all the pertinent facts and evidence relating to a matter so that appropriate action can be taken. Supervisors must make recommendations about whether to forward the case to prosecutors or require additional investigation. Prosecutors must conclude what legal action, if any, to take, or if they must return the case for further investigation. Supervisors, prosecutors, judges, and defense attorneys have often voiced the same complaint: that investigators have displayed an inability to write and fully document a report clearly, concisely and lacking personal opinions.

Report writing is a most demanding and important task for the white-collar crime investigators. The report is often the only evidence as to the work the investigator did and to the manner in which he obtained and preserved evidence. Prosecutions may succeed or fail based on the strength of a case report.

A written report is important for several other reasons. When properly done, the report conveys to the prosecutor all the evidence needed to evaluate the legal status of the case. Based on the report, the prosecutor will decide whether the investigator obtained the evidence legally, and whether that evidence is admissible in court. The prosecutor will then decide whether to commence criminal action by presenting the matter to a grand jury, or to refer the matter to civil or administrative proceedings. Financial crime cases are frequently so complex that they are significant drains on the prosecuting attorney's resources. Prosecutors choose carefully which white-collar criminal cases they will try so to ensure that their limited resources are used to maximum benefit. If the

215

report does not convince a prosecutor that a case is clearly worth trying, he will not prosecute it.

The report can add credibility to the investigation and the case. When an investigator writes a professional and intelligent report, his actions become less questionable. A poorly written report invites criticism and questions from the defense. A truthful report, especially one that includes information favorable to the defense, shows that the investigator was only interested in getting to the truth, despite whether he could file a criminal case.

The fact of a written report forces the white-collar crime investigator to consider his actions before and during the investigation. When the investigator knows he must document his actions, and then present that documentation to his superiors and to prosecutors, he will be more careful to conform to the rules of law and procedure.

A complicated investigation will reveal large amounts of information and evidence that will not be relevant to the matter under investigation. A well-written report omits such immaterial information so that the facts of the case can be clearly and completely understood.

Characteristics of Report Writing

The case report ultimately serves as the basis for the preparation and presentation of a case. To have any value, a report must be logically presented. Otherwise, it will lose effectiveness. The investigator must write the report so the reader can comprehend the full significance of its contents, is convinced of its thoroughness, and is willing to take action based on the facts and evidence presented. An investigator builds an effective presentation on the principles of unity, coherence, emphasis, accuracy, clarity, impartiality, and relevance.

Unity

The principle of unity requires adherence to the main, principal or ultimate idea or purpose and exclusion of all matters that do not prove that idea or purpose. Each sentence, paragraph, and division should help to establish the main point of the report.

"The quality of reports suffers when they must be written according to an arbitrary pattern and the content of reports forced into this structure."[1] The investigator must improvise and adapt a reporting format when writing the investigative report.

The best arrangement for the report is rarely simply to relate the order in which the facts developed. Typically, the investigator will first define the problem or question. Second, he will present the relevant and material results of the investigation logically and understandably. Finally, he will set forth recommendations.

Coherence

Coherence means sticking together. It demands careful planning, critical review, and frequent revision by the investigator. Words, phrases, and clauses should be placed in a sentence so that their relationship is clear and the meaning of the sentence is obvious. Sentences should be clear and continuous from beginning to end.

Each paragraph in a report must have an unmistakable relationship to the whole composition, especially to the paragraph immediately preceding it. The investigator should describe fully each violation, event, or circumstance, and all the supporting facts, before passing to the next aspect of the report.

Emphasis

Emphasis requires the careful placement of words, phrases, and sentences to call attention to the important facts. If the investigator does not emphasize the more significant information, the reader will not retain the essential facts. Important words or phrases should be placed in important positions, at the beginning of a clause or sentence, or at the end. A new topic or idea should be the subject of a new paragraph. The investigator can emphasize important matters by using concrete terms and terse sentences, by numbering, and by indenting a series of important related facts.

The important facts must be clear. If the report is not clear, the prosecutor will invariably have difficulty clarifying the matter at trial. "In the framework of criminal prosecution, unclarity alone is enough to resolve the doubts in favor of defendants."[2]

Accuracy

The investigator must make a timely recording of each official contact in the investigation. Although the investigator cannot repeat a conversation word for word, he must include all relevant facts in the memorandum. He should confirm dates and other supporting information with the interviewee to ensure accuracy. Reconfirmation acts as a precautionary measure to check all facts before writing the report. The investigator must fully and completely describe any attachments to the report.

Clarity

Investigative reports should strive to convey the proper message in the clearest possible language. If necessary, the investigator can quote the interviewee, provided the quotation does not distort the context of the memorandum of interview. The language the investigator chooses for the report should convey the facts, not editorialize.

The investigator should avoid using slang and technical terms in the report. Sometimes, slang terms and technical language may be necessary for clarity in reporting the results of investigations, especially in white-collar crimes. If so, the investigator must define the terms when they first appear.[3]

Abbreviations, when understandable and judiciously used, can contribute to the clarity of a report. The intended meaning must be readily apparent to the readers of the report. If there is any doubt as to meaning, the investigator should not use abbreviations.

Impartiality

Reporting his investigations without bias is imperative for the white-collar crime investigator. "Everything relevant should be included regardless of which side it favors or what it proves or disproves."[4]

Relevance

The white-collar crime investigator must ensure that he includes only matters relevant to the investigation in the details of the report. In most investigations, information is gathered, the relevance of which is not immediately known. In those cases, the investigator should include the information in the report.

The investigator must try to decide, at the outset, what information he will need. Irrelevant information confuses and complicates the written report, and leaves the investigator subject to criticism of his methodology.

Upon the completion of the investigation, the investigator should render a timely report. Timeliness is necessary to ensure accuracy in the report. The longer an investigator waits to prepare the report, the more details he will forget.

Except matters of expert opinion, the investigator should include no opinions in the report. The investigator should be especially careful not to include any statement of opinion about the truthfulness or integrity of any witness. He can show or impeach a witness's veracity through conflicting statements, the testimony of other witnesses, or the presentation of documentary evidence.

The Written Report

Written reports may vary widely in style and format. Each individual law enforcement department has developed its own requirements on report writing. Even within those requirements, however, there is some liberty for individual preference. Lacking an established system of report writing for financial crimes, investigators may need to develop their own format. A recommended format includes a cover page, a case introduction, a description of the suspects, a description of victims and witnesses, a description of the offenses involved, the results of the investigation, a list of the evidence, and a mention of other investigative or administrative agencies with an interest in the case.

Cover Page

The cover page of a report typically includes all pertinent administrative data about a case, including the file number, the dates the investigation opened and closed, a case type, a case classification, a case status, the names of the investigators involved, and the date the report was written.

There are many ways to construct file numbers, and each agency or department has its own way to generate such numbers. It is irrelevant how the numbers are constructed. What is important is that each case has its own unique and logically identifiable number.

The date the investigation opened is the date that the investigator or the agency received the first complaint concerning the allegations. The complaint may come by way of a citizen complaint, in a letter, or through information from an anonymous source. The date the investigation closed is the date the investigator ended the investigation because;

1) he decided there was no criminal violation,
2) he referred the case to an administrative agency, or
3) prosecution has commenced and he anticipates no additional arrests or prosecutions.

The case type categorizes the incident under investigation as criminal, civil, or administrative. The matter under examination can be a combination of the three types. For example, an employee embezzling company funds may be prosecuted criminally, held to be civilly liable, and subject to administrative action such as dismissal.

A case classification categorizes the incident under investigation as a specific criminal offense, such as embezzlement, bank fraud, misapplication of fiduciary property, or bribery.

The case status shows one of three categories: pending, inactive, or closed. The case is pending if the investigation is still ongoing and further reports may be issued. The investigator issues a pending report when the investigation is lengthy, and interim reports are necessary. A case is inactive after all investigation had been completed and the case is forwarded to prosecutors for action. A case is closed when an investigator:

1) determines there has been no criminal violation, and he ends the investigation;
2) decides that the allegations involve an administrative matter, and he forwards the case to the proper administrative agency; or
3) initiates prosecution by complaint or indictment, and he anticipates no additional charges.

The report should include the names of the lead investigator and all assistant investigators on the cover page. The investigators are the main source of information for the prosecutor later if the prosecutor needs additional information or certain points need clarification.

The date the report was written is important. Usually the investigator maintains notes and memoranda throughout the investigation, but only writes the report once the investigation is completed. The report may be written over a period of several days, depending on the complexity of the case. This date should show the date the final corrected copy of the report is completed.

Case Introduction

The case introduction is a short narrative, consisting of one or two paragraphs, explaining briefly the nature of the allegations, the scope of the investigation, what statutes have been violated, and identifying the suspects. If any of the suspects have given a confession, that fact should also be included in the introduction. The investigator should not attempt to include specific information learned during the inquiry in this synopsis.

Description of the Suspects

For purposes of definition, a suspect is the person who most likely committed or assisted in the embezzlement or fraud. Included as suspects are the names of the companies and corporations helping in or used during the embezzlement or fraud.

The investigator should list individual suspects by full name, any aliases, race and sex, date of birth, height and weight, home address, business address, and personal identifier numbers such as driver's license number, social security administration number, Federal Bureau of Investigation number, and state bureau numbers.

If a suspect has been arrested and charged, that information should appear with the suspect's name and identification information. If a suspect has a prior criminal record, that information should appear with the suspect's name.

The report should list each company or corporation by its full name, not by abbreviations. If the business is also known by its initials, the initials may appear as an alias. The report should note the type of business organization: proprietorship, partnership, corporation, or cooperative. The investigator should also note which individuals within each business entity were involved in aiding or abetting embezzlement or fraud. The names of suspects should be listed in block, and separately from the names of victims and witnesses.

Description of the Victims and Witnesses

The investigator should list the victims and witnesses in block, separately from suspects and from one another. The report should identify victims and witnesses by full name, any aliases, race and sex, date of birth, home address, business address, and any known telephone numbers. If, later, a victim or witness becomes a suspect, the investigator should reclassify the name and include it in the suspect section of the report.

Description of the Offenses Involved

In this section, the investigator should list the offenses committed by each individual or business entity, including all charges formally filed and reasonable charges that he may not file.

As an example:

1) John Allen Citizen:	Theft (Felony of the 2nd Degree)
	Misapplication of Fiduciary Property (Felony of the 3rd Degree)
	Criminal Conspiracy (Felony of the 1st Degree)
	Money Laundering (Federal Felony Violation) [Not Filed]
2) Henry Citizen:	Receiving Stolen Property (Felony of the 3rd Degree)
	Criminal Conspiracy (Felony of the 1st Degree)
	Money Laundering (Federal Felony Violation) [Not Filed]
3) James Crook:	Misapplication of Fiduciary Property (Felony of the 3rd Degree)
	Criminal Conspiracy (Felony of the 1st Degree)
4) Widgets, Inc.:	Money Laundering (Federal Felony Violation) [Not Filed]
	Tax Evasion (Federal Felony Violation) [Not Filed]

Results of the Investigation

The result of the investigation is the long narrative detailing the facts of the scheme and of the investigation, and is, by far, the most important section of the written report.

The format of the narrative is nearly impossible to define. The scheme dictates the format of the report. Some schemes will best be reported chronologically, listing the events of each day in the order they occurred. The investigator can report a simple embezzlement scheme in such a manner, listing the losses of each day, and detailing the documentation in support of each loss.

Other schemes may center on specific items of property, such as real estate. Closing a deal to purchase real estate takes several days, and several deals may be developing simultaneously. It may prove more efficient to describe all the details of each individual transaction, one at a time, in the chronological order of each transaction.

Very seldom will the report list the facts in the order in which the investigator learned them. Normally, the facts in white-collar crimes investigations develop in disjointed bits and pieces. The investigator must find a logical method to present the facts to whomever will read the report, be it his supervisor, prosecutors, judges, defense attorneys, or administrative regulators.

In reporting the facts, the investigator must be brief, direct and nonjudgmental in his wording. "Vagueness and wordiness are serious faults in writing investigative reports. Simplicity and directness are not merely assets, but essential elements of effective reporting by investigators."5

When writing the narrative, the investigator should state just one idea or fact per paragraph. The investigator should state only those facts that he can document or support by competent testimony. "Investigators should keep in mind that every statement of an alleged fact in a report must be followed by a reference to an exhibit that supports the statement."6 For example:

John Allen Citizen is the founder and president of Widgets, Incorporated. [Articles of Incorporation (D 1–3) and Deposition of John Allen Citizen (C 116)]

John Allen Citizen has the sole authorization to sign on the Widgets, Incorporated bank account at Last National Bank. [Documents subpoenaed from Last National Bank (F 3–4)]

When one person or business entity suffers a series of losses, the investigator should list, by date, each individual amount lost, along with specific references to documents related to the loss. For example, concerning embezzlement:

Date	Amount of Loss	Check Number	Exhibit Number
01/05/X4	$2,000.00	11,483	F 163
01/30/X4	$1,400.00	12,113	F 793
02/10/X4	$2,100.00	12,410	F 1090

[Documents subpoenaed from Last National Bank (F 35-1196)]

The headings in the above format are flexible and should be worded best to describe and explain the nature of the questioned transactions.

Additionally, the investigator must explain in the narrative why each transaction is fraudulent. If there is but one repeated pattern that applies to all the fraudulent transactions, the investigator must state the pattern and state that all the transactions fall within the pattern. For example:

Henry Citizen is the comptroller and chief accountant of Widgets, Incorporated. [Personnel records of Widgets, Incorporated (G 2) and Deposition of Henry Citizen (H 16)]

Over a period of three months, from January 1, 19X4 to March 31, 19X4, H. Citizen issued a series of twenty-one checks to himself, totaling $47,460.00. [Documents subpoenaed from Last National Bank (F 35-1196)]

John Allen Citizen signed each check. [Documents subpoenaed from Last National Bank (F 35-1196)]

Each check was deposited into the personal bank account of Henry

Citizen at Last National Bank. [Documents subpoenaed from Last National Bank (I 3-31)]

The checks were not issued for H. Citizen's authorized salary. [Personnel records of Widgets, Incorporated (G 19-20)]

H. Citizen charged the checks as an advertising expense to the account of J & J Advertising. [Advertising Expenses Journal of Widgets, Incorporated (E 124–125)]

Ida Noe, the president of J & J Advertising, denies that J & J Advertising received the checks or any of the money from the checks, and she denies that Widgets, Incorporated owed the money to J & J Advertising. [Statement of Ida Noe (J 1)]

A complete listing of each transaction in question should then follow such explanations.

If there is no repeated pattern, and each fraudulent item requires a separate explanation, then the investigator must explain each separate transaction.

List of the Evidence

In preparing the evidence section of the report, the investigator should always start with a brief explanation of the evidence, stating how the investigator obtained the evidence or documents. The investigator should identify as a separate group evidence and documents that he obtained from each witness, or that he secured through a subpoena or search warrant. The investigator must give each page a number for reference. For example:

Table of Evidence

A. Memorandum of Interview—Susan Victim

  Pages 1 to 3—Synopsis of meeting with complaining witness on 01/16/X5 in reference to an embezzlement of funds from Widgets, Incorporated.

B. Corporate Minutes for Widgets, Inc. 19X4

  Pages 1 to 265—Copy of Minutes for Widgets provided by the complaining witness, a stockholder of Widgets, on 01/16/X5.

C. Deposition of John Allen Citizen

  Pages 1 to 293—Certified copy of a deposition taken on 10/19/X4 in relationship to a civil suit filed by the stockholders of Widgets, Incorporated, provided by complaining witness, Victim, on 01/22/X5.

D. Articles of Incorporation of Widgets, Incorporated

  Pages 1 to 3—Certified copy obtained from the Secretary of State on 01/15/X5.

E. Advertising Expenses Journal of Widgets, Incorporated

  Pages 1 to 200—Book 2 of Advertising Expenses Journal for Widgets, Inc., Subpoenaed on 01/12/X5, and returned by Janie Clerk on 01/14/X5.

F. Banking Records of Last National Bank

Pages 1 to 2—Corporate Resolution of Widgets, Inc., authorizing the account

Pages 3 to 4—Signature card for checking account for Widgets, Inc.

Pages 5 to 34—Monthly statements of bank account for Widgets, Inc. for 01/X4 to 03/X4.

Pages 35 to 1196—Copies of checks from Widgets, Inc., bank account. Subpoenaed from Last National Bank on 01/13/X5, and returned by Willie Teller on 01/28/X5.

G. Personal Payroll Records for Henry Boyd Citizen

Pages 1 to 8—Personnel records from Widgets, Inc. Subpoenaed on 01/12/X5, and returned by Janie Clerk on 01/15/X5.

H. Deposition of Henry Boyd Citizen

Pages 1 to 186—Certified copy of a deposition taken on 10/23/X4 in relationship to a civil suit filed by the stockholders of Widgets, Incorporated, provided by complaining witness, Victim, on 01/25/X5.

I. Banking Records of Last National Bank

Pages 1 to 2—Signature card of personal account of Henry Citizen

Pages 2 to 31—Copies of deposits into Henry Citizen's personal checking account. Subpoenaed from Last National Bank on 01/13/X5, and returned by Willie Teller on 01/28/X5.

J. Statement of Ida Noe

Page 1—Sworn statement taken from Ida Noe, President of J & J Advertising on 02/11/X5.

Each item of evidence or each document is identified by letter, to denote the group from which it comes, and by number, to denote the page within the group. For example, a copy of a specific check deposited in Henry Boyd Citizen's account would be designated as I 25 (I for Banking Records of Last National Bank, 25 for the 25th page of the group).

The investigator's work sheets and notes, including receipts for the acceptance and delivery of evidence, should also be classified and included in the evidence section.

Other Interested Agencies

If any other investigative, regulatory, or administrative agency has an interest in the outcome of the case, or has conducted a collateral investigation, the investigator should include that information in the report. If the other interested agency has made a report, the investigator should include a copy of that report with his, if that report s available.

Mistakes in Report Writing

Investigators are subject to making many mistakes in writing investigative reports. Among these is the failure to proofread and revise the report, the statement of conclusions, and the statement of opinions.

Proofreading and Revisions

The importance of revision of the report cannot be overemphasized. The investigator, after completing a report, should set it aside. Two or three days later, he should review the report and decide what changes will improve the report. The investigator should look carefully for:

1) a lack of logic or method in the arrangement of the various parts of the report,
2) omission of important and relevant facts,
3) inaccurate or ambiguous statements,
4) inclusion of unnecessary or irrelevant information,
5) wordiness,
6) poor choice of words or sentence structure,
7) spelling errors, and
8) the statement of conclusion or opinion.

The investigator should make sure that his meaning is clear, and that he has sufficiently developed and documented each theory. In the latter stages of revision, the investigator should continuously ask himself one key question at the end of every paragraph—"How do you know?" Only when the investigator can answer the question by pointing to specific exhibits can he be sure his investigation and report are complete.

Having another investigator or supervisor review the report and make recommendations for improvement may be helpful for the investigator. It is important for the investigator to remember, however, that he alone bears responsibility for the final report.

Discovery

There is no privilege, per se, for an investigator's reports and notes, or for any fraud examination, forensic audit or similar services. There are, however, two general exceptions:

1) If the investigator is conducting an inquiry at the request of an attorney, the report is considered in most courts as an attorney/client work product, and thereby privileged; and
2) If a public authority is conducting the investigation, such as the police or federal agents, the report can be considered privileged.[7]

The investigator should always assume that whatever he writes may be made available to the defense at some time during an investigation or trial. Accordingly, the investigator should try to ensure his report is objective, thorough, and absent of sarcasm or bias.

Case Preparation

Once the case report is completed, the investigator should prepare the case for presentation to a prosecutor. The investigator should include copies of all the information gathered during the investigation. Table 29 contains a guideline of information the investigator should present.

The investigator must carefully sort and store the evidence he has gathered during the investigation. The evidence should be grouped according to its source and subject matter, the pages numbered, and each group of documents packaged together, either in an envelope or box. Each package should then be identified and numbered in the evidence section of the report. The investigator and prosecutor should maintain the evidence in the same condition throughout the investigation and prosecution.

The investigator should make copies of relevant documents, and photograph relevant evidence. Copying all the documents received during an investigation may not be necessary, but the prosecution should have copies of documents relating to every questioned transaction. The investigator may forward copies and photographs to the prosecuting attorney as attachments to the report. "Original documents that will ultimately be offered in evidence during trial should never be attached to the report. They should be retained by the investigator in order to ensure the chain of custody."[8]

The investigator, upon forwarding the report and attachments to the prosecutor, should be prepared for requests for follow-up investigation. Prosecutors are rarely satisfied with the amount of evidence, and, in white-collar cases, they may not even be convinced that a crime has been committed. Defense attorneys, upon reviewing the evidence, will claim that there is no evidence of a crime. If there is evidence of a crime, they will claim that there is insufficient evidence to convict the suspect, or that the investigator obtained the evidence illegally.

The investigator should not despair in these circumstances. It is very important for the investigator to realize, especially in financial investigations, that "no matter how much intelligence and honesty went into the many decisions common to any investigation, the sum total is a subjective impression in the mind of the investigator,"[9] and that means one man's opinion.

Table 29. Guideline for Preparing a Comprehensive Package for the Prosecuting Attorney.

I. Cover Sheet—a title sheet which includes:
  A. A file number
  B. Dates the investigation opened and closed
  C. Case Type
  D. Case Classification
  E. Names of investigators involved
  F. Date the report was written
II. Introductory Statement—a brief narrative which explains:
  A. The nature of the allegations investigated
  B. How the allegation came to the attention of the investigator
  C. The period of time being investigated
  D. The type and total amount of loss
  E. Possible statutes (criminal, civil, and administrative) which were violated
  F. Listing of suspects
  G. Notation of any confessions given by suspects
III. Description of Defendants—a standard identification record may be used, as long as it contains:
  A. Name
  B. Aliases
  C. Addresses (home and business)
  D. Physical description
  E. Place and date of birth
  F. Criminal identification number
  G. Occupation or employers
  H. Associates and accomplices
  I. Prior record
  J. Identification of those who have cooperated or might cooperate with the prosecution
IV. Description of Victims—a standard identification record may be used, as long as it contains:
  A. Name
  B. Address (home and address)
  C. Victim's relationship with the suspects
  D. Loss suffered by the victim
V. Description of Offenses—a listing of suspects detailing;
  A. Charges filed against each suspect
  B. Reasonable charges which have not yet, or may not be, filed
VI. Results of the Investigation—a detailed explanation of all pertinent data concerning the scheme from its conception through its perpetration, to the extent possible describing:
  A. How the scheme was conceived
  B. Who executed the scheme
  C. Where the scheme was put into operation
  D. How long the scheme was in operation
  E. The nature of the scheme, the types of merchandise, services, or fraud involved
  F. Whether the victims can be classified as to economic, social, educational or other backgrounds
  G. The specific loss of each victim and the total losses to all victims

   H. Any additional information which gives a clearer picture of the magnitude, nature and characteristics of the scheme

   I. A narrative description containing the evidence which may possibly be used for development of proof of misrepresentations, fraudulent intent, or other essential elements of the statutes violated. This description should include:

     1. Any occurrence which might lead to a conclusion of criminal intent, including any admissions of the suspects. To this the investigator should attach any diagrammatic outlines of the white-collar crime operation which the investigator may have prepared.

     2. When applicable, each major misrepresentation, false pretense, or false promise which the defendant used in obtaining money or property from the victims.

VII. Evidence — include:

   A. A list of witnesses and a brief narrative of the testimony they can give

   B. A list of documentary and physical evidence associated with each witness

   C. How each item of evidence was obtained, either by interview, search warrant, subpoena, surveillance, questionnaire, etc.

IX. Other Agencies Involved — a brief description of the involvement or interest of other government, law enforcement, or private agencies.

Notes

[1] Wayne K. Bennett and Karen M. Hess, *Criminal Investigation* (St. Paul, MN: West Publishing Co., 1981), p. 259.

[2] U.S. v. Mersky, 361 U.S. 431.

[3] ———, *Financial Investigative Techniques* (Washington, D.C.: Internal Revenue Service, Department of the Treasury, 1986), p. 7-2.

[4] Joseph T. Wells, W. Steve Albrecht, Jack Bologna, Gilbert Geis, and Jack Robertson, *Fraud Examiners' Manual* (Austin, TX: National Association of Certified Fraud Examiners, 1989) Section I, p. 112, quoting Art Buckwalter, *Investigative Methods* (Woburn, MA: Butterworth Publishers, 1984), p. 208.

[5] Bennett and Hess, op cit.

[6] Richard A. Nossen, *The Detection, Investigation and Prosecution of Financial Crimes* (Richmond, VA: Richard A. Nossen & Associates, 1982), p. 116.

[7] Wells et al., op cit., Section I, p. 121.

[8] Nossen, op cit., p. 115.

[9] Bennett and Hess, op cit., p. 293.

APPENDIX A

THE NUMERICAL SYSTEM OF THE AMERICAN BANKERS ASSOCIATION

Index to Prefix Numbers of Cities and States

Numbers 1 to 49 inclusive are Prefixes for Cities
Numbers 50 to 99 inclusive are Prefixes for States

Prefix Numbers of Cities in Numerical Order

1. New York, NY	18. Kansas, MO	35. Houston, TX
2. Chicago, IL	19. Seattle, WA	36. St. Joseph, MO
3. Philadelphia, PA	20. Indianapolis, IN	37. Fort Worth, TX
4. St. Louis, MO	21. Louisville, KY	38. Savannah, GA
5. Boston, MS	22. St. Paul, MN	39. Oklahoma City, OK
6. Cleveland, OH	23. Denver, CO	40. Wichita, KS
7. Baltimore, MD	24. Portland, OR	41. Sioux City, IA
8. Pittsburgh, PA	25. Columbus, OH	42. Pueblo, CO
9. Detroit, MI	26. Memphis, TN	43. Lincoln, NE
10. Buffalo, NY	27. Omaha, NE	44. Topeka, KS
11. San Francisco, CA	28. Spokane, WA	45. Dubuque, IA
12. Milwaukee, WI	29. Albany, NY	46. Galveston, TX
13. Cincinnati, OH	30. San Antonio, TX	47. Cedar Rapids, IA
14. New Orleans, LA	31. Salt Lake City, UT	48. Waco, TX
15. Washington, DC	32. Dallas, TX	49. Muskogee, OK
16. Los Angeles, CA	33. Des Moines, IA	
17. Minneapolis, MN	34. Tacoma, WA	

Prefix Numbers of States in Numerical Order

50. New York	67. South Carolina	84. Louisiana
51. Connecticut	68. Virginia	85. Mississippi
52. Maine	69. West Virginia	86. Oklahoma
53. Massachusetts	70. Illinois	87. Tennessee
54. New Hampshire	71. Indiana	88. Texas
55. New Jersey	72. Iowa	89. Alaska
56. Ohio	73. Kentucky	90. California
57. Rhode Island	74. Michigan	91. Arizona
58. Vermont	75. Minnesota	92. Idaho
59. Hawaii	76. Nebraska	93. Montana
60. Pennsylvania	77. North Dakota	94. Nevada
61. Alabama	78. South Dakota	95. New Mexico

62. Delaware
63. Florida
64. Georgia
65. Maryland
66. North Carolina

79. Wisconsin
80. Missouri
81. Arkansas
82. Colorado
83. Kansas

96. Oregon
97. Utah
98. Washington
99. Wyoming
101. Territories

APPENDIX B

AFFIDAVIT OF FINANCIAL INFORMATION

State of _____)(
County of _____)(

_____, being duly sworn, deposes and says:

My name is _____, my primary residence is
_____, my date of birth is _____,
and my social security number is _____. The following is a complete
and accurate statement, as of _____, of my net worth (assets of whatsoever
kind and nature and wherever situated minus liabilities), income from all sources
and statement of assets transferred of whatsoever kind and nature wherever situated.
In filling out this form I have followed the instructions set out herein.

General Instuctions:

1. Complete all items, marking "None," "Inapplicable," or "Unknown" as
   appropriate.
2. Type or print description of item and amount in the appropriate space.
3. Number each separate item within a specific heading.
4. Furnish additional information as indicated.
5. If additional space is required use a separate rider referring to the category,
   section, letter and/or number and incorporate the rider by specific reference
   within the appropriate section.
6. Under "Jt" column, check if jointly owned with others.
7. Under Amount column insert total purchase price at the time of acquisition.
8. Under My Share column insert percentage of asset owned by deponent.
9. Under Date, list the date the asset was acquired or the debt incurred.
10. Complete one Gross Income From All Sources form, including information
    from each of the last three calendar years (January 1 to December 31) and for
    the current year to date.
11. Attach accurate and complete copies of your federal and state income tax
    returns, including all supporting schedules, for the last three years. If you do
    not have access to such copies, then sign the relevant consent form or forms
    annexed to this Form of Affidavit. This form will not be accepted without
    either the copies or the relevant consents.

ASSETS
Cash Accounts
List financial institution, address,
    account number

	Jt	Amount	My Share	Date

Cash
List financial institution, address,
    account number

	Jt	Amount	My Share	Date

Checking (individual, joint)
List financial institution, address,
    account number

	Jt	Amount	My Share	Date

Savings (individual, joint)
List financial institution, address,
    account number

	Jt	Amount	My Share	Date

Security Deposits, Earnest Money, etc.
List financial institution, address,
    account number

	Jt	Amount	My Share	Date

Short-Term Paper (certificates of deposit, treasury notes)
List financial institution, address,
    account number

	Jt	Amount	My Share	Date

Securities (bonds, notes, mortgages)
List financial institution, address,
    account number

	Jt	Amount	My Share	Date

Equity Securities, Options and Commodity Contracts

Number of Shares	Issuer and Type	Cost	Jt	Amount	My Share	Date
_____	_____	____	___	_____	_____	____
_____	_____	____	___	_____	_____	____
_____	_____	____	___	_____	_____	____

Brokers' Margin Accounts (identify broker, credit balances)

	Jt	Amount	My Share	Date
_____	___	_____	_____	____
_____	___	_____	_____	____
_____	___	_____	_____	____

Loans and Accounts Receivable

Obligor	Maturity Date	Principal Amount	Jt	Market Value	My Share	Date
_____	_____	_____	___	_____	_____	____
_____	_____	_____	___	_____	_____	____
_____	_____	_____	___	_____	_____	____

Value of Interest in any Business (describe investment, giving name and address of company, whether a corporation, partnership, sole proprietorship or trust, your capital contribution, net worth of the business, percent of your interest, and any other information bearing upon valuation including the measure of value used for determination)

	Amount	Date
_____	_____	____
_____	_____	____
_____	_____	____
_____	_____	____
_____	_____	____

Life Insurance (identify whether Term or Whole Life)

Carrier, Policy No.	Beneficiary	Face Value	Cash Value	Owner	Date
_____	_____	_____	_____	_____	____
_____	_____	_____	_____	_____	____
_____	_____	_____	_____	_____	____

Vehicles (boats, planes, trucks, etc.)

Make	Model/Year	Serial #	Jt	Amount	My Share	Date
_____	_____	_____	___	_____	_____	____
_____	_____	_____	___	_____	_____	____
_____	_____	_____	___	_____	_____	____
_____	_____	_____	___	_____	_____	____

Real Estate (include all types of interests such as leaseholds, life estates, at market value; do not deduct mortgage.)

Location & Description	Basis	Jt	Amount	My Share	Date
_____	_____	___	_____	_____	____
_____	_____	___	_____	_____	____
_____	_____	___	_____	_____	____

Vested Interests in Trusts (i.e., pensions, profit sharing, legacies, etc.)

	Jt	Amount	My Share	Date
_____	____	_____	_____	____
_____	____	_____	_____	____
_____	____	_____	_____	____

Deferred Compensation

	Due Date	Jt	Amount	My Share	Date
_____	_____	___	_____	_____	____
_____	_____	___	_____	_____	____

Contingent Interests (for example, stock options, interests subject to life estates, prospective inheritances, date of vesting)

	Jt	Amount	My Share	Date
_____	____	_____	_____	____
_____	____	_____	_____	____
_____	____	_____	_____	____

Jewelry (all items above $500)

	Cost	Jt	Market Value	My Share	Date
_____	_____	___	_____	_____	____
_____	_____	___	_____	_____	____
_____	_____	___	_____	_____	____
_____	_____	___	_____	_____	____

Household Furnishings (list all residences by addresses, market value of furnishings)

	Jt	Amount	My Share	Date
_____	____	_____	_____	____
_____	____	_____	_____	____
_____	____	_____	_____	____
_____	____	_____	_____	____

Art, Antiques, Precious Objects (all items over $500)

	Cost	Jt	Market Value	My Share	Date
_____	_____	___	_____	_____	____
_____	_____	___	_____	_____	____
_____	_____	___	_____	_____	____

Gold and Other Precious Metals
Metal and Form

	Jt	Amount	My Share	Date
_____	____	_____	_____	____
_____	____	_____	_____	____
_____	____	_____	_____	____

Other Assets (for example, tax shelter investments, collections, hobbies, judgments, causes of action, patents, trademarks, copyrights, contract rights and any other assets not herein-above itemized)

	Jt	Amount	My Share	Date

GRAND TOTAL OF ALL ASSETS $_____

_____

LIABILITIES

If jointly with spouse or another, so state, and indicate your share. Attach additional sheets if needed. If payments are due on other than a monthly basis, indicate due dates.

Accounts Payable

Creditor	Date Incurred	Purpose of Debt	Original Amount	Current Amount	Monthly Payment

Notes Payable

Creditor	Date Incurred	Purpose of Debt	Original Amount	Current Amount	Monthly Payment

Installment Accounts Payable

Creditor	Date Incurred	Purpose of Debt	Original Amount	Current Amount	Monthly Payment

Brokers' Margin Accounts

Creditor	Date Incurred	Purpose of Debt	Original Amount	Current Amount	Monthly Payment

Real Estate Mortgages

Creditor	Date Incurred	Purpose of Debt	Original Amount	Current Amount	Monthly Payment

Interest Payable

Creditor	Date Incurred	Purpose of Debt	Original Amount	Current Amount	Monthly Payment

Taxes Payable

Creditor	Date Incurred	Type of Tax	Original Amount	Current Amount	Monthly Payment

Loans on Life Insurance Policies

Creditor	Date Incurred	Purpose of Debt	Original Amount	Current Amount	Monthly Payment

Other Liabilities

Creditor	Date Incurred	Purpose of Debt	Original Amount	Current Amount	Monthly Payment

GRAND TOTAL LIABILITIES $_____

GROSS INCOME FROM ALL SOURCES

State sources of income. Attach additional sheets, if needed. For each category of income, state the total income for an entire calendar year, or this year to date.

Total Income

Gross Income from Calendar Year 19____ $_____
Gross Income from Calendar Year 19____ $_____
Gross Income from Calendar Year 19____ $_____
Gross Income Current Calendar Year to date $_____

Salary or Wages (Set forth the names and addresses of all employers during the three previous calendar years and the total wages paid by each. Indicate overtime earnings separately. Attach W-2's.)

Wages: Employer/Address	Period of Employment	Amount
_____	_____	_____
_____	_____	_____
_____	_____	_____
_____	_____	_____
_____	_____	_____

Current Employer/Address	Period of Employment	Amount
_____	_____	_____

Total Current Salary and Wages $_____
    Weekly _____ Biweekly _____ Monthly _____
    1. Social Security   _____
    2. State/Local Taxes   _____
    3. Federal Taxes   _____
    4. Other deductions (specify)   _____
       Total   _____

Names of Dependents Claimed	Social Security #
_____	_____
_____	_____
_____	_____
_____	_____

Total Number of Dependents   _____

Bonuses, Commissions, Fringe Benefits (use of auto, club memberships, etc., indicate benefits per calendar year)

Describe	Estimated Value
_____	_____
_____	_____
_____	_____
_____	_____

Partnership Income, Royalties, Sales of Assets (including installment payments, indicate benefits per calendar year)

Describe	Estimated Value
_____	_____
_____	_____
_____	_____

Dividends and Interest (per calendar year)

Source   Value

_____   _____

_____   _____

_____   _____

Real Estate Income (describe property and indicate per calendar year)

Property   Amount

_____   _____

_____   _____

_____   _____

Income From Trusts, Profit Sharing or Annuities

Describe   Amount

_____   _____

_____   _____

_____   _____

Pension Income

Source   Amount

_____   _____

_____   _____

_____   _____

Awards, Prizes, Grants

Source   Value

_____   _____

_____   _____

Income From Bequests, Legacies and Gifts

Source   Amount

_____   _____

_____   _____

_____   _____

If your spouse, child or other members of your household is employed or receives income, set forth the name and that person's annual income.

Source   Amount

_____   _____

_____   _____

_____   _____

Total   _____

Social Security Income

Calendar Year   Amount

_____   _____

_____   _____

_____   _____

Disability Benefits

Calendar Year   Amount

_____   _____

_____   _____

_____   _____

Public Assistance Income

Calendar Year   Amount

_____   _____

_____   _____

_____   _____

Income From All Other Sources (including loans)

Source   Amount

_____   _____

_____   _____

_____   _____

_____   _____

GRAND TOTAL INCOME $_____

ASSETS TRANSFERRED

List all assets transferred in any manner on or after [date]. Transfers in the routine course of
    business which resulted in an exchange of assets of substantially equivalent value need
    not be specifically disclosed provided such assets are otherwise identified in the statement
    of net worth.

Description of Property	To Whom Transferred and Relationship to Transferee	Date of Transfer	Value
_____	_____	_____	_____
_____	_____	_____	_____
_____	_____	_____	_____
_____	_____	_____	_____

I, _____, have carefully read the foregoing statement
consisting of ____ pages and a rider consisting of ____ pages annexed hereto and
made part hereof; they are true and correct.

_____

(Signature)

Sworn to before me this ____ day of _____, 19____.

_____

APPENDIX C

AREA ASSIGNMENTS FOR SOCIAL SECURITY NUMBERS

The first three digits of Social Security Administration Numbers (SSN) indicate their assigned areas of issuance.

Number(s)	Area	Number(s)	Area
001–003	New Hampshire	449–467	Texas
004–007	Maine	468–477	Minnesota
008–009	Vermont	478–485	Iowa
010–034	Massachusetts	486–500	Missouri
035–039	Rhode Island	501–502	North Dakota
040–049	Connecticut	503–504	South Dakota
050–134	New York	505–508	Nebraska
135–158	New Jersey	509–515	Kansas
159–211	Pennsylvania	516–517	Montana
212–220	Maryland	518–519	Idaho
221–222	Delaware	520	Wyoming
223–231	Virginia	521–524	Colorado
232–236	West Virginia	525, 585	New Mexico
*232, 237–246	North Carolina	526–527	Arizona
247–251	South Carolina	528–529	Utah
252–260	Georgia	530	Nevada
261–267	Florida	531–539	Washington
268–302	Ohio	540–544	Oregon
303–317	Indiana	545–573	California
318–361	Illinois	574	Alaska
362–386	Michigan	575–576	Hawaii
387–399	Wisconsin	577–579	District of Columbia
400–407	Kentucky	580	Virgin Islands
408–415	Tennessee	**580–584	Puerto Rico
416–424	Alabama	586	Guam
425–428, 587	Mississippi	***586	American Samoa
429–432	Arkansas	***586	Philippine Islands
433–439	Louisiana	700–729	Railroad Retirement
440–448	Oklahoma		Board

*Area 232: Number 30 (middle 2 digits) allocated to North Carolina by transfer from West Virginia.

**Area 580: Numbers 01–18 (middle 2 digits) allocated to the Virgin Islands; numbers 20 and above allocated to Puerto Rico.

***Area 586: Numbers 01–18 (middle 2 digits) allocated to Guam; numbers 20–28 allocated to American Samoa; numbers 60–78 allocated during initial registration of armed service personnel for assignment to those who were natives of the Philippine Islands; numbers 80 and above are not allocated.

APPENDIX D

GUIDE TO SOURCES OF
FINANCIAL INFORMATION

Part I

Types of Information Desired

Type of Information	Refer to Part II
1. Full name	1, 2, 4, 5, 6, 10, 11, 16, 17, 23, 28, 31, 32, 33, 51
2. Address	1, 2, 4, 5, 6, 10, 11, 16, 17, 23, 28, 31, 32, 33, 51, 56
3. Date of birth	2, 3, 8, 13, 23, 31, 32
4. Description	2, 3, 13, 51
5. Photograph	2, 3, 13, 22, 56
6. Occupation	6, 13, 28, 31, 32, 34, 50, 56
7. Marital Status	12, 22, 31, 50, 51
8. Previous addresses and other occupants	32, 33, 56
9. Addresses, whether renting or buying	31
10. Telephone numbers, record of long distance calls	5
11. Sources of income, expenditures, net worth of subject	28
12. Credit charges	15
13. Registered and legal owners of vehicles, previous owners	51
14. Personal and business references, former places of employment	29
15. Stocks bought and sold, profits and losses	30
16. Deeds, grants, mortgages, wills in probate, liens, powers of attorney	55
17. Registration of securities offered for public sale	47
18. Reputation of a business, back issues of city directories	47, 48, 56
19. Business's worth, associates, holdings and ratings	31, 50
20. Persons involved in medical or dental practice, pharmacists, barbers, funeral directors	36
21. Names of post office box holders, return addresses of mail received	4
22. Forwarding addresses	4, 35
23. Marriage license applications	12
24. Names of bride and groom, maiden name of bride	22
25. Divorce information, including names of children, community property, and financial statements	9, 56
26. Parents of a child, occupations and ages	19, 23
27. Disposition of an estate, value of estate, inventory	27

244

28. Name and description of deceased, disposition of
     property on body   24, 26, 27
29. Where death occurred, birth place, names of relatives   24, 56
30. Civil suits, name changes, liens   10
31. Political party affiliation, spouse's name, last place
     registered to vote   6, 56
32. Ship, boat, and yacht registries   38, 39
33. Names and addresses of owners of ships, boats,
     and yachts   38, 39, 54
34. Ownership of aircraft   59
35. Background on horse owners, jockeys, and race track
     employees   7, 56, 60
36. Case histories of welfare recipients   20
37. Student and teacher records   21
38. List of county employees, rates of pay and financial
     records for the county   25
39. Names of hospitals, doctors' names, dates of birth, year
     of graduation, and office addresses   36
40. Bar owners' fingerprints, home addresses, associates
     and employees   45, 65
41. Articles of incorporation   40
42. Copies of telegrams and money orders   34
43. Record of all warrants drawn on the State Treasury;
     accounts of all persons indebted to the State   41
44. Legal description of property, taxes on real property,
     former owners   17
45. Costs of construction   18
46. Dimensions of property, income from property,
     improvements (if any)   16
47. Sources to information in foreign countries   52, 53, 62
48. Anticipated travel to a foreign country by a person and
     vital statistics   13, 56
49. Addresses of aliens   14, 46
50. Alien information, date of entry, date of birth, names
     of spouse and children occupation   14, 46
51. A guide to newspapers and periodicals in the U.S.   37
52. Information on dairies   43
53. Mining, petroleum and gasoline, fish and game   43
54. Records of individuals and firms who have violated
     State and Federal insurance regulations   49, 57, 58
55. Records of individuals and firms who have violated
     State and Federal regulations in commodities traffic   47, 61
56. Companies and individuals doing business in foreign
     countries   63
57. Companies making investments in less developed
     countries   62
58. Credit information on prospective customers of a
     business entity   64

Part II
1. Telephone directories
2. State Department of Justice/Bureau of Identification
3. Federal Bureau of Investigation
4. Post Office
5. Telephone company
6. Registrar of voters
7. State Horse Racing Board
8. County Clerk's Office, Vital Statistics
9. County Clerk's Office, Divorce Records
10. County Clerk's Office, Civil Files
11. County Clerk's Office, Criminal Files
12. County Clerk's Office, Marriage License Applications
13. State Department, Passports Division
14. County Department of Naturalization
15. Credit card companies
16. County Assessor's Office; Title and Abstract Company
17. County Tax Collector's Office; Title and Abstract Company
18. Building Department
19. Health Department
20. Welfare Department
21. School Department
22. County Recorder's Office, Marriage License Section
23. County Recorder's Office, Birth Certificate Section
24. County Recorder's Office, Death Certificate Section
25. County Auditor's Office
26. County Coroner's Office
27. Public Administrator's Office
28. Banks and finance companies
29. Bonding companies
30. Stock brokers
31. Credit reporting agencies
32. Gas and electric companies
33. Water companies
34. Telegraph companies
35. Moving companies
36. American Medical Directory
37. Directory of Newspapers and Periodicals, N. W. Ayer and Sons, Philadelphia
38. Lloyd's Register of Shipping
39. Lloyd's Register of Yachts
40. Secretary of State, Corporate Division
41. State Comptroller
42. State Department of Agriculture
43. Department of Natural Resources
44. Securities and Exchange Commission
45. Alcohol Beverage Control
46. Federal Immigration and Naturalization Service
47. Better Business Bureau
48. Chamber of Commerce

49. American Insurance Company
50. Dun and Bradstreet
51. Department of Motor Vehicles
52. Treasury Department
53. Interpol
54. Harbor Patrol
55. County Recorder's Office
56. Newspaper Library or Newspaper "Morgue"
57. Insurance Crime Prevention Institute
58. Hooper—Holmes Bureau, Inc.
59. Federal Aviation Administration
60. Thoroughbred Racing Protection Bureau, New York
61. Commodities Futures Trading Corporation, Washington, D.C.
62. U.S. Department of Commerce, Washington, D.C.
63. Agency for International Development, Washington, D.C.
64. National Association of Credit Management, New York
65. Distilled Spirits Institute, New York

APPENDIX E

CONSENT TO SEARCH

_____
Date

_____
Location

I, _____, having been informed of my constitutional right not to have a search made of the premises hereinafter mentioned without a search warrant and of my right to refuse to consent to such a search, hereby waive my rights and authorize _____ and _____ to conduct a complete search of my premises located at _____ without a warrant. The above mentioned law enforcement officers are authorized by me to take from my premises any letters, papers, documents, materials or other property which they may desire.

This written permission is being given by me voluntarily and without threats or promises of any kind.

_____
Signature

WITNESSES:

_____   _____

This is to certify that on _____ at _____ the law enforcement officers described above conducted a search of _____. Attached is a list of property removed from the premises.

_____
Signature

WITNESSES:

_____   _____

248

RECEIPT FOR PROPERTY

On _____ the item(s) listed below were:

      _____ Received from
      _____ Returned to
      _____ Released to

(Name)   _____

(Address)   _____

(City/State) _____

Description of Item(s): _____

                        _____

                        _____

                        _____

                        _____

                        _____

                        _____

                        _____

Received by: _____

Received from: _____

APPENDIX F

CUSTOMER CONSENT AND AUTHORIZATION FOR ACCESS TO FINANCIAL RECORDS

I, _____, having read the explanation of my rights which is attached to this form, hereby authorize the (*Name and address of financial institution*) to disclose the following financial records:

to _____, a law enforcement officer, for the following purpose(s): to facilitate a law enforcement investigation.

I understand that this authorization may be revoked by me in writing at any time before my records, as described above, are disclosed, and that this authorization is valid for not more than 90 days from the date of my signature.

_____	_____
Date	Signature
_____	_____
Witness	Address

APPENDIX G

STATEMENT OF RIGHTS

Place: _____
Date: _____
Time: _____

Before we ask you any questions, you must understand your rights.

1) You have the right to remain silent, the right not to answer any questions, and the right not to make a statement.
2) Anything you say can be used against you in court.
3) Anything you say can be used against you at your trial.
4) You have the right to have a lawyer present to advise prior to or during any questioning.
5) If you cannot afford a lawyer, you have the right to have a lawyer appointed to advise you prior to or during any questioning.
6) If you decide to answer questions now, you have the right to terminate the interview at any time.

WAIVER OF RIGHTS

I have read this statement of my rights, and I understand my rights. I am waiving my rights to remain silent and to have a lawyer present to advise me prior to and during the questioning. I am willing to answer questions and to make a statement at this time. I understand and know what I am doing. No promises or threats have been made to me, and no pressure or coercion of any kind has been used against me.

_____
Signature

WITNESSES:

_____

_____   Time: _____

251

GLOSSARY

Abstract — To take or withdraw from; as, to abstract the funds from a bank.
(Sprague v. State, 188 Wis. 432)

Abuse of Trust — The intentional misuse of one's official or fiduciary position, and/or the misuse of privileged information gained by virtue of that position in order to acquire money, property or some privilege to which one is not entitled for oneself, or for another in whom one has an interest.

Acceptance — The taking and receiving of anything in good part, and as it were a tacit agreement to a preceding act, which might have been defeated or avoided if such acceptance had not been made.
(Aetna Inv. Corp. v. Chandler Landscape & Floral Co., 277 Mo.App. 17)

Account — A detailed statement of the mutual demands in the nature of debt and credit between parties, arising out of contracts or some fiduciary relation.
(Portsmouth v. Donaldson, 32 Pa. 202)

Accounting — The act of recording, classifying, and summarizing in a significant manner, and in terms of money, transactions and events which are, in part at least, of a financial character, and interpreting the results thereof.

Accounting Period — The period of time over which an income statement summarizes the changes in an owner's equity.

Accounts Receivable — Contract obligations owing to a person on open account.
(West Virginia Pulp & Paper Co. v. Karnes, 137 Va. 714)

Accounts Payable — Contract obligations owing by a person on open account.
(State Tax Commission v. Shattuck, 44 Ariz. 379)

Accrual Basis — A method of keeping accounts which shows expenses incurred and income earned for a given period, although such expenses and income may not have been actually paid or received in cash.
(Orlando Orange Groves Co. v. Hale, 119 Fla. 159)

Accrued Expenses — Expenses incurred but not yet paid.

Accrued Income — Income earned but not yet received.

Adjusting Entry — An accounting transaction recording the correction of an error, accruals, write-offs, provision for bad debts or depreciation, etc., expressed in the form of a simple journal entry.

Admission — The avowal of a fact or of circumstances from which guilt may be inferred, but only tending to prove the offense charged, and not amounting to a confession of guilt.
(Theis v. State, 164 S.E. 456, 457)

Advance Fee Scheme — A promotion in which assurances of some future benefit are made, but only after the tendering of some partial payment or an advance good

252

faith deposit, by a promoter who has no intention of delivering or performing the benefit.

Affidavit — A written or printed declaration or statement of facts, made voluntarily, and confirmed by the oath or affirmation of the party making it, taken before an officer having the authority to administer such an oath.
(Cox v. Stern, 170 Ill. 442)

Aggregate Theft — The existence of a scheme or a continuing course of conduct to allow aggregation of separate amounts of various acts of theft to increase the degree of the offense may be shown by such factors as: common ownership of the stolen property, similarity of the property and the proximity of time and place of the various incidents of theft.
(Zaiontz v. State, 700 S.W.2d 303)

Alien Corporation — A corporation of another nationality operating in the United States.

Amortization — The operation of paying off bonds, stock, a mortgage, or other indebtedness, commonly of a state or corporation, by installments, or by a sinking fund.
(Bystra v. Federal Land Bank of Columbia, 82 Fla. 472)

Appraise — To fix or set a price or value upon; to fix and state the true value of a thing, and usually in writing.
(Vincent v. German Ins. Co., 120 Iowa 272)

Appropriate — To make a thing one's own; to make a thing the subject of property; to exercise dominion over an object to the extent, and for the purpose, of making it subserve one's own proper use or pleasure.
(People v. Ashworth, 222 N.Y.S. 24)

Artifice — An ingenious contrivance or device of some kind and, when used in a bad sense, it corresponds with trick or fraud.
(US v. Carlin, 44 F.Supp. 940)

Asset — Property or a property right owned by the individual, business, or corporation which is valuable either because it will be converted into cash or because it is expected to benefit future operations and which was acquired at a measurable cost.

Attribute Sampling — Statistical method used to estimate the proportion of items in a population containing a characteristic or attribute of interest.

Audit — An official examination of an account or claim, comparing vouchers, charges, and fixing the balance.

Bad Debt — Accounts that are considered to be uncollectible.

Balance Sheet — A financial statement that reports the assets and equities of a company as of a specified time.

Bailment — A delivery of goods or personal property, by one person to another, in trust for the execution of a special object upon or in relation to such goods, beneficial either to the bailor or bailee or both, and upon a contract, either express or implied, to perform the trust and carry out such object, and thereupon to either redeliver the goods to the bailor or otherwise dispose of the same in conformity with the purpose of the trust.
(Fulcher v. State, 32 Tex.Cr.R. 621)

Bank Deposit Method — An indirect method of proving unknown or illegal sources of funds through an analysis of deposits to all bank accounts, canceled checks, and currency transactions.

Bank Reconciliation — A comparison of the customer's records with the records of the bank, listing differences to bring balances into agreement.

Bank Statement — A document rendered by the bank to the depositor, usually monthly, which reflects deposits and checks which have cleared the bank. These items are listed in chronological order of receipt by the bank.

Banking Violations — Manipulations or arrangements by insiders of banks, savings and loan associations, or credit unions involving embezzlements, self-dealing, and the taking of bribes or special favors to make loans or to refrain from collecting loans. Violations by outsiders include false financial statements, use of fraudulent collateral, check kiting, and similar offenses.

Bankruptcy Fraud — Frauds concerning financial insolvency involving planned thefts and fraudulent concealment.

Beginning Balance — The amount in an account at the start of the accounting period.

Beneficiary — A person having the enjoyment of property of which a trustee or executor has the legal possession.
(Parrott Estate Co. v. McLaughlin, 12 F.Supp. 23)

Best Evidence — "Best evidence" or "primary evidence" includes the best evidence which is available to a party and procurable under the existing situation.
(Best v. Equitable Life Assurance Soc., Mo.App., 299 S.W. 118)

Boiler Room — The use of telephone solicitors to promote fraudulent sales or fraudulent charitable solicitations.

Breach of Contract — Failure, without legal excuse, to perform any promise which forms the whole or part of a contract.
(Friedman v. Katzner, 139 Md. 195)

Business Opportunity Schemes — a fraudulent offer of an opportunity to make a living, or to supplement income by establishing a business, by purchasing franchises, to sell merchandise, or to perform some service.

By-laws — Regulations, ordinances, rules, or laws adopted by an association or corporation or the like for its government.
(Kilgar v. Gratto, 224 Mass. 78)

Capital Expenditure — An expenditure in the nature of an investment for the future.
(Maroon Unison Junior College District v. Gwinn, 106 Cal.App. 12)

Capital Surplus — Property paid into a corporation by shareholders in excess of capital stock liability.
(Commissioner of Corporations and Taxation v. Filoon, 310 Mass. 374)

Cash Basis — A basis of keeping accounts whereby income and expenses are recorded on the books of accounts when received and paid without regard to the period to which they apply.

Cash Flow — The cash flow calculation attempts to measure the actual cash receipts and cash expenses of a firm. Noncash expenses are not included, the principle noncash expense being depreciation.

Caveat Emptor — Let the buyer beware.
(Kellogg Bridge Co. v. Hamilton, 110 US 108)

Chain Referral Schemes — Any scheme in which the victim is induced to part with money or property on the representation that he will make money by inducing others to buy into the same deal.

Charity and Religious Fraud — Frauds arising out of the fund-raising activities of charitable and/or religious groups. Such frauds may commonly be grouped into three categories: (1) the bogus charity or religious group, (2) misrepresentation of association with a charity or religious group, and (3) misrepresentation of the benefits or uses of contributions.

Chart of Accounts — A listing of accounts in balance sheet order, each with a designated order.

Check-Kiting — Any of a variety of frauds against banks which depend for success upon the time it takes for checks to clear the banking system.

Circumstantial Evidence — Evidence of facts or circumstances from which the existence or nonexistence of fact in issue may be inferred.
(People v. Steele, 37 N.Y.S.2d 19,200)

Clear Title — One free from incumbrance, obstruction, burden, or limitation.
(Frank v. Murphy, 64 Ohio App. 501)

Closed Corporation — Corporation owned by a few stockholders, not available for investment by the public.

Closing Entry — One step in transferring the balance of an account to another account; an entry reducing one account to zero and offset by an entry increasing another account by the same amount.

Collateral Frauds — Frauds involving the holding, taking or offering of fictitious or overvalued collateral pursuant to a financial transaction.

Competitive Procurement Fraud — The illegal manipulation of the public or private contracting process. The main forms of competitive procurement frauds include: 1) bid rigging, 2) bid fixing, and 3) bribery or kickbacks.

Competency — The presence of those characteristics, or the absence of those disabilities, which render a witness legally fit and qualified to give testimony in a court of justice; applied, in the same sense, to documents or other written evidence.

Competent Evidence — That which the very nature of the thing to be proven requires, as the production of a writing where its contents are the subject of inquiry.
(Hill v. Hill, 216 Ala. 435)

Confidence Game — Any swindling operation in which advantage is taken of the confidence reposed by the victim in the swindler.
(People v. Blume, 345 Ill. 524)

Confession — A voluntary statement made by a person charged with the commission of a crime or misdemeanor, communicated to another person, wherein he acknowledges himself to be guilty of the offense charged, and discloses the circumstances of the act or the share and participation he had in it.
(Spicer v. Commonwealth, 21 Ky.L.Rep. 528)

Consent — Voluntary agreement by a person in the possession and exercise of sufficient mentality to make an intelligent choice to do something proposed by another.

(People v. Kanglesser, 44 Cal.App. 345)

Consolidated Balance Sheet — Aggregate amounts for the various categories of assets and liabilities of a corporate family.

Contra Account — One of two or more accounts which partially or wholly offset each other.

Conversion — An unauthorized assumption and exercise of the right of ownership over goods or personal chattels belonging to another, to the alteration of their condition or the exclusion of the owner's rights.

(Stickney v. Munro, 44 Me. 197)

Co-operative Association — A union of individuals, commonly laborers, farmers, or small capitalists, formed for the prosecution in common of some productive enterprise, the profits being shared in accordance with the capital or labor contributed by each.

(Mooney v. Farmers' Mercantile & Elevator Co. of Madison, 138 Minn. 199)

Corporation — An artificial person or legal entity created by or under the authority of the laws of a state or nation, composed, in some rare instances, of a single person and his successors, being the incumbents of a particular office, but ordinarily consisting of an association of numerous individuals, who subsist as a body politic under a special denomination, which is regarded in law as having a personality and existence distinct from that of its several members, and which is, by the same authority, vested with the capacity of continuous succession, irrespective of changes in its membership, either in perpetuity or for a limited term of years, and of acting as a unit or single individual in matters relating to the common purpose of the association, within the scope of the powers and authorities conferred upon such bodies by law.

(Dartmouth College v. Woodward, 4 L.Ed. 629)

Corroborating Evidence — Evidence supplementary to that already given and tending to strengthen or confirm it; additional evidence of a different character to the same point.

(Radcliffe v. Chavez, 15 N.M. 258)

Cost Accounting — The process of collecting material, labor, and overhead costs and attaching them to products.

Coupon Redemption Fraud — The returning of discount coupons to manufacturers and merchandisers when there have been no bona fide purchases of the merchandise.

Credit Entry — The record of a decrease in an asset account, or an increase in an equity account.

Credit Card Frauds — Any fraudulent scheme arising out of the application, extension, or use of credit cards.

Creditor — A person to whom a debt is owing by another person who is the debtor.

(Woolverton v. Taylor Co., 43 Ill.App. 424)

Criminal Intent — The intent to commit a crime; malice, as evidenced by a criminal act; an intent to deprive or defraud the true owner of his property.

(People v. Borden's Condensed Milk Co., 165 App.Div. 711)

Current Asset — An asset which is either currently in the form of cash or is expected to be converted into cash within a short period, usually within one year.

Current Liability — An obligation that becomes due within a short time, usually one year.

Debit Entry — The record of an increase in any asset account, or a decrease in an equity account.

Debt — A sum of money due by certain and express agreement; as by bond for a determinate sum, a bill or note, a special bargain, or a rent reserved on a lease, where the amount is fixed and specific, and does not depend upon any subsequent valuation to settle it.

Debt Consolidation Swindles — A fraudulent proposal to provide a service to organize a debtor's assets and income to refinance a heavy debt, usually for a large advance fee.

Deceit — A fraudulent and cheating misrepresentation, artifice, or device, used by one or more persons to deceive and trick another, who is ignorant of the true facts, to the prejudice and damage of the party imposed upon.
(French v. Vining, 102 Mass. 132)

Deception — The act of deceiving; intentional misleading by falsehood spoken or acted.
(Smith v. State, 13 Ala. App. 399)

Deed — A conveyance of realty, a writing signed by the grantor whereby title to realty is transferred from one to another.
(National Fire Ins. Co. v. Patterson, 170 Okl. 593)

Defalcation — The act of a defaulter; misappropriation of trust funds or money held in any fiduciary capacity; failure to properly account for such funds. Usually spoken of officers of corporations or public officials.
(In re Butts, D.C.N.Y., 120 F. 970)

Depletion — An emptying, exhausting, or wasting of assets.
(Arkansas-Louisiana Gas Co. v. City of Texarkana, 17 F.Supp. 447)

Depreciation — The deterioration, or the loss or lessening in value, arising from age, use, and improvements due to better methods.
(Boston & A. R. Co. v. New York Cent. R. Co., 256 Mass. 600)

Direct Evidence — That means of proof which tends to show the existence of a fact in question, without the intervention of the proof of any other fact, and is distinguished from circumstantial evidence, which is often called "indirect."
(State v. Calder, 23 Mont. 504)

Directory Advertising Scheme — Frauds arising from the selling of printing mass advertising services, such as impersonation schemes or limited distribution schemes.

Discount — Amount which the face value of a financial instrument exceeds the sales value.

Discovery Sampling — A sampling design which allows conclusions within a certain percentage confidence level as to whether certain critical errors exist in a population.

Dividend — Portion of the profits distributed to the stockholders.

Documentary Evidence — Evidence supplied by writings and documents of every kind in the widest sense of the term; evidence derived from conventional symbols (such as letters) by which ideas are represented on material substances. Such

evidence as is furnished by written instruments, inscriptions, documents of all kinds and also any inanimate objects admissible for the purpose, as distinguished from "oral" evidence or that delivered by human beings viva voce.
(People v. Purcell, 70 P.2d. 706)

Domestic Corporation — A corporation created by, or organized under, the laws of the state in which it operates.
(In re Grand Lodge, 110 Pa. 613)

Double-Entry Accounting — The type of accounting in which the two aspects of each event (debit and credit) are recorded.

Draft — The common term for a bill of exchange; as being drawn by one person on another.
(Hinnemann v. Rosenback, 39 N.Y. 100)

Duress — Unlawful constraint exercised upon a man whereby he is forced to do some act that he otherwise would not have done.
(Coughlin v. City of Milwaukee, 227 Wis. 35)

Embezzlement — The fraudulent appropriation to his own use or benefit of property or money intrusted to him by another, by a clerk, agent, trustee, public officer, or other person acting in a fiduciary character.
(4 Bl.Comm. 230,231)

Employee Agency Frauds — The fraudulent solicitation of money or fees in order to find employment for, to guarantee the employment of, or to improve the employability of another.

Encumbrance —(Also Incumbrance) A claim, lien, charge, or liability attached to and binding real property.
(Harrison v. Railroad Co., 91 Iowa 114)

Equity —Claims against an asset by the owner.

Escrow —A transaction in which a third party, acting as the agent for the buyer and the seller, carries out instructions of both and assumes the responsibilities of handling all the paperwork and disbursement of funds.

Evidence —Any species of proof, or probative matter, legally presented at the trial of an issue by the act of the parties and through the medium of witnesses, records, documents, concrete objects, etc., for the purpose of inducing belief in the minds of the court or jury as to their contention.
(Hotchkiss v. Newton, 10 Ga. 567)

Expenditure —An expending, a laying out of money; disbursement.
(Grout v. Gates, 97 Vt. 434)

Expense —That which is expended, laid out or consumed; an outlay; charge; cost; price.
(Rowley v. Clarke, 162 Iowa 732)

False Claims —The fraudulent written claims for payment for goods or services not provided as claimed. False claims include: (1) presentation of a bogus claim, (2) misrepresentation of the qualifications of an otherwise ineligible claimant, (3) false representation of the extent of payment or benefits to which the claimant is entitled, or (4) claims for reimbursement for goods and services allegedly provided to nonexistent recipients.

False Entry — An entry in the books of a bank or trust company which is intentionally made to represent what is not true or does not exist, with intent either to deceive its officers or a bank examiner or to defraud the bank or trust company. (Agnew v. U.S., 165 U.S. 36)

False Pretenses — Designed misrepresentation of existing fact or condition whereby a person obtains another's money or goods. (People v. Gould, 363 Ill. 348)

False Representation — A deceitful representation, or one contrary to the fact, made knowingly and with the design and effect of inducing the other party to enter into the contract to which it relates; a declaration of present intention, false when made, to perform an act in the future. (Pease & Elliman v. Wegeman, 299 N.Y.S. 398, 400)

False Statement — Under statutory provision, making it unlawful for an officer or director of a corporation to make any false statement in regard to a corporation's financial condition, the phrase means something more than merely untrue or erroneous, but it implies that the statement is designedly untrue and deceitful, and made with the intention to deceive the person to whom the false statement is made or exhibited. (State v. Johnson, 149 S.C. 138)

False Token — In criminal law, a false document or sign of the existence of a fact.

Feloniously — Proceeding from an evil heart or purpose done with a deliberate intention of committing a crime. (Golden v. Commonwealth, 245 Ky. 19)

Fiduciary — A person holding the character of a trustee, or a character analogous to that of a trustee, in respect to the trust and confidence involved in it and the scrupulous good faith and candor it requires. (Svanoe v. Jurgens, 144 Ill. 507)

FIFO — First in-first out method of inventory valuation which assumes that the goods that enter inventory first are the first to be sold.

Financial Condition — The results conveyed by presenting the assets, liabilities, and capital of an enterprise in the form of a balance sheet.

Financial Interviewing — The systematic questioning of persons who have knowledge of events, those involved, and the evidence surrounding a case under investigation.

Financial Statement — Under the Uniform Commercial Code, a prescribed form filed by a lender with the registrar of deeds or secretary of state giving the name and address of the debtor and the secured party along with the personal property securing the loan.

Fiscal Year — A period of twelve months (not necessarily concurrent with the calendar year) with reference to which appropriations are made and expenditures authorized, and at the end of which accounts are made up and the books balanced. (Shaffer v. Lipinsky, 194 N.C. 1)

Fixed Asset — Tangible property of relatively long life that generally is used in the production of goods and services.

Floating — Appropriating a day's deposits and substituting the following day's deposits to satisfy the accounting. Used in embezzlement schemes.

Foreign Corporation — A corporation created by or under the laws of another state, government, or country.
(In re Grand Lodge, 110 Pa. 613)

Forensic Auditing — Auditing for embezzlement or fraud.

Franchising Fraud — Arise out of business opportunities where individuals invest time or money to obtain a business enterprise, relying on others to provide or supply, at prearranged rates, specified goods and services.

Fraud — An intentional perversion of truth for the purpose of inducing another in reliance upon it to part with some valuable thing belonging to him or to surrender a legal right; a false representation of a matter of fact, whether by words or by conduct, by false or misleading allegations, or by concealment of that which should have been disclosed, which deceives and is intended to deceive another so that he shall act upon it to his legal injury.
(Brainard Dispatch Newspaper Co. v. Crow Wing County, 196 Minn. 194)

Fraud Against Government Benefit Programs — The unlawful application for or receipt of money, property, or benefit from public programs designed to confer such benefits under specific guidelines.

Fraudulent Concealment — The hiding or suppression of a material fact or circumstance which the party is legally or morally bound to disclose.
(Magee v. Insurance Co., 23 L.Ed. 699)

Fraudulent Conversion — Receiving into possession money or property of another and fraudulently withholding, converting, or applying the same to or for one's own use or benefit, or to the use and benefit of any person other than the one to whom the money or property belongs.
(Commonwealth v. Mitchneck, 130 Pa.Super. 433)

Fraudulent Conveyance — A conveyance or transfer of property, the object of which is to defraud a creditor, or hinder or delay him, or to put such property beyond his reach.
(Lockyer v. De Hart, 6 N.J.L. 458)

Fraudulent Representation — A false statement as to material fact, made with intent that another rely thereon, which is believed by another party and on which he relies and by which he is induced to act and does act to his injury, and the statement is fraudulent if the speaker knows the statement to be false or if made with utter disregard of its truth or falsity.
(Osborne v. Simmons, Mo.App., 23 S.W.2d 1102)

General Ledger — A book containing accounts in which are classified, usually in summary form, all transactions of a business enterprise using the double-entry method.

General Partnership — A partnership in which the parties carry on all their trade and business, whatever it may be, for the joint benefit and profit of all the parties concerned, whether the capital stock be limited or not, or the contributions thereto be equal or unequal.
(Bigelow v. Elliot, 3 Fed.Cas. 351)

Ghost Payrolls — A specific form of a false claim wherein fictitious employees are added to the payrolls, and payments to these employees revert to the payroll manipulator.

Goodwill — An intangible asset representing the difference between the purchase price and the value of the tangible assets purchased.

Gross Profit — Sales minus the cost of goods sold.

Hearsay — Evidence not proceeding from the personal knowledge of the witness, but from the mere repetition of what he has heard others say.
(State v. Ah Lee, 18 Or. 540)

Horizontal Analysis — A technique for analyzing the percentage change in individual income statement or balance sheet items from one reporting period to the next.

Hybrid Method — Method of accounting which is a combination of the cash and accrual methods.

Income Statement — An accounting report of the extent to which the owners' equity has increased or decreased during a given period of time, and the specific factors responsible for the change; a statement of revenues and expenses for a given period.

Indirect Methods — Ways of proving unknown or illegal sources of funds which rely upon circumstantial evidence.

Insolvency — The condition of a person who is insolvent; inability to pay one's debts; lack of means to pay one's debts.
(Dewey v. St. Alban's Trust Co., 56 Vt. 475)

Insurance Fraud — Insurance fraud can be broken down into two categories and subclasses:
1. Frauds perpetrated by insurers:
   a. failure to provide promised coverage,
   b. manipulation of risk classes,
   c. embezzlement of funds, or
2. Frauds perpetrated by insureds:
   a. filing of bogus or inflated claims,
   b. false statements to obtain coverage,
   c. bribery or kickbacks to agents to obtain preferential coverage.

Intangible Asset — Such values as accrue to a going business as good will, trademarks, copyrights, franchises, or the like. It exists only in connection with something else, as the good will of the business.
(In re Armour's Estate, 94 A. 284)

Interest — The compensation allowed by law or fixed by the parties for the use or forbearance or detention of money.
(Beach v. Peabody, 188 Ill. 75)

Interrogation — Questioning of suspects and uncooperative witnesses for the purpose of obtaining testimony and evidence or proof of significant omissions.

Interview — Questioning of victims and cooperative witnesses for the purpose of obtaining testimony and evidence or proof of significant omissions.

Inventory — A detailed list of articles of property; a list or schedule, containing a designation or description of each specific article; an itemized list of the various articles constituting a collection, estate, stock in trade, etc., with their established or actual values.
(Lloyd v. Wyckoff, 11 N.J.L. 224)

Investment Fraud — Schemes in which victims, induced by the promises of exceptionally high capital growth or high rates of return, invest money in imprudent or bogus projects or businesses.

Invoice — A list or account of goods or merchandise sent by the merchants to their correspondents at home or abroad, in which the marks of each package, with other particulars, are set forth.
(Merchants' Exch. Co. v. Weisman, 132 Mich. 353)

Joint Venture — An association of two or more persons to carry out a single business enterprise for profit, for which purpose they combine their property, money, effects, skill, and knowledge.
(Foreman v. Lumm, 214 App.Div. 579)

Journal — Preliminary records of transactions kept in chronological order.

Land Fraud — A specie of Investment Fraud involving the sale of land based on extensive misrepresentations of value, quality, facilities, or state of development.

Lapping — The substitution of checks for cash received, generally used in embezzlement schemes.

Larcenous Intent — A larcenous intent exists where a man knowingly takes and carries away the goods of another without any claim or pretense of right, with intent wholly to deprive the owner of them or convert them to his own use.
(Wilson v. State, 18 Tex.App. 274)

Larceny — Felonious stealing, taking, and carrying, leading, riding, or driving away another's personalty, with intent to convert it or to deprive the owner thereof.
(Ledbetter v. State, 24 Ala. App. 447)

Ledger Account — An account that records the changes in value of a particular asset or liability.

Letter of Credit — A document issued by a bank authorizing designated banks to make payments on demand to a specified individual up to a stated total amount.

Liability — The equity of a creditor or that which is owed to another.

Lien — A hold or claim which one person has upon the property of another for some debt or charge.
(Sissman v. Chicago Title & Trust Co., 303 Ill.App. 620)

LIFO — Last in-first out method of inventory valuation which assumes that the goods that enter inventory last are the first to be sold.

Limited Partnership — A partnership consisting of one or more general partners, jointly and severally responsible as ordinary partners, and by whom the business is conducted, and one or more special partners, contributing in cash payments a specific sum as capital to the common stock, and who are not liable for the debts of the partnership beyond the fund so contributed.
(Taylor v. Webster, 39 N.J.L. 104)

Line of Credit — A margin or fixed limit of credit granted by one to another, to the full extent of which the latter may avail himself in his dealings with the former, but which he must not exceed.
(Pittinger v. Southwestern Paper Co. of Fort Worth, 151 S.W.2d 922)

Liquidity — Ability to meet current obligations.

Loan or Lending Fraud — Unlawful practices arising out of lending or borrowing money, such as the failure to disclose information bearing on the extension or granting of a loan, or the misuse or misrepresentation of items of collateral and collateral accounts.

Material — Representation relating to the matter which is so substantial and important as to influence the party to whom it is made.
(McGuire v. Gunn, 133 Kan. 422)

Material Alteration — A material alteration in any written instrument is one which changes its tenor, or its legal meaning and effect; one which causes it to speak a language different in effect from that which it originally spoke.
(Foxworthy v. Colby, 64 Neb. 216)

Material Evidence — Such as is relevant and goes to the substantial matters in dispute, or has a legitimate and effective influence or bearing on the decision of the case.
(Porter v. Valentine, 18 Misc 213)

Means — That through which, or by the help of which, an end is attained; something tending to an object desired; intermediate agency or measure; necessary condition or co-agent; instrument.
(Pope v. Business Mens Assurance Co. of America, 235 Mo.App. 263)

Memorandum of Interview — A written record of an interview embodying something that an investigator desires to fix in memory.

Misapplication — Improper, illegal, wrongful, or corrupt use or application of funds or property.
(Jewett v. U.S., C.C.A.Mass, 41 CCA 88)

Misappropriation — The act of misappropriating or turning to a wrong purpose; a wrong application; a term that does not necessarily mean peculation, although it may mean that.
(Bannon v. Knauss, 57 Ohio App. 228)

Mistake — Some unintentional act, omission, or error arising from ignorance, surprise, imposition, or misplaced confidence.
(Code Ga. para. 3117)

Motive — An inducement, or that which leads or tempts the mind to indulge a criminal act.
(People v. Lewis, 275 N.Y. 33)

Mutual Company — A type of corporation that has no stockholders, but is owned by its customers (most common in insurance and savings associations).

Net Income — Excess of total revenues over total expenditure in a given period.

Net Loss — Excess of total expenditures over total revenues in a given period.

Net Worth — The excess of asset value over creditor claims. Assets − Liabilities = Net Worth (Equity).

Net Worth Analysis — An indirect method of proving unknown or illegal sources of funds by comparing net worth at the beginning and end of a specified period of time.

New Balance — The amount in an account at the end of the accounting period: the difference between the beginning balance plus increases minus the decreases.

Nominal Account — A temporary account for an item appearing on an income statement and closed to a balance sheet account at the end of an accounting period.

Note — A unilateral instrument containing an express and absolute promise of the signer to pay to a specified person on order, or bearer, a definite sum of money at a specified time.
(Shawano Finance Corp. v. Julius, 214 Wis. 637)

Note Receivable — A debt that is evidenced by a note or other written acknowledgment.

Open Corporation — A corporation whose stock is available for investment by the public.

Oral Evidence — Evidence given by word of mouth; the oral testimony of a witness.
(Bates' Ann.St.Ohio 1904)

Owner — The person in whom is vested the ownership, dominion, or title of property; proprietor.
(Garver v. Hawkeye Ins. Co., 69 Iowa 202)

Par — An equality subsisting between the nominal or face value of a bill of exchange, share of stock, etc., and its actual selling value.
(Conover v. Smith, 83 Cal.App. 227)

Parol Evidence Rule — Prevents the introduction of oral evidence or testimony to alter or vary the terms of a written agreement.

Partner — One of the owners of an unincorporated business.

Partnership — An association of two or more persons to carry on as co-owners of a business for profit.
(Schleicker v. Krier, 218 Wis. 376)

Pension Frauds and Abuses — Thefts or fraudulent conversions of pension fund assets either by trustees, employers, or employees.

Percentage Method — An indirect method of proving unknown or illegal sources of funds by using percentages or ratios considered typical of a business under investigation.

Perjury — The willful assertion as to a matter of fact, opinion, belief, or knowledge, made by a witness in a judicial proceeding as part of his evidence, either upon oath or in any form allowed by law to be substituted for an oath, whether such evidence is given in open court, or in an affidavit, or otherwise, such assertion being material to the issue or point of inquiry and known to such witnesses to be false.
(People v. Rendigs, 123 Misc.Rep. 32)

Ponzi Scheme — A general class of frauds in which the promotor uses the money invested by later investors to pay a seemingly high rate of return to earlier investors instead of making the investments represented.

Posting — Transfer of an entry from the journal to a ledger account.

Profit and Loss Account — A temporary account to which are transferred revenue and expense accounts at the end of an accounting period.

Proprietor — One who has the legal right or exclusive title to anything. In many instances it is synonymous with owner.
(State v. F. W. Woolworth Co., 184 Minn. 51)

Proprietorship —An unincorporated business owned by a single person.

Puffing —An expression of opinion by seller not made as a representation of fact. (Gulf Oil Corp. v. Federal Trade Commission, 150 F.2nd 106,109)

Pyramid Scheme —A commercial version of a chain letter, used by promoters in the selling of fraudulent dealerships, franchises, or business opportunity plans.

Quash —To overthrow; to abate; to vacate; to annul; to make void. (Wilson v. Commonwealth, 157 Va. 776)

Question and Answer Statement —A complete transcript of the questions, answers, and statements made by each participant during an interview.

Questioned Document —A writing that has been questioned in whole or in part in respect to its authenticity, identity, or origin.

Random Sampling —Every item or combination of items in a population subject to an audit have an equal probability of being chosen.

Ratio Analysis —The computation of key ratios to compare significant financial statement relationships between reporting periods.

Real Account —An account for an item appearing on a balance sheet; distinguished from a nominal account.

Real Evidence —Evidence furnished by things themselves, on view or inspection, as distinguished from a description of them by the mouth of a witness. (Riggie v. Grand Trunk Ry. Co., 93 Vt. 282)

Registration Statement —A statement describing in detail the financial condition of a corporation, its business, and the reasons it proposes to offer an issue of stocks or bonds to the public.

Relevancy —That quality of evidence which renders it properly applicable in determining the truth and falsity of the matters in issue between the parties to a suit. (1 Greenl.Ev. 49)

Revenue —The income of an individual or private corporation. (Humphrey v. Lang, 169 N.C. 601)

Sampling Risk —The possibility that a sample chosen from a population will not be representative of the population because of chance.

Secondary Evidence —It is that species of evidence which becomes admissible, as being the next best, when the primary or best evidence of the fact in question is lost or inaccessible; as when a witness details orally the contents of an instrument which is lost or destroyed. (Williams v. Davis, 56 Tex. 253)

Secured Creditor —A creditor who holds some special pecuniary assurance of payment of his debt, such as a mortgage or lien. (In re New York Title Mortgage Co., 160 Misc. 67)

Scienter —Knowingly. The term is used in pleading to signify an allegation setting out the defendant's previous knowledge of the cause which led to the injury complained of, or rather his previous knowledge of a state of facts which it was his duty to guard against, and his omission to do which has led to the injury complained of. (People v. Gould, 237 Mich. 156)

Securities Fraud — Fraudulent activities involving the sale, transfer or purchase of securities or of money interests in the business activities of others.

Shell Corporation — A corporation that has no assets or liabilities, simply a charter to do business.

Silent Partner — A partner not liable for debts of the partnership beyond the amount of his or her investment in it, and who does not participate in the management. Also known as a limited partner.

Single Entry Record Keeping — A system of accounting for financial transactions which makes no effort to balance accounts.

Source and Application of Funds — An indirect method of determining unknown or illegal sources of funds by comparison of all known expenditures with all known receipts during a particular period of time.

Stockholder — A person who owns shares of stock in a corporation or joint-stock company.
(Corwith v. Culver, 69 Ill. 502)

Swindling — Cheating and defrauding, grossly with deliberate artifice.
(Chase v. Whitlock, 3 Hill, N.Y., 140)

Subpoena — A mandatory writ or process directed to and requiring one or more persons to appear at a time to come and answer the matters charged against him or them.
(Gondas v. Gondas, 99 N.J.Eq. 473)

Subpoena Duces Tecum — A process by which the court, at the instances of a suitor, commands a witness who has in his possession or control some document or paper that is pertinent to the issues of a pending controversy, to produce it at the trial.
(State ex rel. Everglades Cypress Co. v. Smith, 104 Fla. 91)

Theft — The fraudulent taking of corporeal personal property belonging to another, from his possession, or from the possession of some person holding the same for him, without his consent, with intent to deprive the owner of the value of the same and to appropriate it to the use or benefit of the person taking.
(Quizlow v. State, 1 Tex.App. 65)

Trespass — Doing of unlawful act or of lawful act in unlawful manner to injury of another's person or property.
(Waco Cotton Oil Mill of Waco v. Walker, 103 S.W. 2d 1071)

Trial Balance — A list of the account balances arranged in "balance sheet order" by debits and credits with adjustment columns for entries. Used as a basis for financial statements.

Unit and Volume Method — An indirect method of proving unknown or illegal sources of funds by applying price or profit figures to the known quantity of business.

Variables Sample — A statistical method to determine whether the monetary amount of an account balance is materially misstated.

Verbal Acts — Utterances accompanying some act or conduct to which it is desired to give legal effect are admissible where conduct to be characterized by words is material to issue and equivocal in its nature, and words accompany conduct and aid in giving it legal significance.

(Keefe v. State, 50 Ariz. 295)

Vertical Analysis — A technique for analyzing the relationships between items appearing as lines or the income statement or balance sheet by expressing all the components as percentages.

Vocabularies of Adjustment — An embezzler's use of rationalization and situational ethics to justify and venerate appropriation.

Voluntary — Unconstrained by interference; unimpelled by another's influence; spontaneous; acting of oneself.

(Coker v. State, 199 Ga. 20)

White-Collar Crime — An illegal act or series of illegal acts committed by non-physical means and by concealment or guile, to obtain money or property, to avoid the payment or loss of money or property, or to obtain personal or business advantage.

(42 U.S. Code para 3701 et sequii)

Worksheet — Notes prepared by an accountant as a way of organizing accounting data.

ABBREVIATIONS IN CASE CITATIONS

A.	- Atlantic Reporter
A.2d.	- Atlantic Reporter, Second Series
Ala.	- Alabama Reports
Ala.App.	- Alabama Appellate Court
Ann.St.Ohio	- Annotated Statutes of Ohio
App.D.C.	- Appeals, District of Columbia
App.Div.	- Appellate Division, New York
Ariz.	- Arizona Reports
Bates Ann.St.	- Bates Annotated Revised Statutes, Ohio
Bl.Comm.	- Blackstone's Commentaries
C.C.A.	- United States Circuit Court of Appeals
Cal.	- California Reports
Cal.App.	- California Appellate Reports
Cal.App.2d	- California Appellate Reports, Second Series
Civ.Code S.D.	- Civil Code of South Dakota
Colo.	- Colorado Reports
Conn.	- Connecticut Reports
Cr.L.	- Criminal Law Reporter
F.	- Federal Reporter
F.2d	- Federal Reporter, Second Series
F.Supp.	- Federal Supplement
Fed.Cas.	- Federal Cases
Fl.	- Florida Reports
F.R.E.	- Federal Rules of Evidence
Ga.	- Georgia Reports
Ga.App.	- Georgia Appeals
Greenl.Ev.	- Greenleaf on Evidence
Ill.	- Illinois Reports
Ill.App.	- Illinois Appeal Reports
Iowa	- Iowa Reports
Kan.	- Kansas Reports
Ky.	- Kentucky Reports
Ky.L.Rep.	- Kentucky Law Reporter
L.Ed.	- Lawyers' Edition Supreme Court Reports
Mass.	- Massachusetts Reports
Md.	- Maryland Reports
Me.	- Maine Reports
Mich.	- Michigan Reports
Minn.	- Minnesota Reports
Misc.Rep.	- Miscellaneous Reports, New York
Mo.App.	- Missouri Appeal Reports
Mont.	- Montana Reports
N.C.	- North Carolina Reports

N.E.	- North Eastern Reporter
N.E.2d	- North Eastern Reporter, Second Series
N.J.Eq.	- New Jersey Equity Reports
N.J.L.	- New Jersey Law Reports
N.M.	- New Mexico Reports
N.Y.	- New York Court of Appeals Reports
N.Y.S.	- New York Supplement
N.Y.S.2d	- New York Supplement, Second Series
Neb.	- Nebraska Reports
Ohio App.	- Ohio Appellate Reports
Okl.	- Oklahoma Reports
Okl.Cr.	- Oklahoma Criminal Reports
Or.	- Oregon Reports
P.	- Pacific Reporter
P.2d.	- Pacific Reporter, Second Series
Pa.	- Pennsylvania State Reports
Rich.Eq.	- Richardson's South Carolina Equity Reports
S.C.	- South Carolina Reports
S.D.	- South Dakota Reports
S.E.	- South Eastern Reporter
S.E.2d	- South Eastern Reporter, Second Series
So.2d	- Southern Reporter, Second Series
S.W.	- South Western Reporter
S.W.2d	- South Western Reporter, Second Series
Tex.App.	- Texas Court of Appeals Reports
Tx.Cr.R.	- Texas Criminal Reports
U.S.	- United States Reports
U.S.C.	- United States Code
Va.	- Virginia Reports
Vt.	- Vermont Reports
Wis.	- Wisconsin Reports

BIBLIOGRAPHY

Barmash, Isadore, ed., *Great Business Disasters; Swindlers, Bunglers, and Frauds in American Industry.* Chicago: Playboy Press, 1972.

Bartlett, John, and Emily Morrison Beck, ed., *Familiar Quotations, Fifteenth Edition.* Boston: Little, Brown and Company, 1980.

Bennett, Wayne K., and Karen M. Hess. *Criminal Investigation.* St. Paul, MN: West Publishing Co., 1981.

Bequai, August, "Wanted; The White-Collar Ring," *Student Lawyer.* No. 5. (May, 1977).

Bernstein, Leopold A., *Analysis of Financial Statements.* Homewood IL: Dow Jones-Irwin, 1984.

Bierman, John, "A dictator on trial," *Macleans,* Vol. 101, No. 45 (October 31, 1988), 31.

Bilinski, Andrew, "A Former Era on Trial," *Macleans,* Vol. 101, No. 39 (September 19, 1988), 18.

Black, Henry Campbell, *Black's Law Dictionary Revised, Fourth Edition.* St. Paul, MN: West Publishing Co., 1968.

Bladen, Ashby, "The Texas S&L Massacre," *Forbes,* Vol. 141, No. 6 (March 21, 1988), p. 199.

Bonavita, Fred, "Political consultant fined $7,600, gets probation for petition forgery," *The Houston Post.* Houston, TX: Friday, June 24, 1988.

Brinkley, Homer, Jr., *Master Manipulator.* New York: AMACON, 1985.

Carper, Jean, *Not With a Gun.* New York: Grossman Publishers, 1973.

Chappell, Duncan, "Crime, Law Enforcement, and Penology," *1989 Britannica Book of the Year.* Chicago: Encyclopedia Britannica, Inc., 1989.

Clinard, Marshall B., and Richard Quinney, *Criminal Behavior Systems: A Typology.* New York: Holt, Rinehart and Winston, 1967.

Cole, Patrick E., "Tennis Anyone? Ivan Boesky Does Time," *Business Week,* No. 3049 (April 25, 1988), 70.

Corley, Robert N., and William J. Robert, *Principles of Business Law.* Englewood Cliffs, NJ: Prentice-Hall, Inc., 1975.

Cressey, Donald R., *Other Peoples Money: A Study of the Social Psychology of Embezzlement.* Glencoe, IL: The Free Press, 1953.

——, *Crime in the United States—1992.* Washington, D.C.: Federal Bureau of Investigation, U.S. Department of Justice, 1993.

Dix, George, and M. Michael Sharlot, *Basic Criminal Law, Cases, and Materials.* St. Paul, MN: West Publishing Co., 1980.

Dumaine, Brian, "Beating Bolder Corporate Crooks," *Fortune,* Vol. 117, No. 7 (April 25, 1988), 193.

Edelhertz, Herbert, ed., *The Investigation of White-Collar Crime: A Manual for Law Enforcement Agencies.* Washington, D.C.: US Department of Justice, Law Enforcement Assistance Administration, 1977.

Fenichell, Stephen, *Other People's Money: The Rise and Fall of OPM Leasing Services.* Garden City, NY: Doubleday, 1985.

——, *Financial Investigative Techniques.* Washington, D.C.: Department of the Treasury, Internal Revenue Service, 1986.

Fraser, Lyn M., *Understanding Financial Statements; Through the Maze of a Corporate Annual Report.* Reston, VA: Reston Publishing Co., 1985.

Gibbons, Don C., *Society, Crime, and Criminal Careers: An Introduction to Criminology, Third Edition.* Englewood Cliffs, NJ: Prentice-Hall, Inc., 1977.

Graham, Benjamin and Charles McGalrick, *The Interpretation of Financial Statements.* New York: Harper & Row, 1975.

Greenwood, Peter W., Jan M. Chailcon, and Joan Petersilia, *The Criminal Investigation Process.* Lexington, Mass.: D. C. Heath and Company, 1977.

——, *Guide to Sources of Information.* Washington, D.C.: Department of Justice, Federal Bureau of Investigation, 1987.

Hawkins, Lori, "Employees steal billions, study says," *Austin American-Statesman,* Austin, TX: Tuesday, October 3, 1995.

——, "How to Read a Financial Report," *Narcotics Related Financial Investigative Techniques.* Washington, D.C.: Department of Justice, Federal Bureau of Investigation, 1992.

——, *Introduction to Books and Records.* Washington, D.C.: Department of Justice, Federal Bureau of Investigation, 1981.

Kevitney, Jonathan, "Necessary Payoffs—But Who Really Pays?" *Swindled! Classic Business Frauds of the Seventies.* Princeton, NJ: Dow Jones Books, 1976.

Kinsley, Michael, ed., "Nofzinger's Complaint," *The New Republic,* Vol. 198, No. 10 (March 7, 1988), 8.

Knudten, Richard D., *Crime in a Complex Society: An Introduction to Criminology.* Homewood, IL: The Dorsey Press, 1970.

Kwitney, Jonathan, *The Fountain Pen Conspiracy.* New York, NY: Alfred A. Knopf, 1973.

Lawther, William, "Scandal at the Pentagon," *Maclean,* Vol. 101, No. 27 (June 27, 1988), 25.

Leslie, Donald, Albert Teitlebaum, and Henry Pankratz, "Mathematics of Finance and Statistical Sampling," *Accountants Handbook, Volume I, 6th Edition.* Lee J. Seidler and D. R. Carmichael, eds. New York, NY: John Wiley & Sons, 1981.

Mann, Kenneth, *Defending White-Collar Crime: A Portrait of Attorneys at Work.* New Haven, CT: Yale University Press, 1985.

McCaghy, Charles H., *Deviant Behavior: Crime, Conflict, and Interest Groups.* New York: MacMillan Publishing Co., Inc., 1976.

McCullough, Wm. W., *Sticky Fingers: A Classic Look at America's Fastest Growing Crime.* New York: Amacon, 1981.

——, *Narcotics Related Financial Investigative Techniques.* Quantico, VA: U.S. Department of Justice, Federal Bureau of Investigation, Bureau of Justice Assistance, 1991.

Nettler, Gwynn A., "Embezzlement without problems," *British Journal of Criminology.* 1974.

Nossen, Richard A., *The Detection, Investigation, and Prosecution of Financial Crimes: White Collar, Political, and Racketeering.* Richmond, VA: Richard A. Nossen & Assoc., 1982.

Opatrny, Dennis J., "Women committing more white-collar crime, statistics show," *The Austin American-Statesman.* Austin, TX: Sunday, November 22, 1987.

Parker, Maynard, ed., "At Last, a Verdict Fit for a Queen," *Newsweek,* Vol. CXIV, No. 11 (September 11, 1989), 61.

——, "PTL head gears up for appeal, Bakker to suspend storefront ministry," *The Austin American-Statesman.* Austin, TX: Saturday, October 7, 1989.

Pursley, Robert D., *Introduction to Criminal Justice, Second Edition.* Encino, CA: Glencoe Publishing Co., 1980.

Radelet, Louis A., *The Police and the Community, Fourth Edition.* New York: MacMillan Publishing Co., 1986.

Reckless, Walter C., *The Crime Problem, Fourth Edition.* New York: Meredith Publishing Company, 1967.

Reid, Sue Titus, *Crime and Criminology,* Third Edition. New York: Holt, Rinehart & Winston, 1982.

McCullough, Wm. W., *Sticky Fingers: A Classic Look at America's Fastest Growing Crime.* New York: Amacon, 1981.

——, *Narcotics Related Financial Investigative Techniques.* Quantico, VA: U.S. Department of Justice, Federal Bureau of Investigation, Bureau of Justice Assistance, 1991.

Royal, Robert F., and Steven R. Schutt, *The Gentle Art of Interviewing and Interrogation: A Professional Manual and Guide.* Englewood Cliffs, NJ: Prentice-Hall, Inc., 1976.

Seidler, Lee J., Frederick Andrews, and Marc J. Epstein, *The Equity Funding Papers.* Santa Barbara, CA: John Wiley & Sons, 1978.

Sherrid, Pamela, "The deal Drexel could not refuse," *U.S. News and World Report,* Vol. 106, No. 1 (January 9, 1989), 46.

Stolker, Richard S., *Financial Search Warrants.* Washington, D.C.: U.S. Department of Justice, 1989.

Sutherland, Edwin H., *White Collar Crime.* New York: Holt, Rinehart & Winston, 1961.

Sutherland, Edwin H., *White Collar Crime: The Uncut Version.* New Haven, CT: Yale University Press, 1983.

Sutherland, Edwin H., and Donald R. Cressey, *Principles of Criminology.* New York: J. B. Lippincott Co., 1966.

Sutherland, Edwin H., and Donald R. Cressey, *Criminology, 10th ed.* Philadelphia: J. B. Lippincott Co., 1978.

Wall, James M., ed., "Vatican Challenge," *The Christian Century,* Vol. 105, No. 1 (January 6, 1988), 9.

Wells, Joseph T., W. Steve Albrecht, Jack Bologna, Gilbert Geis, and Jack Robertson, *Fraud Examiners' Manual.* Austin, TX: National Association of Fraud Examiners, 1989.

Wermuth, William C., "Contracts," *Modern American Law.* Chicago, IL: Blackstone College of Law, 1955.

Zeitz, Dorothy, *Women Who Embezzle or Defraud: A Study of Convicted Felons.* New York: Prager Publishers, 1981.

INDEX